Economic Development in Southeast Asia

Economic Development in Southeast Asia

The Chinese Dimension

Yuan-li Wu
Chun-hsi Wu

HOOVER INSTITUTION PRESS
Stanford University, Stanford, California

The Hoover Institution on War, Revolution and Peace, founded at Stanford University in 1919 by the late President Herbert Hoover, is an interdisciplinary research center for advanced study on domestic and international affairs in the twentieth century. The views expressed in its publications are entirely those of the authors and do not necessarily reflect the views of the staff, officers, or Board of Overseers of the Hoover Institution.

Hoover Institution Publication 209

International Standard Book Number: 0–8179–7092-4
Library of Congress Catalog Card Number: 79–2455
Printed in the United States of America

Designed by Elizabeth Gehman

Contents

Tables and Figures

FIGURES

Acknowledgments

This study began as two separate undertakings by the two authors, one focusing on national and historical developments in Southeast Asia affecting the Chinese, the other covering intraregional and international economic developments involving Chinese workers and entrepreneurs. As work by each author progressed independently, it became apparent that the two studies would lend themselves logically to amalgamation. The following work is the outcome of this joint effort.

The authors wish to acknowledge their indebtedness to the Hoover Institution of Stanford University and to the Earhart Foundation for the generous support that has made their respective work possible. They are particularly grateful for the research assistance of Mr. Wang Cheng-chung at the Institute of East Asian Studies, National Chen-chi University in Taipei, and of Mr. H. C. Ling and Miss Thanh Van at the Hoover Institution. A number of China specialists and other scholars, including Professor Wang Gung-wu of the Australian National University, Professor Richard L. Walker of South Carolina, Dr. Ramon Myers at Hoover, and Mr. Ward Smith, formerly of Thailand and Taiwan, have all read the manuscript, and their critical comments have been helpful in more ways than one. Completion of the study in its later stages, when the authors were able for a time to work together at Stanford, owes a great deal to the able and painstaking secretarial assistance of Mrs. Mia Ruhm, to whom the authors wish to express their special thanks. The editorial work of Mrs. Elizabeth Brandt has been particularly exemplary. None of the above persons should of course be held responsible for all the shortcomings of the volume, which are strictly our own.

A great deal of information contained in this volume is derived from interviews and discussions with businessmen and scholars in Southeast Asia during the past several years. Their willingness to help has been indispensable even though their names cannot all be mentioned here. This volume is dedicated to these anonymous contributors to our work and to the Chinese in Southeast Asia.

YUAN-LI WU
CHUN-HSI WU

Introduction

The importance of Southeast Asia in a global economic and political context can be appraised from several points of view. In economic terms, countries in the region offer such divergent experiences and records of growth that an understanding of the underlying reasons for these differences can be beneficial not only to the countries themselves but also to students of economic development and the modernization process in general. For businessmen and foreign investors interested in investment and trade opportunities in the region, the ostensibly comparable but basically dissimilar attitudes of the several countries toward foreign investment, as well as their actual performance, deserve special scrutiny.

From a geopolitical point of view, the peninsular and insular countries of Southeast Asia are located on one of the world's major sea lanes. They command the strategic straits and narrows that link the Indian Ocean and the South and East China Seas to the Pacific. This geographical factor is of particular importance to Japan because the bulk of its fuel and mineral and agricultural raw materials must be brought to its home islands over these very routes. Southeast Asia is itself a major source of supply for these resources, and a large portion of its imports also comes from Japan. During the last quarter century Japan and Southeast Asia have developed a high degree of economic interdependence. the well-being and good will of each are matters of vital concern to the other. From the standpoint of third parties such as the United States and the European Economic Community (EEC), the importance of Japan and Southeast Asia as separate entities is enhanced by this interrelationship.

Another factor should not escape attention: the presence of large numbers of Chinese residents in the area. This makes Southeast Asia of special interest to students of international relations. Given the *potential* political and economic influence that Peking could wield in the region in the long run, although Peking's influence today is relatively limited, the attitude and orientation of the ethnic Chinese has long been of concern to the Southeast Asian countries where they live. A key question, rarely openly articulated, is whether they might become fifth columnists at some critical moment. This fear has contributed to the perception of a Chinese problem in several Southeast Asian countries and has, as a matter of fact, affected their recent foreign and domestic policies.

To sociologists and anthropologists no less than historians and political scientists, the existence of large ethnic-Chinese communities in Southeast Asia and their interaction with the larger societies around them have always been topics of considerable academic interest. It is high time that economists, too, devote attention to the subject. One cannot realistically discuss Southeast Asian economic development or international economic cooperation in the region without inquiring into the changing functions ethnic-Chinese capital, entrepreneurship, and skilled manpower have played in the past and will continue to play in the future. A better appreciation of the roles the Chinese play is needed if local policymakers are to maximize their countries' development potential by harnessing these assets in their midst.

Significant changes have occurred since World War II in the attitudes of ethnic Chinese in Southeast Asia both toward China and toward the countries of their residence. These shifts have occurred simultaneously with political changes in China. The communist takeover of the Chinese mainland in 1949 and the harsh conditions under which the Chinese population has had to live have dampened, to say the least, the enthusiasm of ethnic Chinese in Southeast Asia to return to their ancestral homes. While mainland China has shifted its policies toward ethnic Chinese abroad from time to time, it seems to have been trying to make friends with Southeast Asian countries recently by not exploiting potentially divided loyalties. Needless to say, the Republic of China has shown even greater acceptance of the new roles of ethnic Chinese as Southeast Asians. In an increasing number of cases, the citizenship of ethnic Chinese in Southeast Asian countries has also changed, and many have had to make business and personal readjustments to adapt to changing policies of Southeast Asian governments. As sometimes happens in such instances, the need to adjust to new situations, which began as a necessary condition for survival, has resulted in a long-term improvement in the condition of those successful in making the adjustment: those Chinese who have adapted are, in a sense, stronger today than they were before. They have developed intraregional linkages as well as multinational personal and institutional contacts that did not exist formerly. Such linkages can be immensely useful in furthering regional cooperation and national economic development in Southeast Asia. Awareness and acknowledgment of this new asset would be a useful first step in promoting the economic development, political cohesion, and private and governmental investment opportunities that all Southeast Asian countries seem to desire.

Even those preoccupied with big-power politics, to whom this Chinese aspect may appear unexciting and somewhat trivial, should bear in mind another significant factor affecting the prospects of Southeast Asia. Within the larger geographical context of the Western Pacific, of which Southeast Asia is a part, no single country can claim to be an economic giant and a major military power at the same time. Japan is an economic giant only. The People's Republic of China (PRC) is militarily important but by no means a giant, and it has serious economic handicaps. The absence of a single superpower within the region has two important implications. First, attempts to fill the vacuum may be made by one or both extraregional superpowers, the United States and the Soviet Union. The latter is regarded as an extraregional power because the developed part of the country and the principal locus of its power are in the western part of its Eurasian land mass. Second, the smaller powers in the region have far more room to maneuver and to make individual and multilateral arrangements of their own than they would otherwise possess.

Whatever the countries of Southeast Asia may wish to do in the future, and whatever others who wish Southeast Asia well may envisage as the optimal future for the region, economic development and stability in the individual countries will be a sine qua non. Accordingly, the best use of available resources, both foreign and domestic, is an indispensable condition. In this context ethnic-Chinese resources are assets that should be recognized. Making full use of these is the Chinese dimension in the economic development of the area—a dimension that offers both a challenge and an opportunity to those who acknowledge it in making policy and take advantage of it realistically.

Finally, but by no means as an afterthought, we must not ignore the residents of the Chinese communities themselves. Their number is larger than the populations of some countries or national groups in other parts of the world, sovereign states or not. Their fate is of concern to them and to us on a human level.

1

Economic Growth and Use of Resources

1

The Economic Profile and Conditions of Economic Growth: The Recent Record

In this book we wish to address two questions. First, what are some of the strategic factors spurring economic growth in several Western Pacific countries that the less rapidly developing countries of Southeast Asia might stress to their advantage? Second, how can the latter's policies toward ethnic-Chinese components in their respective populations be modified to enable them to enjoy these same positive conditions for economic development?

In this chapter and the next we will address the first question, with the aid of statistical and other indicators. For this section no detailed knowledge about Chinese communities in Southeast Asia or special insight into their historical development is required. To follow our discussion of the second question, however, the reader must be cognizant of the economic roles ethnic Chinese now play in the individual countries, especially because there are substantial differences among the different countries in spite of a popular tendency to lump all Southeast Asian countries and all Chinese in Southeast Asia together as if we were dealing with totally homogeneous entities. An overview of the current status of Chinese economic activities by country is provided in Chapter 3 as a prelude to the discussion in Chapter 4 of inter-Chinese-community business relations involving more than one country and extending to other parts of the Western Pacific outside Southeast Asia.

The nature of present Chinese economic activities and the interactions of the ethnic Chinese with both the governments of individual Southeast Asian countries and the non-Chinese populations of these countries are current manifestations in a long historical process. Full understanding of the economic roles ethnic Chinese have come to play since World War II requires a review of their activities prior to and during the prewar colonial period. Since a discussion of this subject is unavoidably lengthy, we have segregated it in Part 2. Readers who wish to pursue this subject more thoroughly may find it more instructive to read

Part 2 before turning to Chapter 3 in Part 1. Historians who find economics uninteresting and statistics particularly heavy going may wish to skip Part 1 or its first two chapters and start with the historical supplement.

ECONOMIC GROWTH AND STRUCTURAL DISPARITY

Little can be said at this juncture about the economic prospects of the Indochina states because of the upheavals that have shaken them since 1975 and the present lack of detailed information. They deserve a separate, intensive examination that cannot be provided here.[1] Relatively little can be said about Burma's recent economic development for the simple reason that, as a cynic might say, there has been very little of it. Under its socialist and essentially isolationist government, the Union of Burma managed to keep its economy virtually static during the past decade while the rest of Southeast Asia was in ferment. For the foreseeable future, any discussion of the economic prospects of Southeast Asia must focus on the members of the Association of Southeast Asian Nations (ASEAN): namely, Thailand, Malaysia, Singapore, Indonesia, and the Philippines. These five countries have market economies in which government plays an active role. How well they do is very much affected by the wisdom or inadequacy of government policies.

A casual examination of two sets of economic indicators suffices to show that the Southeast Asian countries listed in Table 1 are at distinctly different stages of

TABLE 1

INDICATORS OF ECONOMIC DEVELOPMENT AND STRUCTURE

	Gross National Product (GNP) Per Capita, 1974 (Current U.S. $)	*Shares of Nonagricultural Sectors in Gross Domestic Product (GDP), 1975 (Percentage)*		
		Manufacturing	Other	Total
ASEAN:				
Singapore	2,120	21.0	78.3	99.3 (1974)
Thailand	300	20.2	52.3	72.5
The Philippines	310	20.4	50.5	70.9
Malaysia	660	16.7	52.3	69.0
Indonesia	150	10.4	50.7	61.1 (1974)
Non-ASEAN:				
Burma	90	10.4	53.7	64.1

SOURCE: Asia Development Bank (ADB), Economic Office, *Key Indicators of Developing Member Countries of ADB*, vol. VII, no. 1 (April 1976): 7 and 9. The ASEAN countries are listed in order of the decreasing share of the nonagricultural sectors in their GDPs. For comparison, the figures for Burma are also included.

economic development and that their internal economic structures diverge widely.

In terms of per-capita GNP, Singapore stands out. As a city-state and a world trade and financial center, it is obviously in a different category from the other developing countries of Southeast Asia, all of which are far more populous and presumably, therefore, less manageable. Singapore is by no means unique, however. We would err seriously if we assumed that a city-state and trade-cum-finance center could not provide an example that larger systems might emulate. Singapore seems an exception only if the other four ASEAN countries are treated as the norm, an incorrect conclusion one might draw by looking at Southeast Asia alone.

A different and more instructive pattern is discernible when we expand our primary list to include the remaining market economies of East Asia. This is done in Table 2, in which the Republics of Korea and China, as well as Hong Kong, are added. (Where data are available, Japan, as a fast-growing country and the most affluent one in Asia,[2] and several nonmarket systems are also listed for additional comparison.) Within this larger context, two groups of developing countries can be distinguished from each other on the basis of their long-term growth rates and per-capita GNPs.

The average annual growth rates shown in the last two columns of Table 2 are based on 1973 as a terminal year because it was the last year before the enormous oil price hike ordered by the Organization of Petroleum Exporting Countries (OPEC) in October, 1973, radically affecting economic conditions in many oil-importing countries. With the exception of Singapore, the Southeast Asian countries were in a distinctly slower-growing group between 1960 and 1973 (see Table 3). During this time Singapore was one of four faster-growing systems: the others were Hong Kong, another city-state and world trade and financial center, and the Republics of Korea and China (ROK and ROC). The highly developed Japanese economy, of course, was equally fast growing.

Table 2 allows us to characterize the economic profiles of the Western Pacific countries in greater detail. First, those countries that increased their output significantly faster than the rest seem to have been less burdened by population growth. Between 1971 and 1975, population growth in Singapore, Taiwan, South Korea, and Hong Kong (the last in spite of a continuous inflow of refugees from mainland China) averaged 2 percent or less each year. In contrast, in the four economically slower-growing Southeast Asian countries, population expansion averaged 2.4–3.1 percent a year during the same period. When these disparate population growth rates are allowed for, the distinction between the two groups of countries becomes even sharper (see Table 4).

Second, these two groups of countries can also be compared with each other in terms of the shares of total output contributed by their respective nonagricultural sectors (see Table 5). From this perspective, conditions in Thailand, the

TABLE 2

AGGREGATE OUTPUT, POPULATION, AND GROWTH RATES IN SOUTHEAST ASIAN NATIONS

		1974 GNP at Market Price (U.S. $ Million)	*1974 Per-Capita GNP at Market Price (Current U.S. $)*	*Average Annual Population Growth (Percentage)*	*Average Annual Real Growth Rate of Per-Capita GNP (Percentage)*		*Average Annual Real GDP Growth Rate (Percentage)*	
				1971–75	1960–73	1965–73	1960–73	1970–73
Southeast Asian market economies	Thailand	12,140	300	3.1	4.8	4.5	7.6	7.3
	Malaysia	7,610	660	2.8	3.9	3.7	6.7	8.4
	The Philippines	13,030	310	2.5	2.3	2.6	6.3	6.5
	Indonesia	18,600	150	2.4	2.4	4.5	4.7	7.6
Other Asian market economies in the Western Pacific	Singapore	4,700	2,120	1.6	7.1	9.4	10.4	12.4
	Hong Kong	6,550	1,540	2.0	7.0	5.8	9.1	7.6
	ROK	15,800	470	1.7	7.1	8.7	9.3	11.3
	ROC	11,370	720	1.9	6.9	7.3	9.7	11.8
	Japan	425,880	3,880	1.2	8.2	10.0	9.6	8.7
Southeast Asian nonmarket economies	North Vietnam	3,000	130	. . .[a]	. . .	. . .	. . .	. . .
	South Vietnam	3,440	170	2.7	0.6	−0.7	2.8	2.8
	Cambodia	570	70	2.8	. . .	. . .	. . .	. . .
	Laos	220	70	2.5	. . .	. . .	. . .	. . .
	Burma	2,710	90	2.2	0.7	0.7	2.0	2.0
People's Republic of China (PRC)		223,000	240	2.3	3.6	4.0	5.7	6.6

SOURCES: ADB, *Key Indicators*, vol. VII, no. 1 (April 1976): 3 and 7; United Nations, *Yearbook of National Accounts Statistics*, vol. 1, (New York, 1976), p. 775; *U.N. Statistical Yearbook, 1974;* International Monetary Fund and the World Bank Group, *Finance and Development* 10, no. 1, (March 1973); *The World Bank Atlas* (Washington, D.C., 1975); Federal Reserve Bank of San Francisco, *Pacific Basin Economic Indicators* 1, no. 1 (1976). For estimates for the PRC, see *Handbook of Economic Statistics, 1975* (Washington, D.C., 1975), pp. 15, 23, 26, 41, and (1976), p. 1.

[a] . . . is the symbol employed here and throughout all tables to indicate "no information."—Ed.

TABLE 3

THE RECORD OF PERFORMANCE 1960–73 IN EAST AND SOUTHEAST ASIA
(Per-Capita GNP in 1974)

	Very Affluent ($3,500–$5,000)	Affluent ($1,500–$2,500)	More Developed ($450–$750)	Less Developed ($150–$350)
Faster-growth countries (approximately 9–10 percent per annum in real GDP):	Japan	Singapore Hong Kong	ROC ROK	–
Slower-growth countries (approximately 5–7.5 percent per annum in real GDP):	–	–	Malaysia	Thailand The Philippines Indonesia

TABLE 4

THE RECORD OF PER-CAPITA GROWTH IN 1960–73, EAST AND SOUTHEAST ASIA

	Very Affluent ($3,500–$5,000)	Affluent ($1,500–$2,500)	More Developed ($450–$750)	Less Developed ($150–$350)
Faster-growth countries (approximately 7 percent per annum in per-capita real output)	Japan	Singapore Hong Kong	ROK ROC	–
Slower-growth countries (approximately 2.3–4.8 percent per annum in per-capita real output)	–	–	Malaysia	Thailand The Philippines Indonesia

Philippines and, to a lesser extent, Malaysia in 1975 were comparable to those in the ROC in 1965 or in Korea in 1970. The same comparison may be made for conditions in Indonesia in 1975 and in Korea in 1965. Thus approximately a decade of development seems to separate Indonesia from South Korea and the other Southeast Asian countries (except Singapore) from Taiwan. In contrast, Singapore and Hong Kong bear a strong resemblance to each other and are conspicuously different structurally from the other Southeast Asian economies.

TABLE 5

SECTORAL SHARES IN GROSS DOMESTIC PRODUCT (GDP)
(Percentages)

Manufacturing				*Total Nonagriculture*			
	1975		1965		1975		1965
The Philippines	20.4	ROC	19.9	Thailand	72.5	ROC	73.1
Thailand	20.2			The Philippines	70.9		
Malaysia	16.7			Malaysia	69.0		
Indonesia	10.4	ROK*	12.0	Indonesia	61.1	ROK*	57.2
Singapore	21.0 (1974)	Singapore	15.3	Singapore	99.3 (1974)	Singapore	96.7
Hong Kong	28.5	Hong Kong	. . .	Hong Kong	98.2 (1972)	Hong Kong	. . .

SOURCE: ADB, *Key Indicators,* vol. VII, no. 1 (April 1976): 9.
*The sectoral shares for Korea in 1970 were: manufacturing, 19.1 percent; nonagriculture, 68.9 percent.

The figures in Table 5 should not be interpreted mechanically. They by no means imply that it will take the Southeast Asian countries (except Singapore) some five to ten years to reach a stage of economic development comparable to that of present-day Taiwan or South Korea. What they do mean is that the four economically faster-growing countries managed to forge ahead far more rapidly, both quantitatively and in terms of changing emphasis in economic sectors than did the four slower-growing Southeast Asian countries, and that it would take the latter time to catch up. Given favorable conditions, the actual time required might be substantially less, particularly in view of the considerably greater natural resources that are actually available in these lesser-developed countries.

AVAILABILITY OF NATURAL RESOURCES

The availability of food and energy products is usually considered of crucial importance to a developing economy. Among the five ASEAN nations, only Thailand is a large exporter of rice and corn. Between 1962 and 1971, net exports were 27 percent of the country's total grain production.[3] During the same period, Indonesia and the Philippines were only marginally dependent upon imports, which made up approximately 2 percent and 6 percent, respectively, of their total food-grain supply. Only Malaysia derived a larger proportion (30 percent) of its food grains from imports than did two members of the faster-growing group, the ROK (16 percent) and the ROC (7 percent), not to mention Japan (18 percent). The most extreme case, the virtually 100-percent dependence of Singapore and

Hong Kong on food-grain imports, obviously did not hamper the phenomenal economic expansion of the two city-states.

During 1972 and 1973, immediately before the oil crisis of the winter of 1973–74, three ASEAN countries—Thailand, the Philippines, and Singapore—imported 100 percent of their total supplies of crude oil, as did Hong Kong, South Korea, and, for most practical purposes, Taiwan and Japan. Even Malaysia, which grew faster than the other countries in the economically slower-growing group, was dependent upon imports for nearly 40 percent of its total crude-oil supply in 1972 and 1973. On the other hand, Indonesia, the slowest-growing member of ASEAN in real gross domestic product (GDP) between 1960 and 1973, exported more than 60 percent of its total crude-oil supply during this period.

Tables 6 and 7 present data on production and net import (or export) of selected cereals and tubers as well as of crude oil in the same comparative framework. Table 8 registers the total and per-capita volume of proven and probable reserves of crude oil and coal. Table 9 presents the production and net import (or export) figures for selected metals and ores. These statistics are given here to reinforce an incontrovertible fact: the availability of natural resources does not guarantee economic development. Conversely, and perhaps more important, the absence of domestic natural resources is by no means an insurmountable barrier to economic development—even to very rapid economic

TABLE 6

NET IMPORTS AS PERCENTAGE OF TOTAL FOOD GRAINS
(Average of 1962–71)

	Total Food Grain	Rice	Wheat	Corn	Soybeans
Singapore	100	100	- - -[a]	- - -	- - -
Hong Kong	100	100	100	- - -	100
Malaysia	30	26	100	- - -	- - -
Japan	18	- - -	80	- - -	91
ROK	16	7	73	- - -	- - -
ROC	7	- - -	99	91	90
The Philippines	6	4	100	- - -	. . .
Indonesia	2	3	- - -	- - -	- - -
Thailand	-27	-15	- - -	-689	- - -
PRC[b]	2	-1	16	. . .	. . .

SOURCE: Food and Agriculture Organization (F.A.O.), *Production Yearbook, 1974*, (Washington, D.C., 1975). Estimates for the PRC are derived from U.S. Department of Agriculture, Economic Research Service, Foreign Agricultural Report No. 111, *The Agricultural Situation in the People's Republic of China and Other Communist Asian Countries, Review of 1974 and Outlook for 1975*, (Washington, D.C.), pp. 3, 9–10.

NOTE: Countries are listed in decreasing order of their total imports.

[a] - - - is the symbol employed here and throughout all tables to indicate "nil"–Ed.

[b] 1973 only. PRC food-grain statistics include those for potatoes and sweet potatoes at one quarter of their gross weight.

TABLE 7

NET IMPORTS AS PERCENTAGE OF CRUDE-OIL SUPPLY, 1970–73

	1970	1971	1972	1973
Indonesia	-58.9	-54.7	-60.4	-63.4
Malaysia	88.1	64.6	39.3	37.6
ROC	97.6	97.0	...	...
Japan	99.3	99.2	99.5	99.5
Thailand	99.5	99.6	99.7	99.2
Hong Kong	100.0	100.0	100.0	100.0
Singapore	100.0	100.0	100.0	100.0
The Philippines	100.0	100.0	100.0	100.0
ROK	100.0	100.0	100.0	100.0

SOURCES: United Nations, *World Energy Supplies, 1970–73,* series J, no. 18, tables 2 and 7 (New York, 1975), pp. 26–34 and 68–72. For the Republic of China, 1968–69, see U.S. Department of Interior, Bureau of Mines, *Minerals Yearbook, 1970,* vol. 3, pp. 731–33. For 1970–72, see ibid., 1972, vol. 3, pp. 771–74.

NOTE: Countries are arranged in increasing order of imports.

growth. The pattern does not change if we include such agricultural products as rubber, palm oil, and copra.

The record of the last fifteen years shows that the resource-poor economies in the Western Pacific performed noticeably better up to the eve of the oil crisis than the resource-rich countries. ASEAN members (excluding Singapore) are in the latter category. It appears that the rate of economic development depends on how well a nation makes use of all the resources it possesses (especially its human resources) rather than merely on the amount of natural, material resources to be found within its borders. Moreover, a slow-growing raw-material-exporting country may owe its export to its slow growth, which keeps domestic consumption low.

CAPITAL FORMATION AND FOREIGN FINANCING

One of the more obvious ways to determine national growth rates is to find the proportion of current output devoted to capital formation. In the years from 1960 to 1973, there was a substantial and widening difference in this index between the slower-growing Southeast Asian countries (again excluding Singapore) and the faster-growing countries. The ratio of gross *fixed* capital formation to GDP in 1960 was between 8 and 15 percent in Thailand, Malaysia, the Philippines, and Indonesia (see Table 10). During the same year, the corresponding range for Singapore, Taiwan, and South Korea (no data are available for Hong Kong) was only slightly higher—11 to 17 percent. However, by 1973, a pre-oil-crisis boom year for most countries, the ratio had risen to about 18 to 21 percent for the four slower-growing Southeast Asian countries and from 24 percent to well over 30 percent for the faster-growing group (Table 10).

TABLE 8

RESERVES OF SELECTED ENERGY RESOURCES

		Crude Oil[a]		*Coal*[b]	
	Population (Millions) 1975	Total (Millions of Barrels)	Per Capita (Barrels)	Total (Million Metric Tons)	Per Capita (Metric Tons)
Thailand	42.28	10[f]	0.23	. . .	. . .
Malaysia	11.97	2,000[e]	167.0	. . .	. . .
The Philippines	41.83	. . .	. . .	27	0.65
Indonesia	132.22	15,000[e]	113.4	2,123[g]	16.06
ROK	34.02[j]	. . .	. . .	500[k]	14.7
ROC	16.0[i]	18.4[j]	182.5	224[i]	14.0
Japan	111.0[d]	22,714[l]	204.6	7,080[h]	63.8
Burma	30.17	67.8	2.25	. . .	. . .
PRC	935[c]	20,000[e]	21.4	80,000[g]	85.6

SOURCES:

[a]U.S. Department of Interior, Bureau of Mines, *Minerals Yearbook*, vol. 3: *Area Reports International, 1971* (Washington, D.C., 1973), pp. 179, 221, 377, 393, 405, 465, 523, 559, 637, 661, 781, 793, and 1075;

[b]*International Petroleum Encyclopedia, 1974* (Tulsa, Okla.,: Petroleum Publishing Co., 1975), pp. 72–90;

[c]*People's Republic of China, Handbook of Economic Indicators* (Washington, D.C., 1976), p. 1;

[d]Bureau of Statistics, Office of the Prime Minister, *Monthly Statistics of Japan* (Tokyo, Sept. 1976), p. 6;

[e]Office of Economic Research, *Statistical Survey, International Oil Developments* (Washington, D.C., 1976), p. 4;

[f]*Sekiyū kaihatsu kankei shiryō* [Data on Oil Development] (Tokyo: Petroleum Producers Federation, 1974), p. 49;

[g]*Handbook of Economic Statistics* (Washington, D.C., 1976), p. 78;

[h]Bureau of Statistics, Office of the Prime Minister, *Japan Statistical Yearbook, 1973–74* (Tokyo, 1974), p. 163; Also reported as 19,248 million tons (World Power conference, 1968). The latter was cited in Kagaku Gijutsu-chō Shigen Chōsakai, *shōrai no shigen mondai* [Future of Resource Problems] (Tokyo, 1971), p. 36;

[i]Directorate General of Budget, Accounting and Statistics, *Monthly Bulletin of Statistics, the Republic of China* (Taipei) 2, no. 9 (September 1976), p. 5; and Directorate-General of Budget, Accounting and Statistics, *Statistical Yearbook of the Republic of China, 1975* (Taipei), p. 108;

[j]ADB, *Key Indicators*, vol. VII, no. 1 (April 1976): 102.

[k]Also reported as 1,185 million tons (World Power Conference 1968); ibid., p. 36;

[l]Kōzan Sekitankyoku, *Shigen Mondai No Tembō* [Perspective of Resource Problems] (Tokyo: Tsūshō Sangyōshō, 1971), p. 370.

A similar picture emerges from a comparison of the ratio of gross capital formation (fixed capital formation plus change in stock) to GDP (Table 10). In this case, however, because of involuntary accumulation of stocks of exportable primary products that are not saleable in some years, an unusually high ratio may develop occasionally in countries of slow economic growth. This seems to have been the case, for example, in Thailand in 1970 and 1975, in the Philippines in 1975, and in Malaysia in 1974 and 1975. However, the ratio was distinctly higher in the faster-growing countries both in 1975, a recession year in many developed countries, and in 1973, a boom year. In 1975, the

TABLE 9

OUTPUT AND NET EXPORT OF SELECTED METALS AND ORES
(Thousand Metric Tons)

	Output	Net Export	1970	1971	1972	1970–72 Average
Thailand	Iron-ore concentrate		13	24	16	17.7
	Lead concentrate		1	1	2	1.3
	Tin concentrate		22	22	22	22.0
		Tin concentrate	...	...	...	...
		Tin metal	22	22	22	22.0
Malaysia		Tin metal	92	87	90	89.7
East: Sarawak	Iron-ore concentrate		2,516	532	296	1,114.7
West: Peninsular Malaysia	Tin concentrate		74	75	77	75.3
	Bauxite concentrate		1,139	978	1,076	1,064.3
		Tin metal	92	87	90	44.8
		Iron-ore concentrate	4,901	879	371	1,780.3
The Philippines	Iron-ore concentrate		1,166	1,381	1,359	1,302.0
	Copper concentrate		160	189	214	187.6
		Copper	632	815	823	756.7
Indonesia	Tin concentrate		19	20	22	20.3
	Bauxite concentrate		1,229	1,238	1,278	1,248.3
		Tin concentrate	14	18	11	14.3
ROK	Iron-ore concentrate		300	222	207	243.0
	Lead-ore concentrate		11	11	9	10.3
		Iron-ore concentrate	515	421	475	470.3

TABLE 9 (Cont.)

Japan	Iron-ore concentrate	916	826	783	841.7
	Copper-ore concentrate	120	120	112	117.3
	Lead-ore concentrate	64	71	63	66.0
	Tin concentrate	793	788	873	818.0
	Zinc-ore concentrate	280	294	281	285.0
	Iron and Steel	17,539	23,618	21,374	20,843.7

SOURCES: United Nations, *Statistical Yearbook for Asia and the Pacific, 1973* (Bangkok, 1973). Data for Thailand are on pp. 387–95; for Malaysia on pp. 235–60; for the Philippines on pp. 336–44; for Indonesia on pp. 140–49; for Japan on pp. 175–86; and for the Republic of Korea on pp. 211–21.

NOTE: Estimated figures for the PRC, according to Wang Kung-ping, *The People's Republic of China: A New Industrial Power with a Strong Mineral Base* (Washington, D.C.: U.S. Department of Interior, Bureau of Mines, 1975), p. 7; and U.S. Congress, Joint Economic Committee, *China: A Reassessment of the Economy*, 94th Cong., 1st sess., July 10, 1975, p. 647, are as follows:

Output for 1970 of Selected Metals and Ores (Thousand Metric Tons):

Coal	350,000	Lead, refined	100
Crude petroleum	22,000*	Zinc, refined	100
Refined petroleum	21,000	Manganese ore	1,000
Iron ore	44,000	Tungsten, content of concentrate	7
Pig iron	22,000	Antimony	12
Steel ingot	18,000	Tin	20
Rolled steel	14,000	Cement	15,000
Aluminum	130	Salt	15,000
Copper, refined	100		

*Close to 1.6 million barrels a day in 1975, including shale oil.

Exports of Metals (U.S. $ Million):

	1970	1971	1972
Iron and steel	40	65	65
Nonferrous metals	25	45	30

TABLE 10

CAPITAL-FORMATION RATES

	Gross Fixed Capital Formation as Percentage of GDP			Gross Capital Formation as Percentage of GDP				
	1960	1970	1973	1965	1970	1973	1974	1975
Thailand	14.0	26.2	21.1	21.6	29.5	24.3	24.4	25.3
Malaysia	11.0	15.9	15.9 (1971)	...	17.4	16.5	20.5	20.4
The Philippines	15.0	18.0	18.0	21.2	19.9	16.8	19.1	27.3
Indonesia	8.0	14.0	18.0	...	15.5	17.9	19.8	19.8 (1974)
Singapore	13.0 (1961)	33.0	34.0	21.8	36.7	35.3	39.3	39.3 (1974)
Hong Kong	...	20.0	23.0 (1972)	26.9	19.0	21.9	20.5	20.5 (1974)
ROK	11.0	25.0	24.0	12.9	27.3	26.0	28.6	26.0
ROC	17.0	22.0	26.0	23.0	26.1	27.4	38.3	37.0
Japan	23.0	35.0	37.0	33.0	39.0	40.0	38.0	32.0
South Vietnam	8.0	8.0	9.0	12.7	18.7	16.8	14.8	14.8 (1974)
Cambodia	...	...	...	14.6	...	...	...	...
Burma	...	11.3	...	17.9	14.2	8.7	9.0	9.8

SOURCES: United Nations, *Statistical Yearbook, 1975*, pp. 559–612; Economic Planning Council, Republic of China, *Taiwan Statistical Data Book, 1975*, (Taiwan, 1975), pp. 29 and 40; ADB, *Key Indicators*, vol. VII, no. 1 (April 1976): 10; Economic Planning Agency, Japanese Government, *Japanese Economic Indicators*, January 1961, no. 107; January 1966, no. 167; January 1971, no. 227; January 1975, no. 275; January 1976, no. 287.

NOTE: Gross capital formation in the PRC is usually estimated at 20–25 percent of GNP. No data are available for North Vietnam and Laos.

faster-growing countries showed higher ratios (26 percent for the ROK and 37 percent for the ROC) than the slower-moving ones (20 to 27 percent). In 1973, the ratios were 22–35 percent in the faster-growing countries; and 17–24 percent in the slower-growing nations.

A priori, a country that accumulates capital assets slowly does so because funds for capital formation are not readily forthcoming from domestic sources and/or because the inflow of foreign capital is limited. In the case of the slower-growing ASEAN countries, substantial inflows of foreign resources did not prevent lower overall capital-formation rates. The resultant dependence upon foreign financing for capital formation does not appear to be an appropriate or a complete answer to a serious problem.

Table 11 lists the net inflow of foreign resources in the form of (1) private foreign investment; (2) total foreign private capital, which is the sum of item (1) and net private export credit; and (3) grants and loans from foreign governments and multilateral agencies.

Malaysia, the Philippines, and Indonesia were recipients of foreign private investment comparable to corresponding inflows into Singapore, Hong Kong, South Korea, and Taiwan. Indonesia was an especially notable recipient of large private foreign investment, including considerable oil money. Thailand was the principal exception to the strong dependence on foreign financing for capital formation, as measured by these indicators. We can get an even clearer picture of the degree of dependence on foreign financing over and above the needs of capital formation—covering also the financing of current imports and debt servicing—from the sum of items (2) and (3) above, which represents the total inflow of foreign resources.

The last two columns in Table 12 provide a quick comparison of the relative dependence for financing of the two sets of developing market systems in the Western Pacific on private foreign investment and on net total inflow of foreign resources. The higher the figure, the greater is the country's dependence on foreign financing, both in relation to private foreign investment only (column IV) and in relation to the maintenance of all current imports and general economic activity (column V). The figures within the blocked areas are generally higher. Among the four slower-growing economies of Southeast Asia, Thailand was least dependent upon foreign money in both 1973, a boom year, and 1974, a year of economic slowdown. In the faster-growing group, the ROC was the least dependent in both years. Indonesia, the slowest-growing country in Southeast Asia between 1960 and 1973, was the most dependent upon foreign-capital inflow. Malaysia was second. The underlying reason was the smaller proportion of current production that these countries were willing and able to devote to capital formation.

One of the reasons Thailand enjoyed an exceptionally favorable position in this respect was the receipt, in recent years, of foreign-exchange earnings from

TABLE 11

NET INFLOW OF FOREIGN RESOURCES, 1973–74 (Value in U.S. $ Million; Percentages in Terms of GDP)

	1973								
		Net Flow of Private Capital				*Net Flow from Governments and Multi-lateral Agencies*		*Total Net Flow*	
				Net Private Investment					
	GDP	Value	Percentage	Value	Percentage	Value	Percentage	Value	Percentage
Thailand	10,561	148.22	1.4	26.71	0.3	54.28	0.5	202.50	1.9
Malaysia	6,885	144.80	2.1	137.57	2.0	73.78	1.1	218.58	3.2
The Philippines	10,593	2.93	0.03	61.12	0.6	265.1	2.5	268.03	2.5
Indonesia	16,272	557.04	3.4	389.78	2.4	662.92	4.1	1,219.96	7.5
Singapore	4,178	149.79	3.6	105.25	2.5	81.21	1.9	231.00	5.6
Hong Kong	6,022	140.97	2.3	150.75	2.5	159.0	2.6	299.97	5.0
ROK	12,477	331.65	2.6	225.16	1.8	430.26	3.4	761.91	6.1
ROC	10,229	101.14	1.0	60.34	0.6	99.9	1.0	201.04	2.0
North Vietnam	. . .	. . .	. . .	. . .	. . .	. . .	. . .	. . .	. . .
South Vietnam	2,713	−10.44	−0.4	−2.93	−0.1	446.0	16.4	435.56	16.1
Cambodia	626*	−4.28	−0.7	−0.66	−0.1	144.93	23.2	140.65	22.5
Laos	249*	−5.14	−2.1	−1.36	−0.5	75.39	30.3	70.25	28.2
Burma	2,415	16.81	0.7	0.33	0.01	65.89	2.7	82.70	3.4
Thailand	13,253	31.63	0.2	37.80	0.3	105.88	0.8	137.51	1.03
Malaysia	8,734	106.97	1.2	81.63	0.9	116.13	1.32	223.10	2.6
The Philippines	14,172	163.19	1.15	114.17	0.8	164.07	1.15	327.26	2.3
Indonesia	23,701	297.50	1.3	204.13	0.9	740.11	3.1	1,037.61	4.3
Singapore	5,592	65.75	1.2	74.63	1.3	69.26	1.2	135.01	2.4
Hong Kong	6,989	32.90	0.4	73.32	1.04	29.87	0.4	62.77	0.9
ROK	14,142	184.27	1.3	105.38	0.7	378.69	2.6	562.96	3.9
ROC	13,808	213.55	1.5	99.02	0.7	137.2	0.9	350.75	2.5
North Vietnam	3,000*	. . .	. . .	. . .	. . .	. . .	. . .	. . .	. . .
South Vietnam	3,253	3.05	0.09	9.72	0.2	673.86	20.7	676.91	20.8
Cambodia	570*	−0.69	−0.12	1.59	0.3	308.1	54.0	307.42	54.0
Laos	220*	2.99	1.36	1.17	0.5	60.66	27.5	63.65	30.0
Burma	3,088	1.66	0.05	2.37	0.07	63.56	2.05	65.22	2.1

SOURCE: ADB, *Key Indicators,* vol. VII, no. 1 (April 1976): 29–31.

NOTE: Japan is a net capital exporting country. The PRC has had only trade credit, as well as medium-term credit in the form of deferred payments.

*GNP

TABLE 12

FOREIGN-RESOURCES INFLOW IN RELATION TO GROSS CAPITAL FORMATION

	Gross Domestic Capital Formation as Percentage of GDP (I)		*Net Private Foreign Investment as Percentage of GDP (II)*		*Total Inflow of Foreign Resources as Percentage of GDP (III)*		*(II)/(I) (Percentage) (IV)*		*(III)/(I) (Percentage) (V)*	
	1973	1974	1973	1974	1973	1974	1973	1974	1973	1974
Thailand	24.3	24.4	0.3	0.3	1.9	1.03	1.2	1.2	7.8	4.2
Malaysia	16.5	20.5	2.0	0.9	3.2	2.6	12.1	4.4	19.4	12.7
The Philippines	16.8	19.1	0.6	0.8	2.5	2.3	3.6	4.2	14.9	12.0
Indonesia	17.9	19.8	2.4	0.9	7.5	4.3	13.4	4.5	41.9	21.7
Singapore	35.3	39.3	2.5	1.3	5.6	2.4	7.1	3.3	15.9	6.1
Hong Kong	21.9	20.5*	2.5	1.04	5.0	0.9	11.4	5.1*	22.8	4.4*
ROK	26.0	28.6	1.8	0.7	6.1	3.9	6.9	2.4	23.5	13.6
ROC	27.4	38.3	0.6	0.7	2.0	2.5	2.2	1.8	7.3	6.5

SOURCE: Table 11.
*Preliminary figures.

large numbers of U.S. servicemen operating from Thai bases during the Vietnam war. Their removal in 1976 could change the economic pattern. Good prices for Thai primary-product exports in some years also helped. Among the faster-growing countries, the high ratios in column V for Hong Kong in 1973 and South Korea in 1973 and 1974 reflected large trade credits.

FOREIGN-TRADE ORIENTATION, DIRECTIONS OF TRADE, THE DEBT-SERVICE RATIO, AND INTERNATIONAL LIQUIDITY

Foreign-Trade Orientation and Capital Inflow

Although the inflow of foreign resources from other governments or multilateral agencies is partly influenced by politico-strategic considerations, the international flow of private capital, both short- and long-term, is governed by expectations of appropriate returns. In particular, foreign lenders and investors are interested in the prospect of earning and then remitting homeward, when they so desire, dividend and interest income. The attractiveness of any country to foreign capital is critically affected by an evaluation of its attitude toward business, especially foreign business, its ability to earn foreign exchange and meet foreign claims, and its susceptibility to sudden capital flight on a large scale. Without a detailed analysis of the balance of payments and the structure of foreign assets and liabilities of the individual Southeast Asian countries, we can nevertheless appraise their external economic status by looking at a few statistics.

The data employed for this purpose in Table 13 are (1) the ratio of foreign trade to GNP, which serves as an indication of the degree of external orientation of the economy; (2) the foreign-debt-service ratio, which is an indicator of the extent to which export earnings are committed to servicing existing public debts; and (3) the number of months of imports official international reserves can cover, which is a good indicator of the foreign-exchange authorities' ability to meet short-term exigencies with their own resources and, therefore, of their ability to call on foreign commercial credit. The following observations can be made on the basis of these data:

First, on the eve of the oil crisis, Thailand, the Philippines, and Indonesia were all significantly less foreign-trade oriented than South Korea and Taiwan, not to mention Singapore and Hong Kong, whose economic well-being is totally based on external trade. Among slower-growing Southeast Asian nations, Malaysia was also highly trade oriented.

Japan's relatively low trade-to-GNP ratio is especially illuminating. Although Japan's foreign trade is extremely large—75.2 billion current U.S. dollars in 1973 and $113.6 billion in 1975—its GNP is even larger, dwarfing the very high

TABLE 13

INDICATORS OF FOREIGN-TRADE ORIENTATION AND INTERNATIONAL LIQUIDITY

	External Public Debt, Outstanding End of 1974 ($ Million)	Debt-Service Ratio, 1974 (Percentage)	Official International Reserves, End of 1975 ($ Million)	Months of Imports Covered by Official Reserves, 1975	Exports and Imports GNP (Percentage) 1973	1974
Thailand	1,123.1	1.9	1,785	6.5	42.1	42.2
Malaysia	2,189.5	2.4	1,524	5.3	89.8	101.7
The Philippines	1,996.0	5.2	1,360	4.8	38.5	40.5
Indonesia	8,693.2	9.4 (1973)	586	1.5	34.6	50.1
Singapore	641.6	0.7	3,015 (Oct.)	4.4	217.4	267.3*
Hong Kong	22.0	0.01	1,078 (March 1974)	1.9	179.4	186.2*
ROK	6,150.0	10.6	1,550	2.9	65.6	80.8
ROC	2,577.1	1.7	1,169	2.4	89.2	90.5
South Vietnam	291.6	2.8	201 (March)	. . .	22.7	22.7
Cambodia	. . .	52.1 (1972)	. . .	. . .	. . .	. . .
Laos	. . .	. . .		. . .	25.0	24.3
Burma	455.4	28.5 (1973)	134	5.7	11.3	4.6

SOURCES: ADB, *Key Indicators*, vol. VII, no. 1 (April 1976): 33–39; For Singapore's GNP, see Chief Statistician, Dept. of Statistics, *Yearbook of Statistics, Singapore 1975/76* (Singapore, 1976).

NOTE: In 1975 the Exports and Imports:GNP ratios for Malaysia was 90.3 percent; for the Philippines, 37.9 percent; for Singapore, 238.5 percent; and for the ROC, 78.2 percent. For Japan, the ratio of Exports and Imports:GNP in 1973 was 21 percent. The official international reserves at the end of 1975 were $12.8 billion. This was equivalent to 2.6 months of imports.

*GDP is used.

trade volume. The highly developed Japanese economy has an extremely large domestic sector that can both sustain a predominant portion of aggregate demand and supply the goods demanded. A country in which the domestic sector is not developed can neither generate sufficient private demand nor, without the injection of foreign material and human resources, supply sufficient goods to meet demand.

Directions of Trade

Second, in slower-growing countries that are less oriented towards external trade, lagging performance in the domestic sector is also reflected in a relatively small share of intraregional trade. As the figures in Table 14 show, the volume of intraregional imports among ASEAN members was less than that of imports from the United States and Japan both before and since the oil crisis, and also less than that of imports from the EEC countries during the latter period. The volume of intraregional exports, on the other hand, was less than that of exports to Japan both before and since the oil crisis and also to the United States in the latter period. The magnitudes and changes in these trade shares reflect the dependence of the ASEAN members on investments and supplies of industrial goods from Japan and Western nations, their exports of primary products, including oil, and the changing terms of trade since the oil crisis. The significant tilt in foreign trade toward a few industrialized countries is of some concern to those who are suspicious of multinational companies headquartered in those same countries.

With more economic development and the appearance of new industries and consumption patterns, ASEAN members will doubtless trade more with each other and with other developing countries in adjacent areas. The likelihood of such a development will be greater if intraregional, especially interisland, shipping can develop quickly at decreasing cost.

Debt Service and International Liquidity

Countries that have received heavy inflows of foreign capital—such as Indonesia among the slower-growing countries of Southeast Asia or South Korea among the faster-growing countries of East Asia—are more likely than others to be burdened with heavier debt service. In 1974, the debt-service ratio, defined as the ratio of debt-service payments on external public debt to total export of goods and nonfactor services, was 10.6 percent for South Korea. The corresponding ratio for Indonesia was 9.4 percent in 1973. This rose to 13.8 percent in 1976 as a result of serious mismanagement on the part of Pertamina, the government oil monopoly. The debt-service ratio has generally been much lower for the faster-growing countries of Singapore, Hong Kong, and Taiwan than it has for Thailand, Malaysia, and the Philippines,[4] where foreign-capital inflow is a major factor in financing economic growth. This situation emphasizes the need to

TABLE 14

SHARES OF ASEAN MEMBERS, JAPAN, THE UNITED STATES, AND THE EEC IN ASEAN'S TRADE WITH THE WORLD, 1971–73 AND 1974–75

	Share of Total ASEAN Imports from World (Percentage)		*Share of Total ASEAN Exports to World (Percentage)*	
Sources of Imports/ Destinations of Exports	1971–73 Average	1974–75 Average	1971–73 Average	1974–75 Average
Intra-ASEAN	13.5	12.9	18.3	15.8
Japan	25.0	23.6	25.5	28.1
United States	14.9	14.7	17.1	19.5
European Economic Community (EEC)	12.6	15.5	15.3	12.5

SOURCE: Appendix A

expand export earnings and to increase the volume of direct private investment rather than loans so that fixed burdens on the balance of payments are reduced.

One characteristic of the four slower-growing Southeast Asian countries is the large share of their total exports a few commodities make up. In 1973, for example, 46.2 percent of Malaysia's total exports were composed of rubber (34.0 percent) and tin metal and concentrate (12.2 percent).[5] In the Philippines during the same year, logs and lumber, copper concentrate, and sugar were responsible for 19.2 percent, 16.4 percent, and 15.6 percent, respectively, or a total of 51.2 percent, of the country's exports. On a comparable scale, 40.9 percent of Thailand's total exports in 1973 were accounted for by rice (11.2 percent), corn (9.2 percent), rubber (14.2 percent), and tin (6.3 percent, both metal and concentrate). In Indonesia, wood and rubber were responsible for 17.9 percent and 12.2 percent of total exports, respectively—with crude oil and petroleum products accounting for another 51.1 percent. Following the phenomenal rise of petroleum prices since the last quarter of 1973, the potential plight of exporters of other primary products may be underestimated. Some products are inherently susceptible to large price fluctuations. Furthermore, demand for them has been adversely affected by the worldwide recession to which the sharp increase in oil prices contributed significantly. The price data in Table 15 illustrate this situation.

The same situation can be examined from the perspective of the overall terms of trade. The variations in 1973 and 1974, with 1970 as base, are noted in Table 16.

Primary-product prices were much higher in 1973 and 1974, benefiting such exporting countries as Malaysia, the Philippines, and Thailand and, in the case of petroleum, especially Indonesia. The GDP growth rates of these countries increased, but their terms of trade were adversely affected by the simultaneous

TABLE 15

PRICE INDICES OF SELECTED PRIMARY EXPORT COMMODITIES
(1972 = 100)

	1973	1974	1975
Rice	232	360	240
Corn	174	235	213
Sugar	115	331	271
Copra	251	471	183
Palm oil	173	307	198
Rubber	195	214	164
Logs	194	177	166
Tin	128	218	182
Copper	165	191	115
Petroleum	142	514	565

SOURCE: International Bank for Reconstruction and Development (IBRD), *World Economic Indicators,* March 2, 1976, quoted in ADB, *Key Indicators,* vol. VII, no. 1 (April 1976): 27. The figures have been converted from the original 1967–69 base to a 1972 base.

TABLE 16

TERMS OF TRADE
(1970 = 100)

	1973	1974
Thailand	121.3	100.6
Malaysia	87.0	84.0
The Philippines	90.3	96.9
Indonesia	. . .	. . .
Singapore	106.0	104.8
Hong Kong	106.7	102.9
ROK	93.6	76.2
ROC	91.6	86.5

SOURCE: ADB, *Key Indicators,* vol. VII, no. 1 (April 1976): 28. The terms of trade are defined as the percentage unit-value index of exports to unit-value index of imports.

price increases of imported manufactures. Hence to minimize price fluctuations, as well as the effects of adverse changes in the terms of trade, expansion of exports must be accompanied by an increase in the share of manufactures. This requires long-term readjustments of the economic structure by sector, assuming that the infrastructure is adequate for sectoral changes. To expand the manufacturing sector, plus the infrastructure where necessary, the inflow of foreign capital and the rate of capital formation as a whole must be raised. Foreign loans and grants are probably needed for the expansion of the infrastructure, while foreign private direct investment may be the ideal method to expand the manufacturing industry.

FOREIGN INVESTMENT AND EXPORT EXPANSION

In the initial years of a country's economic development, export expansion in new manufactures is likely to benefit greatly if foreign investors are themselves directly involved in selling their own products outside the host countries. Where foreign investors have entered a country for the purpose of lowering their cost of production below the levels in their own countries, sale of products in the investors' home markets presents little problem.[6] Some investors may also seek to sell the products in third-country markets. This was the case with United States and Japanese investors in Taiwan, South Korea, and Hong Kong during the last decade. In the early 1970s the same situation was occurring increasingly in Thailand, Malaysia, Indonesia, and the Philippines. Exports from the manufacturing sector will expand more rapidly in Southeast Asia if foreign direct investment grows at a faster rate.

Although full information on direct private foreign investment is not available for all Southeast Asian countries over a large number of years, a high positive correlation is indicated between the growth of such investment and exports. Figures A-1 – A-4 in Appendix A are scatter diagrams that show the increase in annual exports in recent years, together with the corresponding rise of private direct investment (measured in cumulative values) for Thailand, the Philippines, Malaysia, and Indonesia.[7] A more complete data series is available for Taiwan. Figure A-5 gives evidence for a strong correlation between the growth of private direct foreign investment and Taiwan's exports. Foreign investors in Taiwan accounted for a major portion of exports, so the strong correlation was in fact an indication of causation. We are probably justified in assuming that the same would be true for Thailand, Malaysia, Indonesia, and the Philippines, and that an increase in private direct foreign investment would be, under present conditions, a precondition for any large increase in exports in the short run.

LABOR PRODUCTIVITY AND THE SUPPLY OF SKILLED LABOR

Financial resources, international market connections, and the availability of equipment and raw materials are not the only indispensable factors in economic development. The human element is, perhaps, even more critical. If labor-intensive projects dominate the expanding sectors of an economy in the early phase of its development, a supply of willing and reliable workers is essential. The health and literacy of these workers are important considerations.

As the economy develops further and production shifts toward industries requiring greater skills, a steady supply of skilled labor, including both technicians and managerial personnel, becomes increasingly important. Such a supply depends on the nature and distribution of educational opportunities and the response of the young to available opportunities.

Table 17 presents four sets of indicators of public health. Infant mortality rates are included because a high rate could conceivably affect the supply of female labor. Inadequate public-health facilities probably imply higher absenteeism and lower productivity. The slower-developing countries of Southeast Asia were found to be in a far worse condition than the faster-growing countries of East Asia and Singapore, although life expectancy was low only in Indonesia. The exceptions (see the figures blocked off in Table 17) are South Korea (ROK) in the latter group and the Philippines in the former, in the categories of persons per hospital bed and per physician, and Malaysia, in the category of persons per hospital bed.

Table 18 presents three indicators of the state of education. Perhaps the most serious disadvantage suffered by the slower-growing Southeast Asian countries is a low enrollment ratio in secondary schools; students in this age group are the primary source of supply for future skilled workers and technicians. This is most noticeable in Thailand and Indonesia, but Malaysia also has a low literacy rate and should be counted among these nations.

To the extent that foreign capital and technology are not forthcoming in adequate quantities, the rates of economic growth and export expansion are likely to be affected immediately, and to the extent that the supply of skilled workers and technicians cannot be assured in the future, continuation of economic growth and a shift away from highly labor-intensive production will be threatened sooner or later. Mutatis mutandis, what is said of skilled workers, technicians, and junior managerial staff also applies to middle- and higher-level engineers and executives, as well as entrepreneurs of modern businesses.

CONDITIONS FOR CONTINUED GROWTH

Virtually all the slower-growing countries of Southeast Asia were doing better in the early 1970s than in the 1960s. As Table 19 shows, their real-GDP growth rates all peaked in 1973. Unsettled domestic political conditions in the early 1960s were major reasons for the poor earlier performances, especially in Indonesia (before September 1965) and the Philippines (before 1971). However, changing prices for a few primary products were equally responsible for the varying fortunes. Good prices accounted for the high growth rates in 1973, but the boom was not to last. To reduce fluctuations and to resume and sustain growth at a higher level, certain underlying conditions must be changed for the better.[8] The following must be achieved: fuller use of available domestic resources, a higher rate of effective capital formation,[9] a larger and steadier inflow of foreign

TABLE 17

INDICATORS OF PUBLIC HEALTH

		Life Expectancy (Years)		*Infant Mortality*		*Persons per Hospital Bed*		*Persons Per Physician*	
		Male	Female	(Per 1,000 Live Births)					
Thailand	1967	64.8	66.9	1972	27	1973	1,345	1973	8,522
Malaysia	1972	63.4*	68.0*	1972	38*	1973	344	1973	4,573
The Philippines	1970–75	60.0		1972	68	1973	785	1972	1,157
Indonesia	1960	47.5		1962	125	1971	1,452	1971	25,847
Singapore	1970	65.1	70.0	1974	17	1974	282	1974	1,400
Hong Kong	1971	67.4	75.0	1974	17	1974	249	1974	1,560
ROK	1970	63.0	67.0	Not specified	41	1972	1,987	1973	3,013
ROC	1973	66.7	72.2	1973	14	1973	563	1973	1,702

SOURCE: ADB, *Key Indicators*, vol. VII, no. 1 (April 1976): 4.

*West Malaysia only

TABLE 18

INDICATORS OF THE STATE OF EDUCATION

	Primary-School Enrollment Ratio[a] (Percentage of School-Age Population)		*Secondary-School* Enrollment Ratio[a] (Percentage of School-Age Population)		*Literacy Rate* (Percentage of Population)	
Thailand	1968	81	1968	13	1970	79
Malaysia	1974	94	1974	39	1970	61[b]
The Philippines	1971–72	86	1967	42	1972	83
Indonesia	1970	71	1970	12	1971	60
Singapore	1974	69	1974	62	1974	76
Hong Kong	1971	85	1970	46	1971	83
ROK	1970	84	1970	41	1970	88
ROC	1975	99	1972–73	61	1974	87

SOURCE: ADB, *Key Indicators*, vol. VII, no. 1 (April 1976):5.

[a]The age groups on which the ratios are based vary from country to country.

[b]West Malaysia.

TABLE 19

ANNUAL REAL GDP GROWTH RATES, 1970–75

	Country	1970	1971	1972	1973	1974	1975
Southeast Asian market economies	Thailand	7.3	6.9	4.2	10.5	3.2	6.4
	Malaysia	. . .	6.2	5.8	13.3	7.7	0.5
	The Philippines	6.0	5.9	4.8	9.2	5.0	5.7
	Indonesia	7.6	7.0	8.3	11.3	7.4	. . .
Other Asian market economies in the western Pacific	Singapore	13.7	12.5	13.4	11.4	6.2	4.2
	Hong Kong	5.7	3.3	7.2	13.7	0.8	. . .
	ROK	8.6	9.8	7.3	16.9	8.7	8.0
	ROC[a]	10.9	11.5	11.9	12.0	0.6	2.0
	Japan	10.9	7.3	9.0	10.9	−1.2	3.6
Southeast Asian nonmarket economies	South Vietnam	7.8	3.8	2.0	2.8	−2.0	. . .
	Cambodia	−9.5	−8.0	−2.3	−18.9	−5.3	. . .
	Laos	4.9	3.9	3.9	−1.2	1.7	. . .
	Burma	5.0	4.1	2.4	−0.4	4.5	3.5
PRC		. . .	. . .	10.6	3.9	5.8	

SOURCES: ADB, *Key Indicators*, vol. VII, no. 1 (April 1976): 8; *United Nations Statistical Yearbook, 1974*; the *World Bank Atlas*, 1975; *Finance and Development*, 1975; Dept. of Economic and Social Affairs, Statistical Office of the United Nations, *Yearbook of National Accounts Statistics, 1975*, vol. I: *Individual Data*, (New York: United Nations, 1976), p. 775.

NOTES: The GDP real growth rates have the following bases:

Burma, 1969–70 (fiscal year)
Cambodia, GNP, 1960
ROC, 1971
Hong Kong, 1966
Indonesia, 1960 and 1973 (new series)
ROK, 1970
Laos, GNP, 1964
Malaysia, 1970
The Philippines, 1967
Singapore, 1968
South Vietnam, 1960
Thailand, 1962
Japan, 1970

The real GDP growth rate of the PRC was estimated at 10.6 percent in 1972, 3.9 percent in 1973, and 5.8 percent in 1974.

[a]The preliminary estimate of Taiwan's GDP growth rate in 1976 is slightly over 10 percent.

capital, greater emphasis on the manufacturing sector, a stronger orientation toward exports, and a policy covering employment and development of human resources consistent with these goals. Chapters 2 and 3 will examine how well and rationally, or how poorly and perversely, the Southeast Asian countries have answered these questions in the past with respect to a major component of their domestic capital, enterprise, and manpower, the ethnic Chinese.

2

Effective Use of Domestic and Foreign Resources: The Chinese Dimension

We suggested in the preceding chapter that lack of effectiveness in the use of domestic resources has been an important factor in the relatively sluggish economic growth of several Southeast Asian countries. This has accentuated their dependence upon the inflow of foreign capital, which, given the need to service past foreign credits and direct investments, never seems to be sufficient. Besides, foreign resources are not always a perfect substitute for domestic effort because effective use of the former depends upon adequate support from the latter.

In these circumstances, a natural question is whether large portions of domestic natural and human resources have not been used to the best advantage—specifically ethnic-Chinese capital, labor, and entrepreneurship. Are these elements of significant magnitude to merit attention? How effectively have they been harnessed in the interest of economic development?

THE MAGNITUDE OF ETHNIC-CHINESE ENTERPRISES

Some Preliminary Indications

The importance of Chinese enterprise to the future economic development of Southeast Asia can be gauged on two levels: (1) domestic capital accumulation and (2) the supply of skilled labor, technicians, management, and entrepreneurship. Before going into detail it will be useful to review the traditional perception of the role of ethnic Chinese in the national economies of Southeast Asia. This popular impression of the scope of Chinese business interest in the area is incomplete, and for that reason somewhat misleading.

Consider first such accounts of Chinese enterprise in Southeast Asia as that in the June 1, 1974, issue of *The Economist*.[1] It states: "Fourteen million Overseas Chinese are the most formidable economic power in Asia outside Japan.

85 percent of them were born in the countries in which they now live. They have no territory of their own except in Singapore, but they are united across many borders by a common language, culture and heritage. They operate economically rather like a huge multi-national corporation with its own conduct."

The position of the Chinese in individual Southeast Asian economies has been characterized in other sources in various ways, as the next few paragraphs show.

Singapore

According to Louis Kraar writing in *Fortune,*[2] the entrepôt trade of Singapore, where Chinese constitute three quarters of the population, is exclusively in their hands. Since the end of Sukarno's "confrontation" and the establishment of greater stability under Suharto, the Chinese are again investing in Indonesia from their Singapore base. Trade between Indonesia and Singapore has reached very large proportions and the Chinese are responsible for approximately 80 percent of it, as well as for the same proportion of trade between Malaysia and Singapore.

Malaysia

In 1970, Chinese enterprises accounted for 22.5 percent of the outstanding stocks of limited companies in West Malaysia, compared with 1.9 percent for Malays, 60.7 percent for foreigners, and 14.9 percent for other Malaysian residents, including the Malaysian federal and state governments and statutory bodies. In terms of fixed assets owned by corporations in the modern industrial sector, the relative distribution, as shown below, gave the Chinese 26.2 percent, the Malays 0.9 percent, foreigners 57.2 percent, Indians 0.1 percent, and other residents 15.6 percent.[3] In addition, the Chinese, who constitute 36 percent of the population, are said to control 85 percent of retail trade.[4] Malaysian government sources have stated that 90 percent of the Malaysian economy was controlled by the Chinese at the beginning of this decade.[5]

Indonesia

Here it is reported that the Chinese control well over 50 percent of wholesale trade.[6] They may hold the same proportion of retail trade, although Chinese businessmen are now barred from retailing in rural areas. Chinese entrepreneurs are said to be frequently in partnership with high government officials and military personnel, and both sides have reportedly prospered through the alliance.[7]

The Philippines

Although Chinese constitute only 2 percent of the population of the Philippines, *The Economist* has reported that only the same small percentage of the country's business can claim to have no Chinese connection whatsoever.[8] This report is probably exaggerated. According to S. C. Liao's study on capital investment in the Philippines, 26.5 percent of all investment between 1945 and mid-1956 was of Chinese origin. The corresponding figure for investment by Filipinos was 69 percent.[9] In Liao's view, in spite of a nearly 50 percent increase during this period in the amount of Chinese investment in the Philippines, the relative position of the Chinese had declined. In 1955, however, Chinese business enterprises were still responsible for 16 percent of nonagricultural employment, excluding the professions, the service sector, and government employment.

Thailand

The Chinese in Thailand are well assimilated. Persons of ethnic-Chinese origin control the large banks and the principal exports of the country—rice, tea, rubber and timber—and appear to dominate the areas of distribution and manufacturing. More than 79 percent of students at the Chulalongkorn and Tammasat Universities—the two most prestigious national institutions—are Chinese or of mixed, part-Chinese parentage. Because of the thorough assimilation, many high government officials and politicians are also of Chinese descent.

Chinese versus Foreign Capital

A more comprehensive overview can be obtained from an estimate of ethnic-Chinese capital in Southeast Asia. (For our purpose, the term ethnic Chinese includes both those who regard themselves as Chinese and those who are regarded by others in their respective societies as Chinese. Capital includes productive capital only, excluding personal effects and residential housing.) A number of such estimates with varying coverages have been made at different times (see Table 20). One of the most recent is that of Ho I-wu (Table 21), which gives a total of $3,159 million for the ASEAN members and $3,820 for all Southeast Asia, including Burma and the Indochina states; it was made in 1969 on the basis of a survey supplemented by data from the individual countries. Two earlier estimates by Fukuda (1930) and Callis (1937) also deserve attention.

Ho's estimate, when adjusted to correct some of the more obvious undervaluations, provides us with a basis from which an estimate can be derived for 1975 for the ASEAN countries. The details of this forward projection are presented in Appendix B. There are three principal adjustments. First, Ho's estimate for Malaysia is replaced by an alternative estimate for 1975 based on the Third Malaysian Plan (1976–80). Second, his estimate for the Philippines seems to have grossly understated Chinese-owned stock in the commercial sector. An alternative figure for the 1969 baseline capital stock has been provided. Third, a more recent estimate (1972), derived from private Thai banking circles, is available for Chinese-owned capital stock in Thailand. The baseline figures for

TABLE 20

SELECTED ESTIMATES OF CHINESE CAPITAL IN SOUTHEAST ASIA
(Current U.S. $)

	Vietnam	Cambodia	Laos	Thailand	Malaysia and Singapore	The Philippines	Indonesia	Burma	Total
Shōzō Fukuda (1930)	126.9	...	...	251.3	264	101.3	333.3	...	1,077.4
H. G. Callis (1937)	80	...	...	100	200	100	150	14	644
China Yearbook (1948)	0.5	...	...	212.8	1,761.3	...	550.3	100.5	2,625.4
Wu Ku (1960)	150	...	...	600	1,200	400	900	70	3,320
Yu Chung-hsün (1968)	80	...	...	700	1,200	500	400	50	2,930
Ho I-wu (1969)	430	55	40.1	412	1,470	573.5	704	135	3,819.6

SOURCES: Shōzō Fukuda, *Kakyō keizai ron* [Treatise on Overseas Chinese Economy] (Tokyo: Ganshōdō, 1940), p. 101; Helmut G. Callis, *Foreign Capital in Southeast Asia* (New York: Institute of Pacific Relations, 1942), pp. 8, 21, 57, 69, 85, and 96: *Chung-hua nien-chien, 1948* [China Yearbook] (Nanking: Chun-hua nien-chien she, 1948), pp. 1915–1923; Naosaku Uchida, *Tōnan ajia no kakyō*] Overseas Chinese in Southeast Asia], p. 116, quoted in Yu Chung-hsun,*Kakyo keizai no kenkyū* [A study on Overseas Chinese Economy] (Tokyo: Ajia keizai kenkyūjo, 1969); Wu Ku, *Tang-ch'ien Tung-nan-ya hua-ch'iao tsai-ching chih ku-chi* [An Estimate of Overseas Chinese Capital Investment in Southeast Asia] (Hong Kong: Ching-chi tao-pao, 1960), no. 657, p. 11; Yu Chung-hsun, *Kakyō keizai no kenkyū*, p. 173; Ho I-wu, *Hua-ch'iao ching-chi yen-chiu*] A Study on Overseas Chinese Economy] (Taipei: Overseas Chinese Affairs Commission, 1966, pp. 49–50.

NOTE: In addition to the above, an estimate by W. E. Willmott in *The Chinese in Cambodia* (Vancouver, Canada: University of British Columbia, 1967) placed the figure for Cambodia at $200–400 million. For the Philippines a 1955 estimate by Huang Ming-teh gave a total of $750 million—considerably higher than the other estimates.

TABLE 21

TOTAL CHINESE CAPITAL INVESTMENT IN SOUTHEAST ASIA, 1969
(Value in U.S. $ Million)

	Thailand		*Malaysia*		*The Philippines*		*Indonesia*		*Singapore*		*South Vietnam*		*Cambodia*		*Burma*	
	Value	Per-centage	Value	Per-centage	Value	Per-centage	Value	Per-centage	Value	Per-centage	Value	Per-centage	Value	Per-centage	Value	Per-centage
Primary	73.0	17.7	250.0	35.7	10.0	1.7	---	---	70.0	9.0	100.0	23.3	5.0	9.1	---	---
Secondary	125.0	30.3	150.0	21.4	288.7	50.4	230.0	32.7	200.0	26.0	150.0	34.8	10.0	18.2	50.0	37.0
Tertiary	214.0	52.0	300.0	42.9	274.7	47.9	474.0	67.3	500.0	65.0	180.0	41.9	40.0	72.7	85.0	63.0
Total	412.0	100.0	700.0	100.0	573.4[a]	100.0	704.0	100.0	770.0	100.0	430.0	100.0	55.0	100.0	135.0	100.0

	Total ASEAN		*Total Southeast Asia*	
	Value	Per-centage	Value	Per-centage
Primary	403.0	12.76	508.0	13.44
Secondary	993.7	31.45	1,203.7	31.85
Tertiary	1,762.7	55.79	2,067.7	54.71
Total	3,159.4	100.0	3,779.4	100.0

SOURCE: See Table 2 (estimates made by Ho I-wu.)

[a]The figure for the Philippines includes as Chinese only those who are not citizens.

individual countries have been projected forward to 1975 on the assumption that the initial Chinese-owned capital stock was augmented between 1970 and 1975, through reinvestment at rates commensurate with the known Chinese propensity to invest and with rising income during this period. The result is shown in Table 22.

The magnitudes involved cannot be appreciated without a consideration of foreign direct investments in the five Southeast Asian countries, plus Hong Kong, Taiwan, and South Korea, during the last two decades or so (see Table 23). The components, which are of different dates, yield a cumulative total of about U.S. $10 billion by the mid-1970s in noncommunist East and Southeast Asia. The amount for the ASEAN member countries alone is no more than $7.8 billion, and if Singapore is excluded, the total value of foreign direct investment in the remaining four ASEAN countries drops to $6.4 billion in an area with ethnic-Chinese capital of $11.7 billion. Although additional foreign investments had been greater in these countries in earlier years, and there has been an especially large recent influx of Japanese investment,[10] Chinese investment in Southeast Asia definitely constitutes a substantial proportion of the region's entire capital. This would have been true even if we had had to rely solely on the $3.8 billion figure Ho gave for 1969.

Chinese Human Resources

The importance of ethnic-Chinese human resources to the economic development of Southeast Asia is equally inescapable. In Thailand, for example, there were more ethnic Chinese than ethnic Thais in the mid-high- and mid-low-status segments of the labor force: 52.5 percent Chinese versus 47.5 percent Thais in the first category and 72.2 percent Chinese versus 27.8 percent Thais in the second. In contrast, there were more than twice as many Thais as there were Chinese in the highest segment of the labor force—65.5 percent and 34.5 percent respectively—and slightly more ethnic Thais than Chinese in the lowest segment—50.9 percent versus 49.1 percent.[11] Chinese form a large segment of

TABLE 22

Ethnic-Chinese Capital, End of 1975
(U.S. $ Billion)

Singapore	4.6
Thailand	3.7
Malaysia	3.7
Indonesia	2.6
The Philippines	2.0
Total	16.6

TABLE 23

DISTRIBUTION OF CUMULATIVE FOREIGN DIRECT INVESTMENT IN SELECTED COUNTRIES BY COUNTRY OF INVESTOR
(Percentage)

Country	Date and Coverage	U.S. Capital	Japanese Capital	Other	Total	Total Value (U.S. $ Million)
Thailand	1960 to March 31, 1975; "Promoted Investments" less withdrawals	14.5	41.7	43.8	100.0	186.1
The Philippines	Feb. 21, 1970, to Dec. 31, 1975; amount committed.	44.0	23.9	32.1	100.0	493.0
Indonesia	Jan. 1967 to March 31, 1976; includes investment in oil	19.0	41.5	39.5	100.0	5,047.8
Malaysia	Cumulative to 1975	...	...	...	100.0	730.0
Singapore	End of 1975; gross fixed assets in manufacturing	33.7	11.4	54.9	100.0	1,366.7
Hong Kong	To end of 1974; manufacturing only	44.2	19.2	36.6	100.0	320.5
ROK	To end of March 1973	36.8	55.9	7.3	100.0	458.4
ROC	1952–75 inclusive	33.4	17.2	49.4	100.0	1,405.2
Total ASEAN		...	...	...	100.0	7,823.6
Grand Total		...	...	...	100.0	10,007.7

SOURCES: The above data are derived from official statistics contained in releases of the Department of Commerce and Industry, Hong Kong; the Economic Development Board, Singapore; the Ministry of Economic Affairs, Republic of China; the Economic Planning Board, Investment Promotion Office, Republic of Korea; the Central Bank of the Philippines; the Board of Investments, Indonesia (adjusted for withdrawals); the Board of Investment, Thailand; and the Federal Industrial Development Authority, Malaysia. Note that some of the foreign-investment data include investments by ethnic Chinese who are foreign nationals that have entered the individual countries as foreign investments.

the middle class of business entrepreneurs, technical and managerial personnel, and skilled workers.

While Malays hold the political and policymaking positions within the federal government in Malaysia, there was a majority of Chinese in the technical and professional services in the 1960s, as the figures in Table 24 illustrate.

Many more Chinese than Malays are enrolled in engineering and the physical and biological sciences at the college level (see Table 25). Chinese have been drawn to those fields where they can more readily survive without political power or backing. The same distribution for today's college students will tend to perpetuate this condition in the future.

Less detailed information is available on the relative importance of ethnic Chinese in the total labor force in different occupations and on different levels of

TABLE 24

NUMBER OF SENIOR MEMBERS IN GOVERNMENT SERVICE IN WEST MALAYSIA, 1962

	Civil Service	Medical Service	Educational Service
Malay	219	78	74
Chinese	17	347	131

	Technical and Professional	
	Scientific Background	Nonscientific Background
Malay	183	115
Chinese	539	176

SOURCE: Robert O. Tilman, *Bureaucratic Transition in Malaya* (Durham, N.C.: Duke University Press, 1964), pp. 70–75.

TABLE 25

DISTRIBUTION OF STUDENTS AT THE UNIVERSITY OF MALAYA, 1971–72, BY FACULTY AND RACE
(Percentage)

Faculty	Malays	Chinese	Indians	Others	Total
Arts	69.33	20.21	9.06	1.40	100.00
Economics and administration	40.15	45.85	12.70	1.22	100.00
Education	35.31	50.77	12.78	1.14	100.00
Pre-Engineering	6.12	89.52	3.94	0.44	100.00
Engineering	2.33	90.69	2.33	4.65	100.00
Agriculture	38.98	53.01	7.83	0.28	100.00
Medicine	24.01	62.53	11.92	1.54	100.00
Sciences	10.24	81.43	7.44	0.21	100.00

SOURCE: University of Malaya, *Annual Report 1971–72* (Kuala Lumpur: Economy Printers, 1973). Totals may not add to 100 due to rounding.

employment. In the industrial labor forces of all Southeast Asian countries except Singapore, however, ethnic Chinese are rarely found below the level of floor foreman, and their wages are accordingly much higher than those of workers native to those countries—a situation that is readily observable.

In terms of employment by industry, Table 26 shows that, in general, the proportion of ethnic Chinese employed in the secondary and tertiary industries in Southeast Asia is far larger than the proportion of workers in the labor force as a whole. Within ASEAN the only significant exception is Singapore, probably as a result of the presence of large numbers of non-Chinese personnel (many of them Western) in the foreign-trade and service industries.

It would be most difficult to replace the ethnic Chinese in the labor force—not to mention ethnic-Chinese capital—in the economic life of Southeast Asia. In practice, the functions of the Chinese entrepreneur and technician and those of the Chinese rentier, or supplier of capital, are inseparable. Attempts to dislodge the Chinese from certain fields of employment cannot fail to disrupt the operation of Chinese capital.

SOUTHEAST ASIAN POLICIES TOWARD ETHNIC-CHINESE BUSINESS AND LABOR

In view of these considerations, what would be the most logical policy for a Southeast Asian government intent on rapid economic development? Given the amount of ethnic-Chinese capital in Southeast Asia and the key part Chinese workers, professionals, and entrepreneurs play in the economy, as well as the importance of Chinese material and human resources as essential domestic resources in the countries in question, the answer is obvious. First, production through the use of these resources should be maximized. Second, the less productive segments of the economy should be induced to increase their productivity. Third, ways should be found for the more productive segments to aid the less productive so that the existing disparity between them will be gradually reduced. However, this last goal must not be achieved in a way that has an adverse effect on attainment of the first objective: if the two are in conflict, a solution can be reached only by appealing to the values of the society and to the principles of the political authorities, which presumably reflect the value system. We shall now see how the Southeast Asian countries have in fact dealt with this aspect of their development.

Indigenization

In the contemporary American scene, the term affirmative action means the use of legislative, administrative, and political measures to improve the

TABLE 26

DISTRIBUTION OF THE OVERALL LABOR FORCE AND OF CHINESE EMPLOYMENT

	Thailand		The Philippines		Indonesia		Malaysia		Singapore		Hong Kong		Burma	
	1969	(1957)	1972	(1957)	1971	(1940)	1975	(1975)	1975	(1973)	1971	(1971)	1973	(. . .)
Primary	78.1	(8.0)	54.2	(–)	60.5	(30.8)	59.2	(26.4)	0.5	(0.4)	4.0	(4.0)	66.3	(. . .)
Secondary	4.6	(22.0)	11.1	(11.5)	22.2[a]	(20.0)	15.2	(32.1)	35.1	(45.3)	48.0	(53.9)	7.0	(. . .)
Tertiary	17.3)	(70.0)	34.6	(88.5)	17.2	(49.2)	25.6	(41.5)	64.4	(54.2)	48.0	(42.1)	26.7	(. . .)
Total	100.0	(100.0)	100.0[b]	(100.0)	100.0[b]	(100.0)	100.0	(100.0)	100.0	(100.0)[b]	100.0	(100.0)	(100.0)	(. . .)

SOURCES: ADB, *Key Indicators,* vol. V, no. 2 (October 1974): 5; Singapore Chief Statistician, Dept. of Statistics, *Yearbook of Statistics, Singapore 1973/74,* pp. 27 and 28; Hong Kong, Dept. of Census and Statistics, *Hong Kong Social and Economic Trends, 1968–72* (Hong Kong, 1973), p. 18; Naikaku Kambō Chōsashitsu, *Tōnan Ajia yōran, 1974* (Tokyo), pp. 8–26.

NOTES: The Chinese employment figures and years of data are given in parentheses.

[a]The Indonesian manufacturing sector accounts for 7.5 percent of the labor force.

[b]Components to not add up to 100 because of rounding.

economic and overall social position of racial minorities in relation to the rest of the society. The measures employed can be, and are, both positive and negative. Among positive measures are special programs of education, job training, and easy credit. Examples of negative measures are such practices as setting special quotas for members of specified minorities and lowering standards in dispensing scarce goods and opportunities to favored groups. In the latter case, since the resources or opportunities available are limited, reserving a portion for one group larger than it would receive without such intervention discriminates against other groups not so favored.

What the authorities in the Southeast Asian countries (excluding Singapore) have done since World War II—and even before that—can be described as standing the U.S. type of affirmative action on its head. In varying degrees, ethnic-Chinese minorities have been the target of discriminatory legislative, administrative, and political measures aimed at the betterment of the economic position of the majority indigenous races. In the United States, since the cost of the policy is borne, in the first instance at any rate, mostly by the majority, the economic burden on it is relatively small. Since the reverse is true in Southeast Asia, the burden of this policy on the Chinese minority is severe. The relevant question in the present context is how such a policy has prevented the effective use of available domestic resources in furthering economic growth.

Generally speaking, restrictive measures directed against the ethnic Chinese can be divided into five categories:

1. Outright exclusion from certain specified industries and occupations;
2. Transfer, under government decree, of specified proportions of equity in existing Chinese businesses to indigenous stockholders as partners;
3. Sharing of control of existing Chinese enterprises with new indigenous directors and managers;
4. Setting of smaller quotas for the ethnic Chinese or their businesses in issuing business licenses, allocating foreign exchange to importers where there is exchange control, admitting students to universities and professional schools, accepting applications for government and private jobs, and so on; and
5. Imposing special obligations on Chinese firms in terms of deposit requirements for various purposes, supplying of funds to indigenous buyers for the acquisition of equity in Chinese-owned businesses, training of indigenous workers and managerial personnel (the latter sometimes to assume control of the very same enterprises), and so on. The restrictive measures against the Chinese are supplemented by positive support of indigenous businesses or potential businessmen, mostly by providing special credit facilities and larger quotas of various kinds.

The following are some examples of measures from each of the preceding categories (for details see Appendix C). The list is by no means exhaustive.

1. *Exclusion*: A 1957 Indonesian decree excluding alien Chinese from fifteen industries, mostly in light manufacturing; the November 1959 Indonesian Government Regulation No. 10 excluding alien Chinese from retailing in rural areas below the regency level; the 1954 Philippine Republic Act No. 1180 providing for the Filipinization of alien retail establishments; exclusion of alien Chinese in Thailand from specified occupations.
2. *Transfer of Equity*: Measures requiring transfer of 50 percent of the equity of nonindigenous-owned firms in the fifteen specified industries in Indonesia referred to under "Exclusion" to indigenous (*Pribumi*) owners, and of varying proportions of alien-owned firms to Malaysians and from nonindigenous Malaysians to indigenous Malaysians (that is, *Bumiputras*).
3. *Sharing of Control*: The 1950 *Benteng* program of Indonesia giving favorable foreign-exchange allocations only to firms under predominantly indigenous Indonesian management—generally applied in all those cases in category (2).
4. *Quota Setting*: Most common in Malaysia, but also part of the *Benteng* program in Indonesia; Philippine foreign-exchange allocation to importers from 1949 to 1962.
5. *Special Requirements and Treatment*: Existing in many forms in four ASEAN countries (not Singapore).

Examples of special credit facilities for the establishment of new enterprises or the acquisition of existing Chinese enterprises by new indigenous owners can be found in Malaysia, the Philippines, and Indonesia. (There is no such special treatment in Thailand.)

Some Economic Consequences

What are the important economic consequences when such restrictive measures are applied to an ethnic minority like the Chinese?

First, when long-established enterprises are ousted from certain industries in which they are presumably more efficient (1) than they would be elsewhere and (2) than their inexperienced replacements, the short-run effects are bound to be adverse. Businesses forced to move into a different industry are likely to suffer a net loss of output, assuming that they succeed in making the change, and new entrants are likely to be less productive, if they can be found. Changes of this kind obviously lead to a reduction of total output in the economy.

Second, if the effort to replace ethnic Chinese workers and enterprises by indigenous ones fails to provide 100 percent replacement within a reasonably short time, other industries that supply or buy from the industries and enterprises affected will in turn suffer from dislocation. This is an example of adverse economic impact through both forward and backward linkages. The special and very large role played by Chinese enterprises in distribution and transportation assures a large adverse economic impact when it is accompanied by only partially successful replacement efforts.

Third, where a decline in total output occurs in an important sector and is followed by a wider dislocation for some time, the fall in income will affect aggregate demand and the entire domestic market.

Fourth, insofar as ethnic-Chinese businesses suffer either a complete loss of income or reduced income because of the higher costs and lower revenues, their ability to save will decline. Their indigenous replacements may not be able to replace the lost savings. The net effect will be a lower rate of domestic savings as a source of funds for capital formation. Government aid cannot make up more of the lost investment than it could provide in the absence of these indigenization efforts. Hence, dependence upon foreign financing will increase.

Fifth, when faced with discriminatory practices and lowered profit horizons, the Chinese businessmen affected are likely to move to less restricted or more promising pursuits—for instance, from retailing to manufacturing. They might also choose to move to more promising or less restrictive countries. The latter alternative, of course, entails the flight of capital, skilled workers, and managerial personnel, compounding the scarcity of these resources in the original countries.

Sixth, there are two potentially offsetting factors that could reduce the adverse impact:

First, there might be a long-term improvement in productivity, capacity to invest, and managerial ability on the part of the indigenous population—the result that proponents of the reverse-affirmative-action policy in Southeast Asian countries hope for. The likelihood of such a development remains, however, to be determined empirically. Thus far, conclusive evidence is lacking. Furthermore, the length of time that must elapse before such a net favorable development can be felt is crucial. Other disruptive events could occur if the beneficial effects are too long in coming.

Second, if two assumptions—that ethnic Chinese enterprises have been monopolistic and that such practices have been responsible for the lagging performance of indigenous entrepreneurs—are correct, then the removal or weakening of Chinese competition could conceivably result in a sizable expansion of indigenous enterprises. After surmounting the Chinese barrier, indigenous enterprises could become significantly more productive than the Chinese businesses that had previously stood in their way. As we shall see later, the first assumption is partly true insofar as the various social, speech-group, emigrant, and other associations to which Chinese businessmen belonged exercised social and other sanctions against individual Chinese businessmen who were overzealous in competing with other members of the same associations.[12] These sanctions did not apply, however, to dealings with indigenous competitors. It is far less certain, however, that the second assumption is correct. There were other reasons for lagging performance on the part of indigenous businesses. Besides, it is by no means clear that reverse discrimination is the best way to correct the effects of past discrimination. A combination of positive measures to aid indigenous businessmen (such as loans and education) with rules against restraint of trade by any group, Chinese or not, appears a better solution.

Attraction of Foreign Capital versus Restriction of Ethnic-Chinese Capital

Restrictions on ethnic-Chinese economic activity have sometimes been concealed under anti-alien legislation. In Thailand, Indonesia, and the Philippines, for example, some restrictions were directed against aliens. Since most noncitizens were Chinese, however, the effect of these restrictions was anti-Chinese. This effect was heightened by further sanctions that often made it particularly difficult for Chinese residents to acquire citizenship—a situation that existed in the Philippines until recently.[13] Measures that discriminate against the *peranakans* (nonindigenous Indonesians) in Indonesia,[14] as well as the racial-quota system of Malaysia, are unashamedly directed against the ethnic Chinese.

In general, ethnic-Chinese capital and enterprises have been subjected to restrictions normally reserved for alien interests following the tenets of economic nationalism. At the same time, the same countries that have instituted these restrictions have sought to augment the inflow of private foreign investment as well as foreign resources in other forms (for details see Appendix C).[15] More specifically, foreign investments that would promote exports have been welcomed, while ethnic-Chinese enterprises especially adapted to intraregional trade have been targets of discrimination. Similarly, foreign investments that would add to forward or backward linkages in the economic structure have been courted at the same time that strenuous attempts have been made to reduce or eliminate distribution by Chinese entrepreneurs. While foreign managerial and technical personnel, along with foreign capital, have been eagerly sought, equally qualified ethnic Chinese have often been given a strong incentive to leave the country through the denial of equal opportunity in employment and education. There seems to have been fundamental inconsistency, if not perverseness, in policy. The degree of dependence on foreign capital for economic development has been unnecessarily increased.

It can, perhaps, be argued that the kind of foreign capital and technology required by these developing countries is not what the ethnic Chinese supply. This point is worth closer examination, but it ignores the catalytic function modern Chinese financial and economic interests can perform or have performed.[16] It also overlooks the fact that some foreign enterprises, notably Japanese ones, would like to have local ethnic-Chinese partners.[17] A most important point is the impression made on foreign investors by a nation that discriminates against selected domestic investors. Capriciousness and arbitrariness are surely not traits a country should display when inviting foreign investment.

Fortunately, both for the Southeast Asian countries and for the ethnic Chinese in the region, the realization is growing among national authorities that a truly equal treatment for all races in a plural society is the only rational approach. The sources of the problems this policy must overcome, as well as its rewards, will be considered in the next chapters.

Loopholes and Side Effects

The statistical overview of the last chapter amply demonstrated the lower economic growth rates since 1960 of the Southeast Asian countries (excluding Singapore) in comparison with Singapore, South Korea, Taiwan, and Hong Kong. However, the disruptive economic effects of the restrictive measures aimed at the ethnic Chinese have been at least partially offset by positive developments, such as increases in foreign investments. These effects have also been reduced by the failure to implement the restrictions fully in some cases as a result of modifications or practical adaptations of policy. For example, where ethnic Chinese are no longer permitted to pursue given economic activities, indigenous persons have frequently been found to front for them. This practice is sometimes known as the Ali Baba arrangement. The Bumiputra Ali fronts for Baba, the Chinese, at a suitable rate of compensation. In some instances, the real Chinese owner has even become a nominal employee. The front man is sometimes known as the dummy. (In the Philippines, for instance, antidummy measures have been enacted precisely to deal with this situation.)

Ethnic-Chinese enterprises have also been converted nominally into joint ventures through the participation of socially, and often politically, prominent indigenous figures as directors, partners, or principal officers. Politicians and military men often play this role, at varying levels. Again, suitable emoluments are entailed.

Finally, ethnic-Chinese businessmen have taken their capital out of the country, sometimes along with members of their families. Once these businesses have been established outside, in *one or more* other countries, funds begin to flow back into the original country as foreign capital, which is then awarded many of the benefits designed to attract foreign investors. The attraction these countries offer to non-Chinese foreign investors can be equally alluring to the Chinese if they are considered foreign investors instead of second-class citizens.

One effect of these subterfuges has been the emergence of a new rentier class composed of politicians, generals, and other persons who occupy less august positions in a given social and political hierarchy. Their function is to forestall really damaging effects on aggregate output and resource allocation by preventing the full implementation of restrictive measures. In a sense, the degree of contraction in potential output is reduced by an act of income and/or wealth transfer in favor of a select group. Each time enactment of a new restrictive measure is threatened, another type of service supplying the know-how and social or political connections needed to arrange exemption from it is provided. This has resulted in a built-in tendency to invent more rules and restrictions from which exemptions can then be sold. Despite the inevitable increase in cost to ethnic-Chinese businesses, these enterprises can purchase exemption and protection, and in many cases survive. Business operations become more cumbersome and time-consuming, however, and the adverse effect extends beyond the Chinese enterprises.

Another by-product of the alliance system developed between Chinese businessmen and indigenous bureaucrats, generals, and politicians is its effect on income distribution and, through that distribution, on development. Income distribution in the society as a whole can easily become less equitable as a result of all these adjustments. If this happens, national consensus or the lack of it and political stability will be adversely affected, which may in turn affect the availability of external resources and the rate of growth itself. Needless to say, it would be best for all concerned, except the recipients of the transfer income, to remove the need for subterfuge by abolishing the restrictions.

Some Unanswered Questions

The preceding discussion leads to some interesting questions. Not the least of these is whether the apparent perversity in policymaking has a good explanation. If ethnic-Chinese resources are regarded as domestic resources by the countries of domicile, then optimal utilization of domestic resources should include them. On the other hand, if ethnic-Chinese resources are regarded as foreign resources, they should be treated as such. Failure to accept the first interpretation would unnecessarily raise the demand for foreign resources. Failure to accept the second—assuming, of course, that the first is rejected—implies discrimination on the basis of domicile and/or race and raises doubt about the future prospects of all foreign capital in the countries in question.

The timing of the more restrictive anti-Chinese measures provides an explanation of sorts for their imposition. They all date from the post-World War II period, when the formerly colonial territories of Southeast Asia became independent, highly nationalistic states. Not surprisingly, in this climate the Chinese, even long-term residents, were considered foreign, particularly because in many areas the Chinese were associated in the native mind with the former colonial administrations or at least with an economic order in which the indigenous peoples were at the bottom of the pile. A reasoned approach to long-term problems would have been unlikely under the circumstances. However, even if there is an understandable reason to treat ethnic-Chinese resources as neither foreign nor indigenous ones but a special type, it does not follow that that explanation will remain valid indefinitely. Circumstances can change so that past reasons are no longer applicable.

The following chapter will trace the historical development of Chinese economic activities in the individual countries.

3

The Evolution of Chinese Economic Activities and of Local Attitudes Toward Them

SOME ECONOMIC RAMIFICATIONS OF NATIONALISM, POLITICS, AND HISTORY

Several basic factors must be borne in mind if one is to understand the attitudes of Southeast Asian countries toward the ethnic Chinese and Chinese business and the manner in which Chinese economic activities and business interests have attained their present magnitude and pervasiveness. These factors are (1) nationalistic sentiments in states that became independent only after World War II; (2) the perception of China and of the ethnic Chinese by the new Southeast Asian political elites, (3) the historical evolution of the economic roles of ethnic-Chinese communities in the individual countries, and (4) the responses of ethnic Chinese to restrictive policies adopted against them.

Post-World War II Nationalism and Policies

With the exception of Thailand, all the Southeast Asian countries gained independence after World War II, some after protracted military conflict. Many of the political leaders who came to power after independence had had years of experience in movements of national independence. While close economic ties continued to exist between the former colonies and the erstwhile colonial powers, the single most treasured possession of the new states was their independence and the right to determine their own political and economic futures. This nationalistic zeal allowed no distinction to be made with respect to the source of foreign intervention. Ethnic-Chinese communities have suffered for two reasons. First, their residents were thought to be aliens who desired to return to

China and who had no real roots in the countries of their domicile. Second, they were, and to some extent still are, suspected of being potential fifth columnists for an ambitious China.

In the past, the Chinese government regarded all overseas Chinese as Chinese citizens. While this is no longer the prevailing policy in either the Republic of China or the People's Republic, the traditional policies as others understood them made the Chinese suspect in the eyes of the nationalists in the newly independent states. One of the most difficult and urgent tasks for these new countries was, and still is, to create a national identity capable of transcending the separate identities of the different communities in the plural societies of all Southeast Asian countries. To the new governments the unassimilated ethnic Chinese appeared to be a major obstacle to attainment of this goal.

The natural suspicions directed at the ethnic Chinese were aggravated by any Chinese foreign policies that hinted at either military expansion or political subversion. Because of the ROC's small size and unavoidably weaker international position even before 1971, when it lost its seat in the United Nations, Taipei has, of course, been much less a source of concern than Peking. Peking's dualistic approach to foreign relations permits political support for insurgent or subversive movements in a country with which it maintains normal state-to-state relations. This policy has produced not only uneasiness among countries in Southeast Asia, but bitter experience as well. Both Malaysia and Indonesia, the two countries that still impose the most restrictions on the ethnic Chinese, have suffered grievously from Peking-supported insurgency.[1] The September 1965 coup in Indonesia and the continuing activities of Peking-supported guerrillas in Malaysia are examples.

Still another factor responsible for anti-Chinese attitudes is conflict of economic interests. Among those who have gained political power in Southeast Asia are a relatively small number of Western-educated members of the middle class who by virtue of their education are, and consider themselves, qualified to take over both the political and the economic functions of the former colonial interests. The withdrawal of the colonial government has removed an adjudicating influence and left the ethnic Chinese to deal directly with this expanding middle class and the indigenous government. Furthermore, at the time of the withdrawal of colonial political control and a major portion of colonial economic interests, the ethnic Chinese temporarily filled an economic vacuum. This key role further aroused the antipathy of the local population; economic conflict and anti-Chinese political sentiments have fed upon each other. It is not surprising that some newly independent countries of Southeast Asia are anxious to develop an independent and autonomous economic system and to secure a more advantageous place in it for their local majority races at the expense of both the colonial powers and the ethnic Chinese or, more generally, alien Asiatics.[2]

The Evolving Economic Functions of Ethnic Chinese in the Plural Societies of Southeast Asia

That ethnic-Chinese communities have had to bear the brunt of nascent nationalism is, of course, partly a reflection of the economic roles they played in the past. Without going into detail at this point,[3] we will briefly indicate the economic function of the Chinese in a Southeast Asian plural society.[4] An important characteristic of such societies is the coexistence within the larger group of component national groups, each with its own cultural background and social order. Because these different elements are not fully assimilated, they lack both a common national consciousness and a set of commonly accepted cultural or political values. Since all the ethnic groups are engaged in economic activities, however, their point of contact is the marketplace. In Southeast Asia from the beginning of the colonial period to the years immediately after World War II, three types of economic structure coexisted, albeit sometimes uncomfortably—the capitalist system of the West, the commercial institutions of the Chinese, and the agricultural economy of the native peoples.

These three layers of the Southeast Asian economy formed a socioeconomic pyramid.[5] Industrial production was in the hands of Europeans accustomed to large-scale machine production of standardized products. They managed the larger enterprises, including factories, mines, and plantations, and controlled material resources and trade on a large scale. They enjoyed special privileges and political protection as citizens of the colonial powers: thus their place was at the apex of the pyramid. Chinese businessmen were in the middle. They began their economic ascent by engaging in retailing, transportation, and buying and selling in general; they also provided agricultural credit. In these ways they succeeded in developing direct and close relations with local producers as well as consumers; and these contacts brought certain advantages over the years, including intermarriage with the indigenous population, linguistic ability, and familiarity with the economic conditions and ways of life of different segments of the local rural society. These advantages enabled them to compete more successfully with other foreign businessmen from both Asia and Europe. The indigenous population formed the bottom layer of the economic pyramid. It supplied the bulk of the labor force and provided a market for consumer goods.

In its economically underdeveloped condition, rural Southeast Asia was deficient in agricultural credit facilities. The small indigenous farmer needed credit to purchase seeds, fertilizer, and equipment; he also needed consumption loans to tide him over the period before the harvest. Chinese merchants who lived among the indigenous farmers provided loans when needed, with interest and principal payments usually made in farm produce. At the same time, since rural transportation was also underdeveloped, the collection of farm products in small quantities, as well as their sorting, processing, and transportation, were tasks the

Chinese network of trade and transportation could perform. It was the Chinese merchant who, over a period of several centuries, brought farm products to the cities and thence to the export market, and carried industrial products back to the rural sector. Some Chinese became rich thereby because they performed a necessary economic function and because competitors were not on the scene. They were often criticized, however, by both the ruling class and the indigenous middle class as exploiters who took their pound of flesh twice, once through interest as providers of farm credit and again through profit in distribution.[6]

The ethnic Chinese more than held their own economically during this period because they had managed to adapt to prevailing conditions. Apart from being frugal and hard-working, they developed community-wide organizations that supported economic activity. Family associations and groups of persons from the same provinces or speech groups provided multiple channels for cooperation. Capital accumulation was made easier,[7] guarantors could be found for loans, and timely market information, indispensable to successful competition, could be readily obtained. This kind of mutual assistance was lacking among the indigenous populations. The nuclear-family business management practiced by the latter was less efficient than the organized business procedures of the ethnic Chinese based on the extended family.

A highly developed system of business ethics was a natural concomitant of the cooperative activities of these Chinese entrepreneurs. Personal trust and credibility were highly treasured assets in the business community, both among those in the same trade and between members of different trades. The aim of such business ethics was to safeguard not only one's own business, but also the interests of other members of the extended Chinese communities. The indigenous peoples whose social organization was less tightly knit had no equivalent system.

The natural resources and agricultural products of Southeast Asia were of considerable interest to Western colonial investors. Consequently, the development of large-scale enterprises was fairly rapid. The indigenous society, however, remained at the level of a subsistence economy. Surplus farm labor, scattered plots, and the backward production of the natives stood in sharp contrast to the developed money economy of the European colonials. The Chinese were intermediaries, providing a necessary bridge between the European and the native systems. This is why Chinese communities were allowed to exist in Southeast Asia during the colonial period.[8]

The advent of Southeast Asian political independence removed the Europeans from their privileged colonial positions. Since this change more or less eliminated a major component in the triple-tiered economic structure, one immediate effect was severe economic dislocation. The ethnic Chinese, whose position had depended on maintaining an orderly link between the colonial elite and the indigenous society, now faced adjustment to a new situation.

Adaptability and Transformation

During the colonial period, the Chinese were content with their status and not particularly interested in political and social developments in the countries where they resided. In general, they favored nonparticipation and noninterference in domestic political disputes and activities. Their attention was focused primarily on how best to adapt to their environment, including particularly the need to conform to the policies of the colonial governments on the one hand and the need to live in peace with the indigenous population on the other. Above all, of course, they sought economic opportunities.

Chinese activities were concentrated in the commercial, service, financial, and industrial sectors. Nonagricultural employment exceeded agricultural employment by a large margin. The relatively few Chinese who were directly engaged in agriculture worked primarily in rubber, pineapples, sugar, pepper, and truck farming, producing exclusively crops for the commercial market. The cultivation of food grains for subsistence was left in the hands of the indigenous population, while the Chinese, for the greater part, worked as traders, moneylenders, and entrepreneurs. This pattern of occupational distribution is clearly shown in statistics Fukuda provided for the prewar period that cover both employment and capital investment.[9]

Although the discrepancies in income and wealth between the more successful Chinese and the local population aroused envy, the lives and property of the Chinese were protected by the colonial governments. This protection was useful but perhaps less than essential because the position of the Chinese depended less on privilege than on their abilities and their usefulness in developing Southeast Asian economies. They enjoyed other advantages as well, notably their adaptability and even their relative mobility; if their existence seemed threatened and no other alternative was available, they could shift to new areas where conditions seemed more promising. In the normal course, however, their services were valued by the majority at both ends of the economic spectrum; thus Chinese ethnic subcommunities enjoyed relative stability prior to World War II.

The postwar disintegration of the colonial system meant the disappearance of the economic support provided by the erstwhile colonial powers. This created a serious disequilibrium in production and marketing, affecting the export of primary products, which were the mainstay of the monoculture economies in Southeast Asia. Under pressure from nationalist economic interests, the Chinese sought, or were forced, to reduce their marketing activities and shift their investments to industrial and manufacturing enterprises for which the developing countries felt a more urgent demand. They also diversified geographically. As a result of these adjustments, there has been a distinct increase in the Chinese share in industry and mining, while their stake in commercial and agricultural activities has declined proportionately. This can be seen by comparing the patterns of distribution of employment and investment presented in Tables 21 and 26 in Chapter 2 with those of 1930 (see the tables in footnote 9 of this chapter).

Chinese businesses in Southeast Asia span a wide range of sizes and modes of operation. Not all Chinese in Southeast Asia are rich. Nor are all Chinese businesses large and modern. Many small and medium-sized ethnic-Chinese enterprises are still bound by traditional individualism and familial relations; these are far more numerous than large, modern firms. Their proprietors tend to favor self-sufficiency and exhibit psychological traits that are usually associated with subsistence farmers. They are conservative or even backward in organization, capital structure, and management.

As the data in Table 27 show, proprietorships and partnerships are still the dominant forms of organization for ethnic-Chinese enterprises. This reflects historical precedents: the majority of small Chinese businesses were established with personal savings accumulated over long periods. The successful immigrant Chinese worker saved his money to open a small business which he hoped to pass on to his children, generation after generation. He did not wish to see others step into the family business. Even today one can find many father-and-son combinations or companies owned by brothers. If these single-family enterprises expanded at all, it was normally through marriages with persons from the same emigrant areas. This was also the manner in which individual proprietorships became partnerships.

The great majority of the small businesses are engaged in retailing or the service trades, including restaurants, laundries, hairdressing shops, and market stalls. Both sales and capital tend to be limited. In Malaysia, Chinese operators account for 85 percent of retailing.[10] The corresponding proportion in the Philippines is 75 percent;[11] in Thailand, Vietnam, Indonesia, and Cambodia the Chinese share exceeds 70 percent. A survey by Taku Suyama[12] of 6,043 retail sales permits in Singapore in 1974 shows that 1,640 permits were issued to eating and drinking

TABLE 27

CHINESE ENTERPRISES BY TYPE OF ORGANIZATION
(Percentage)

	Singapore (1957)	West Malaysia (1957)	The Philippines (1964)	Thailand (1970)
Proprietorships	40.0	...	57.0	...
Partnerships	10.2	94.9	34.0	66.6
Corporations	9.8	5.1	9.0	33.4
Not classified	40.0	...	...	...

SOURCES: For Singapore, Malaysia, and Thailand, see Yu Chung-hsün, *Kakyō keizai no kenkyū*, p. 180; for the Philippines, see Schubert S. C. Liao, ed., *Chinese Participation in Philippine Culture and Economy* (Manila: Published by the Author, 1964), p. 234.

establishments, 1,059 to fruit stalls, 858 to shops selling coffee and other beverages, 685 to dry-goods stores, 647 to bakeries, 442 to laundry and cleaning shops, 162 to ice cream parlors, and 12 to other kinds of businesses. The patterns elsewhere are similar.

Excluding entrepôt trade, 74.6 percent of the total imports of Singapore and Malaysia in 1956 was accounted for by European importers.[13] Chinese trading houses were responsible for only 10.1 percent; another 2.2 percent was handled by Indians. The two major exports of Cambodia—rubber and pepper—were both marketed by European businesses. In the Philippines, Chinese foreign-trade firms handle only 13 percent of the total. All in all, ethnic-Chinese firms in Southeast Asia have found themselves unable to compete with European, Japanese, and other foreign traders in trade outside the region.

Individual ethnic-Chinese entrepreneurs have managed to make extraordinary strides, however, in specific areas. An oft-cited example is Oei Tiong Ham, a onetime sugar king from Indonesia. At one time, some twenty of Oei's rubber, banking, and shipping enterprises were in operation all over the world. When Oei's Indonesian assets were nationalized by Sukarno, they were valued at 4 billion rupiah (then equivalent to U.S. $90 million).[14] In Vietnam, Hui Bon Hoa, who built his fortune on a monopoly in pawnbroking under French rule, became the wealthiest Chinese in Saigon. Even after the fall of South Vietnam, his enterprise, the Cong Ty Xa Hoi Kim Long, has remained active in Southeast Asia and Hong Kong. Aw Boon Haw of Tiger Balm fame built his fortune first in Burma and then in Singapore. He later moved from the drug business to banking and publishing. Aw founded newspapers that have become familiar household names in Asia. Tan Kah Kee of Malaysia was well known in the rubber industry, as was Fong Seong in tin mining. Lok Yawe and his son, and Lee Kuang Chian, son-in-law of Tan Kah Kee, all became millionaire industrialists in recent times. Many others have followed in their footsteps and have attained international reputations.

THE CURRENT ECONOMIC CONDITION OF CHINESE COMMUNITIES: A TOUR D'HORIZON

The general observations in the preceding section need to be supplemented by a closer examination of the conditions faced by Chinese communities in individual countries. The following account deals first with the background and current economic condition of Chinese in each of the four ASEAN member countries. This is followed by a summary of conditions in the communist or socialist countries of Indochina and Burma. Conditions in Singapore and Hong Kong, where ethnic-Chinese residents are a majority instead of a minority as in the other countries, will be covered in the next chapter.

Official policies dealing with Chinese residents vary considerably among the four ASEAN nations. Malaysia and Indonesia have the most discriminatory rules—these are applied even when the Chinese are legally citizens of the country. Thailand discriminates against aliens but not against Thai citizens, whose hope is that they will become assimilated. The Philippines also lacks any formal policies of discrimination against citizens of Chinese descent, but until recently it was both difficult and costly for alien Chinese to acquire Filipino citizenship.

The Plural Society of Malaysia

The Early Period. The Chinese have been in Malaya for many centuries. A fourteenth-century account of Chinese living in Tumasik (present-day Singapore) was one of the early records.[15] It was not until after 1786, however, when the British East India Company leased Penang, and the settlement of Singapore by Raffles in 1819, that sizable ethnic-Chinese communities began to appear in this area.[16] Large-scale Chinese immigration into Malaya under the contract-labor system began toward the end of the nineteenth century and continued into the beginning of the twentieth. A significant, if gradual, change in the composition of the population took place after World War I. From only 215 Chinese females to every 1,000 males in 1911, the proportion had risen by 1957 to 926 to every 1,000.[17] This change in sex ratio, together with continued immigration, helps to account for a steady rise in the Chinese population of Malaya and the increasing percentage of locally born residents. The total Chinese population in the Federated States of Malaya rose from 856,000 in 1921, when only 20.9 percent were born locally, to 1,885,000 in 1947, when 63.5 percent were locally born.[18] The corresponding figures in 1957 were 2,334,000 and 75.5 percent.

Chinese began planting rubber and mining tin in Malaya during the nineteenth century. By 1931, 162,200 Chinese were reportedly engaged in planting and cutting rubber, while another 70,700 Chinese workers were mining tin.[19] Of an estimated total Chinese-owned capital of M $493 million (Malaysian dollars) in 1931, tin mining and rubber plantations accounted for 64.5 percent; the remaining 35.5 percent was invested in commercial establishments.[20] During the 1930s, the Chinese were overtaken by the Europeans in tin mining as a result of the Westerners' modern technology and larger-scale production.[21]

A 1928 ordinance restricting immigration was followed by the Alien Ordinance of 1933. These laws sharply curtailed new immigration, slowing the expansion of the Chinese labor force, but the large immigrant community of Chinese already there remained. It was composed of several speech groups, of which the Hokkiens were the most numerous.[22]

Fukuda's 1930 survey, which covered both Malaya and Singapore,[23] found that 39 percent of Chinese employment was still concentrated in primary industry; the remaining 61 percent was about equally divided between the secondary and tertiary sectors. On the eve of World War II, economic control of the area was almost entirely in Chinese and Western hands. Helmut G. Callis estimated Chinese investment in Malaya and Singapore in 1937 at U.S. $200 million, compared with a Western investment of $454.5 million,[24] of which more than 70 percent was British. Chinese entrepreneurs were often employed by British companies as compradors responsible for purchasing exportable goods and for selling imports on the local market on behalf of their employers. This system, an institution since the establishment of the East India Company, was abolished only after World War II.

Post-World War II Development. The end of World War II saw a succession of major political changes. First, Malaya became independent after a period of emergency that lasted twelve years. The Federation of Malaysia was finally formed in 1963, and in 1965 Singapore became a separate state outside the federation. Within the plural society of Malaysia, from which Singapore has been excluded, the Malays (Bumiputras) claim a special position, while non-Malays (primarily ethnic Chinese) cling tenaciously to their legitimate interests and acquired rights. The Malay claim to primacy and the efforts of other ethnic communities to protect their own interests caused repeated conflicts that exploded into a major open clash on May 13, 1969.[25] Until then moderate and far-sighted Malay leaders like Tunku Rahman had thought of building Malaysia's future on three pillars: the retention of political power by the Malays, the continued development of business and credit by the Chinese, and a greater role for the Indians as workers. As the federation's first prime minister, the Tunku was optimistic about the prospect that Malaysian prosperity could be built on this basis, even though internal communist-inspired insurgency had not yet been completely eradicated. As a matter of fact, ethnic Chinese in Malaysia did prosper during the 1950s and 1960s. Their economic condition was relatively stable there in comparison with their position in other Southeast Asian areas.

West Malaysia had a population of 10.4 million in 1975. Of these 5.5 million were Malays and 3.7 million were Chinese; the rest were Indians, Pakistanis, and others. Although the Malays constitute a majority, Chinese and Westerners dominate the nation's economy. This is especially true in the modern sector and for larger enterprises (see Tables 28 and 29).

The Chinese may possess a greater potential for further economic development than the Malays. An important reason is that Chinese stay in school longer. Reflecting the fact that Chinese traditionally encourage their children to obtain advanced education, more Chinese than Malay students are enrolled in science and technology courses, whereas more Malay than Chinese students major in the arts. Reports on student enrollment in the University of Malaya in the 1971–72 academic year indicate that while the number of Malays enrolled (3,738) was

TABLE 28

OWNERSHIP OF SHARE CAPITAL OF LIMITED COMPANIES, BY RACE AND INDUSTRIAL SECTOR—PENINSULAR MALAYSIA, 1970

	Malay		*Chinese*		*Indian*		*Foreign*		*Totals*[a]	
	M $	Percentage	M $	Percentage	M $	Percentage	M $	Percentage	M $	Percentage
Agriculture, forestry, and fisheries	13,724	0.9	177,438	22.4	16,191	0.1	1,079,714	75.3	1,432,400	100
Mining and quarrying	3,876	0.7	91,557	16.8	2,488	0.4	393,910	72.4	543,497	100
Manufacturing	33,650	2.5	296,363	22.0	8,880	0.7	804,282	59.6	1,348,245	100
Construction	1,258	2.2	30,855	52.8	447	0.8	19,937	24.1	58,419	100
Transportation and communications	10,875	13.3	35,498	43.4	1,903	2.3	9,845	12.0	81,887	100
Commerce	4,715	0.8	184,461	30.4	4,711	0.7	384,549	63.5	605,164	100
Banking and insurance	21,164	3.3	155,581	24.3	4,434	0.6	332,790	52.2	636,850	100
Others	13,349	2.3	220,330	37.8	13,348	2.3	182,862	31.4	582,516	100
Total	102,611	1.9	1,192,083	22.5	52,402	1.0	3,207,889	60.7	5,288,978	100

SOURCE: Atan bin Long, "Majority-Minority Situation: Malaysia" (Paper presented at the Manila conference on the Majority-Minority Situation in Southeast Asia organized by ASAIHL, May 3–10, 1974).

[a]Totals include share capital ownership by federal and state governments and statutory bodies and other Malaysian residents (individuals and nominee and locally controlled companies), amounting to about $734 million. The racial shares in each sector exclude these two groups.

TABLE 29

OWNERSHIP OF ASSETS IN MODERN AGRICULTURE AND INDUSTRY—PENINSULAR MALAYSIA, 1970

	Modern Agriculture[a] *Corporate Sector*		*Planted Acreage Noncorporate sector*		*Industry*[b] *(Fixed Assets)* *Corporate Sector*		*Noncorporate Sector*	
	Thousands of acres	Percentage	Thousands of acres	Percentage	M $ Million	Percentage	M $ Million	Percentage
Malaysians:								
Malays	5.0	0.3	349.3	47.1	11.2	0.9	3.9	2.3
Chinese	457.0	25.9	243.3	32.8	342.3	26.2	158.0	92.2
Indians	4.9	0.3	74.8	10.1	1.5	0.1	3.9	2.3
Others	48.1	2.7	13.2	1.8	187.2	14.3	1.4	0.8
Government[c]	–	–	17.0	2.3	17.5	1.3	–	–
Total Malaysians	515.0	29.2	697.6	94.1	559.7	42.8	167.2	97.6
Non-Malaysians	1,249.6	70.8	44.0	5.9	747.3	57.2	4.1	2.4
Total	1,764.6	100.0	741.6	100.0	1,307.0	100.0	171.3	100.0
Percentage of Total Planted Acres/ Fixed Assets		70.4		29.6		87.4		12.6

SOURCE: Same as Table 28.

[a]Modern agriculture covers estate acreage under rubber, oil palm, coconut, and tea. Ownership is indicated in terms of total planted acreage.

[b]The industry sector covers manufacturing, construction, and mining. Ownership is stated in terms of fixed assets.

[c]Government ownership of seventeen thousand acres in modern agriculture is included in the noncorporate sector, while the ownership of $17.5 million of fixed assets in industry is included in the corporate sector.

about equal to the number of Chinese (3,892), there were marked differences in their distribution by discipline. There were only 29 Malays versus 448 Chinese in the engineering faculty. In the faculty of science, there were 147 Malays and 1,169 Chinese, and in the school of medicine, 157 Malays and 409 Chinese. There were also more Chinese than Malays in economics, administration, education, and agriculture, although the differences were smaller. Only in the faculty of arts was there a large majority of Malays—2,481 of them, compared with only 723 Chinese.[26]

The disparity in average income that follows from the substantial differences between these two groups, economic conditions and educational specialization is compounded by differences in the distribution pattern within each community. In 1970, the average monthly income per person was M $68 for Chinese, M $57 for Indians, and M $34 for Malays. The mean household income per month was M $387 for Chinese, M $310 for Indians, and M $179 for Malays. In 1970, 40.3 percent of Malay households in peninsular Malaysia had a monthly income of less than M $100, and 74 percent had a monthly income of less than M $200. In the Chinese community, 8.3 percent of all households had a monthly income of less than M $100 and 33.3 percent had a monthly income of less than M $200.[27] Data in the Third Malaysian Plan (1976–80)[28] show 26 percent of Chinese households below the poverty line, compared with 65 percent of Malay households. Earlier statistics covering the Chinese alone indicate that 30 percent of Chinese households were extremely poor; 35 percent could just make do; 30 percent could be regarded as in the middle class, and 5 percent were well off.[29] It appears, however, that although the Chinese were better off than Malays as a whole, rich Malays were far wealthier than their poor confreres. Thus the Malay community suffers not only from relative poverty in comparison with the ethnic-Chinese and Indian communities, but also from gross disparities in income distribution among the Malays themselves.

Disruptions of the rural economy during the communist emergency forced many Chinese to move to safer urban areas. Commerce in the rural sector was greatly affected, and the adverse effect was felt in reduced exports. West Malaysia suffers from excessive dependence upon primary-product exports. Tin (metal and ore), rubber, palm oil, coconut oil, and timber are still among the most important exports: in 1975 they accounted for 68.3 percent of the total.[30] International price fluctuations have a major impact on Malaysian economic prosperity, and the economic condition of the Chinese community is affected in turn. There is no immediate prospect of a permanent change for the better unless exports can be diversified to include a larger proportion of manufactured goods, and the domestic economy can be substantially expanded.

The dominance of Chinese and Westerners in the Malaysian economy is further shown by the distribution by race of ownership of the larger limited companies. In 1970, ownership in West Malaysian corporations, including government corporations, was 2.4 percent Malay, 27.2 percent Chinese, and 63.3 percent Western.[31] Modern Chinese businessmen have broken away from their comprador position to operate independently of Western companies; they have also left their traditional district and speech-group organizations and are moving toward cooperation with Western capital.[32] Furthermore, by shifting their capital from commercial to industrial enterprises, they have greatly expanded the scope of their economic activity.

Restructuring the Distribution of Ownership. In an attempt to correct economic disparities between Bumiputras and non-Bumiputras, the Malaysian government has embarked upon an energetic policy to restructure the economy in terms of ownership by race. To quote from the Second Malaysian Plan (1971–75), "The government has set a target that within a period of 29 years, Malays and other indigenous people will manage and own at least 30 percent of the total commercial and industrial activities in all categories and scales of operation."[33] Among the desired changes are the transfer of enterprises operated by Western companies to Malaysians (including both Bumiputras or native sons and non-Bumiputras) and additional transfers of equity specifically to the Bumiputras. The end result sought by 1990 is to have Malaysians in control of 70 percent of the country's economic activity and to reserve three sevenths of the 70 percent (that is, 30 percent of the total) for Bumiputras. These targets are to be attained by gradually acquiring stock in foreign companies for redistribution to Malaysians and by reserving for the Bumiputras a share in newly formed foreign enterprises. These new enterprises will necessarily be joint ventures, therefore, in which foreign ownership will be limited to 30 percent, Bumiputras will have another 30 percent, and non-Bumiputra Malaysians will hold 40 percent.

In pursuing this objective, the Malaysian government had acquired, from 1971 through August 1975, M $199 million worth of stock in foreign enterprises. Of this amount, M $503.6 million, plus other stock held by government corporations, was resold to the Bumiputras.[34] A number of state corporations have been established to promote this program. They include the Bumiputra Trust Bank (MARA), which gives loans to Malays who wish to engage in industrial and business activities of various kinds; the Urban Development Authority (UDA), which supports urban housing and commercial development by Malays; and the State Economic Development Corporation (SEDC), which actively purchases stock in foreign companies.

According to official data provided by the Federal Industrial Development Authority (FIDA), equity participation in approved projects under the authority of FIDA was distributed in 1971 and 1974 as shown in Table 30. The 1974 figures are clearly in accordance with the prescribed targets, but they do not show whether there are Bumiputras fronting for non-Bumiputras; nor do these

TABLE 30

EQUITY DISTRIBUTION BY RACE AND NATIONALITY IN FIDA-APPROVED PROJECTS, MALAYSIA
(Percentage)

	Bumiputras	Non-Bumiputras	Foreigners
1971	16.0	66.9	17.1
1974	33.0	33.1	33.9

figures include previously established enterprises. One rather cynical estimate puts the proportion of real Bumiputra equity as closer to 3 percent than to the 33 percent given in the official figures.

A number of indications, nonetheless, suggest that the balance between the Malays' special position and the acquired rights of the other ethnic communities has been tilted in the Malays' favor. The quota system in government appointments, the reserved-admission quotas for Malays in institutions of higher learning, and the issuance of special licenses for Malay business operations mentioned in Appendix C are all examples. Limitation of educational opportunities threatens the dominant position of the Chinese in the professions, and the large inflow of Malays into urban areas and the government requirement that 50 percent of private industrial and business employment consist of Malays are posing a serious threat to middle- and working-class Chinese. The flight of Chinese capital since 1969 in response to these measures presages a potentially large loss of confidence in the country's economic future and the place of the ethnic Chinese in it. Any attempt to force through the proposed transfers of ownership or any redistribution that favors the very rich may create conditions under which political stability will be seriously threatened. An alliance of discontented Malays with embittered Chinese could well provide mass support for renewed militant activity. Hence the timely formulation of a racially more harmonious policy is a necessary condition for accelerated economic growth.

Chinese in Indonesia

Before World War II. Long before the Dutch arrived in present-day Indonesia in 1596, Chinese traders had been active in the area. Already during the T'ang dynasty (618–907 A.D.) in China, Chinese businessmen traded porcelain, silk, and tea for cloves, pepper, and other local products. At the end of the Sung dynasty (960–1279), when the Indies were ruled by the Madjapahit dynasty (1238–1419), Chinese were known to be living in the country and economic relations between China and the Indies were quite developed. The voyages (1405–33) of Admiral Cheng-ho in the Ming dynasty were also instrumental in promoting trade. The Dutch succeeded in acquiring a monopoly on trading rights toward the end of the sixteenth century, however, and founded the Dutch East India Company in 1602. Batavia was established in 1619. During the seventeenth century, while the East India Company monopolized foreign trade, retailing was left to the Chinese; their commercial position as intermediaries between the Europeans and the local population became well established during this period. Chinese businessmen soon expanded from commercial activities into farming and manufacturing. A Chinese, So Bing Kong, became the first kapitan in charge of Chinese affairs, serving concurrently as the Dutch businessmen's comprador.

When the expanding operations of the Chinese started to infringe upon Dutch interests, restrictive measures were introduced, beginning in 1727. Many Chinese were massacred in 1740.[35] Nevertheless, Chinese immigration was encouraged afterward and those who came managed to prosper. A system of compulsory crop culture was introduced by the Dutch government in 1730. Indigenous farmers were instructed to plant coffee, sugar, and tobacco, with the crops from one fifth of the cultivated land constituting a tax payment. The system was finally abolished in 1870, and a policy of free enterprise in crop cultivation was introduced in its place. Considerable Western capital then came into the country, and the eonomic influence of the Chinese increased with it.

Tin mining began in the Indies in 1864; this industry, together with rubber plantations, required large numbers of contract laborers, many of whom went to Sumatra. Between 1888 and 1931, 305,000 Chinese workers came from Swatow and Hong Kong.[36] It was during this period that a Chinese commercial network spread over Java and the other islands.[37]

The Japanese took Indonesia in August 1940, ushering in an occupation under which Chinese interests were severely damaged. As Victor Purcell pointed out, "the vicissitudes suffered by the Overseas Chinese in this period, consequent on the new pattern of force operating in the region, were more painful in Indonesia than in any other country in Southeast Asia. However, their fate did not end with the return to peace."[38]

Size and Socioeconomic Characteristics of the Chinese Community in Indonesia

A 1930 census found 1,233,214 ethnic Chinese in Indonesia. Of this number, 756,172 had been born locally.[39] A distinction was made between Indonesian citizens (*wanga negara Indonesia* or WNI) and noncitizens (*wanga negara asing* or WNA) in the 1961 and 1971 censuses. Ethnic Chinese who held Indonesian citizenship were carried as Indonesian citizens and no longer listed separately. According to Indonesian immigration authorities in 1973, 1,097,875 alien Chinese were living in the country.[40] Students of Chinese affairs in

Indonesia usually make no distinction between citizens and noncitizens, however, preferring to employ the 1930 census figure as a basis for projection. Using an annual growth rate of 2 to 2.3 percent and allowing for net immigration, Purcell estimated the total number of ethnic Chinese in 1960 at 2.5 million.[41] Skinner's estimate for 1965 was 2,750,000. President Suharto used a round number of 2.5 million Chinese in Indonesia both in his 1968 speech in Japan on Indonesia's Chinese problem and in a February 17, 1971, interview in Jakarta in which he noted the need to utilize the 2.5 million Indonesian Chinese since they were like other Indonesians. Suharto was evidently thinking of Chinese who were Indonesian citizens, excluding, therefore, the alien Chinese. If the latter were added to his figure, then the ethnic-Chinese population should have been between 2.5 and 3.5 million in the late 1960s.

We need to bear in mind that considerable Chinese emigration from Indonesia took place under Sukarno's rule. These emigrants left for Hong Kong, Singapore, and Taiwan; some even went to Holland or South and Central America. As many as 96,000 Chinese left Indonesia for mainland China between February and April 1960 [42] as a result of a November 1959 law forbidding Chinese retailing in the villages. Although there was in fact virtually no new Chinese immigration into Indonesia after World War II, some of those who went to China in 1960 returned to Indonesia after 1967 when Suharto was firmly in power and conditions in Indonesia had stabilized. Accordingly, an estimate of 3.25 million ethnic Chinese at the end of 1974 seems plausible.

Hokkiens constitute the large majority of the ethnic Chinese in Indonesia. This phenomenon is to be explained by their early start and by the marked tendency of dialect and clan groups to concentrate in given areas. According to the 1930 census statistics, Hokkiens accounted for 50 percent of ethnic Chinese in Indonesia, followed by Hakkas (16.5 percent), Kwongfus or Cantonese (11.5 percent), and Teochius (7.5 percent). The remainder came from other provinces of China, including a large number from Hainan. Among the Hokkiens, those from Ch'üan-chou, Chang-chou, and Amoy in southern Fukien were economically dominant. Since World War II, immigrants from Fu-ch'ing and Hsing-hua—both in Fukien—have also become more prosperous, rivaling those from southern Fukien. As in other parts of Southeast Asia, the development of Chinese business interests in Indonesia has followed district, speech, and family association groupings with some overlapping. According to an April 1972 report of the Jakarta Chinese Chamber of Commerce, the Hokkien group was active in rubber, copra, coffee, pepper, tobacco, and other indigenous products, as well as in import and export, rubber and plastic processing, textiles, knitwares, weaving, garments, glassware, earthenware, tea processing, drugs, gold and jewelry, bicycles, trishaw (three-wheeled pedicabs), printing, hotels, the entertainment business, and finance. The Cantonese and Hakkas, on the other hand, were involved in rice milling, lumber mills, machine shops, soap factories, bakeries, food canning, furniture, hardware, tailoring, photo stores, coffee shops, truck farming, poultry, and restaurants. As clothiers and sellers of piece goods and dry goods, they tended to overlap in occupation with the first group. Overlapping also occurs in printing, plastic products, and the entertainment business. More recent immigrants from Taiwan have become involved in transportation or have established hotels, restaurants, and many new manufacturing concerns for which they have imported capital and equipment, including the production of electrical appliances, paper and wood products, steel, nuts and bolts, and lumber. Those from Kiangsu and Chekiang are engaged in making and selling optical supplies, clocks and watches, shoes, gifts, and books. Immigrants from Hupei seem to have concentrated in dentistry. The Shantung immigrants are sellers of piece goods.

Developments in the Post-Sukarno Period. A favorable climate for foreign investment under Suharto encouraged Chinese from Hong Kong, Singapore, Malaysia, the Philippines, and Taiwan to form joint ventures in their original fields with ethnic Chinese in Indonesia. Subsidiaries, branches, and new enterprises have sprung up, and these newcomers have contributed considerably to the modernization of Indonesian business practices. They are involved in a wide variety of manufactured consumer products: among them tobacco, canned foods, vegetable oil, animal feeds, cosmetics, drugs, wheat flour, electrical wiring, kilns, cement and steel, aluminum wares, stainless-steel appliances, thermos bottles, textiles, garments, and many others.

President Suharto was quoted as having said on February 17, 1971, that the 2.5 million Chinese in Indonesia controlled wealth out of proportion to their numbers. Accordingly, he continued, the Indonesian government would do all within its power to encourage and promote indigenous enterprise in the hope that indigenous entrepreneurs and ethnic Chinese in Indonesia would eventually be on a par, each owning about 50 percent of the total wealth of the country.

Previous estimates of Chinese investment in Indonesia include those of E. Helfferich in 1921, Fukuda in 1930, and Helmut G. Callis in 1937. Helfferich estimated it at 340 million Dutch florins (Dfl). Fukuda's estimate, as we noted earlier, was 654.8 million guilders. The Callis estimate was U.S. $150 million, which at 1937 exchange rates (£1 to 10.69 guilders and, roughly, £1 to $5) was considerably lower than the previous two. A February 27, 1972, report indicated that investment by alien Chinese in Indonesia in all sectors, including commerce, manufacturing, the tourist trade, transportation, and forest products, had reached $800 million. Our estimate for 1975, given in Appendix B, is $2.3 billion.

As many as three hundred thousand Chinese reportedly lost their lives during the 1965 communist-inspired coup and its aftermath. In spite of this serious loss of life and property, the recovery of Chinese enterprises has been phenomenal. Their widespread economic activities, with differing specializations by individual groups, have contributed to their ability to survive. Kraar's statements about "the most formidable economic power in Asia, outside of Japan,"[43] or "a nation of 21 million . . . remarkably resilient, industrious people . . . the most modern, adaptable group in their part of the world" are not exaggerated insofar as the ethnic Chinese in Indonesia are concerned.

Chinese Investment in the Commercial Sector. The July 1959 registration of aliens in Indonesia recorded a total of 109,736 alien-Chinese commercial establishments with an aggregate investment of $765 million (see Table 31).

Many Chinese businesses maintain close connections with Singapore and Hong Kong through branches and agencies. In the years since 1967 they have received considerable commercial credit from affiliates and correspondents in these two trade and financial centers. Importers obtain supplies from Hong Kong and Singapore on credit, repaying only upon the sale of the products in Indonesia. Letters of credit are issued in advance to enable buyers in Indonesia to purchase local products for export. Chinese investors have entered into many new joint ventures with local entrepreneurs, and this in turn has benefited other Chinese businessmen and retailers. As of 1974, the number of Chinese commercial establishments had risen to 150,000 firms, of which a majority (120,000) consisted of retail businesses.[44]

Chinese Industrial Investment. A 1953 directory of the Chinese Chamber of Commerce in Indonesia listed some 2,000 ethnic-Chinese industrial enterprises of varying size. Of these about one quarter (512 firms) were located in Jakarta or its environs. Some Chinese enterprises previously nationalized under the Sukarno regime were returned to their owners after 1967. These, together with new Chinese-owned enterprises, have prospered under Suharto.

The Indonesian Central Bureau of Statistics[45] reported 102 joint ventures involving Indonesian and Chinese participation between 1967 and mid-1971. Some of these businesses, listed by the source of Chinese funds outside

TABLE 31

ALIEN-CHINESE BUSINESS IN INDONESIA BY TYPE AND CAPITAL INVESTMENT, 1959

	Number of Firms	Estimated Capital Investment (U.S. $ Million)
Foreign trade and wholesale merchants	962	96.20
Proprietors of medium-sized businesses	24,991	249.91
Retailers	83,783	418.91
Total	109,736	765.02

SOURCE: *Hua-ch'iao ching-chi nien-chien, 1971* [Overseas Chinese Economy Yearbook] (Taipei: World Chinese Traders Convention Liaison Office).

TABLE 32

JOINT CHINESE-INDONESIAN BUSINESS PROJECTS FORMED IN 1967–71

Source of Chinese Funds	Number of Projects	Capital Investments (U.S. $ Million)
Hong Kong	53	101.4
Singapore	27	50.5
Malaysia	22	35.5
Total	102	187.4

Indonesia, also attracted non-Chinese foreign capital and technology. The bureau's statistics are given in Table 32.

It should be noted that only projects of some scale that had been formally approved as foreign investments are included in these data. Many other smaller enterprises have been established jointly with Indonesian citizens of Chinese origin on an informal basis outside the purview of the foreign-investment regulations. In addition, private businesses in Taiwan have made investments of approximately $16 million, according to a 1975 report of the Jakarta Chinese Chamber of Commerce.

Chinese in the Agricultural Sector. There were 1,502 large farms or plantations in Indonesia in 1957, according to the Indonesian government.[46] About one fifth of these (314), accounting for 236,000 of 2,231,000 acres of farmland, were Chinese owned. Their principal crops were sugar cane, rubber, coconut, coffee, tobacco, and pepper, all intended for the commercial market. More recently, Chinese investors have entered the lumber business, mostly working with other Chinese interests in Southeast Asia, Hong Kong, and Taiwan. Although Chinese-owned undertakings are smaller in scale than those of Japanese and European firms, the logging operations of these non-Chinese firms are frequently performed by Chinese contractors using indigenous labor. One interesting example in this field is a joint venture between ethnic Chinese in Indonesia and Taiwan, backed by Japanese loan financing for the purchase of logging equipment.

Some fifty thousand ethnic Chinese are engaged in fishing—mostly poor fishermen who are unable to purchase new equipment. Even this sector, however, has begun to attract the attention of enterprising businessmen confident of the prospects for an Indonesian fishing industry.

Indonesian Policy toward Chinese Enterprises. Discrimination against Chinese enterprises during the Sukarno period focused on the commercial sector. Special bank credits and preferential allocations of import licenses and foreign exchanges to indigenous businesses, an expanding list of goods that only indigenous Indonesians were allowed to import under a 1950 program, and high deposit requirements for alien importers were among the restrictive measures that led to the closing of nearly a thousand Chinese import houses. These measures were paralleled by the confiscation of Chinese-owned rice mills and by the ousting of Chinese retailers, since 1959, from rural areas.[47]

The Suharto administration's basic policy toward Chinese was first outlined in a June 1967 instruction of the presidium of the cabinet (No. 37.U/IN/6.1967). The conditions, in brief, were: (1) no residence permits would be issued to new Chinese immigrants to enable them to work or go into a business; (2) resident aliens must apply for work permits to find employment or to open businesses; (3) efforts would be made to mobilize alien capital invested in Indonesia (this excluded capital that entered Indonesia as foreign capital under the current foreign-investment law); and (4) aliens might apply for naturalization and become Indonesian citizens.

A few months after making this policy statement, President Suharto announced in a March 29, 1968, speech in Japan that Indonesia planned to make full use of alien-Chinese capital during the next ten to thirty years. A law passed in the same year stipulated that foreign capital in commercial enterprises should pass into Indonesian ownership within ten years unless it had originally been invested in a joint venture. Foreign capital in other productive enterprises would be similarly treated within thirty years. Alien-Chinese commercial activities would also be eliminated by 1997, excluding those financed by foreign capital that had originally been remitted to Indonesia for this purpose. A 1972 speech by Suharto indicated that Indonesia would like to transfer foreign equity to indigenous ownership via a government-sponsored stock market, thus going beyond the mere encouragement of Indonesian enterprises. Furthermore, while advocating equal opportunity during the period of economic construction for both Pribumis and non-Pribumis, Suharto also announced that regulations would be devised to enable non-Pribumi entrepreneurs to sell their 50 percent of stock to the government for resale to the Pribumis. A subsequent explanatory statement noted that the transfer should leave the foreign investors with no more than 49 percent of equity, while Indonesian citizens must possess 51 percent.

As we can see from the preceding account, there has been a gradual shift of position under the Suharto government. The need to seek the full cooperation of ethnic-Chinese capital and enterprise is increasingly being acknowledged. There is also growing recognition that Indonesianization should proceed at least partly through the acquisition of Indonesian citizenship by ethnic-Chinese entrepreneurs and capitalists, and that all Indonesian citizens should be treated equally, regardless of racial origin. Of course, equal treatment has not been fully realized, and ambiguity and equivocation remain. Nevertheless, the present position is a substantial departure from the views espoused by the strongly nationalist Assaat movement. Founded in March 1956 at an all-Indonesian national congress in Surabaya, this movement was openly anti-Chinese. "Even though the anti-Chinese tide has been stopped and there is a positive policy toward the solution of this problem," wrote Lie Tek Tjeng in 1970, "discrimination in one form or another against the ethnic Chinese will continue during our present generation as a result of the chaotic economic situation, local conditions, economic and other rivalries, prejudices, etc., and it may be difficult for those experiencing this to take the long view and see it in terms of decades, if not centuries."[48] Will events prove Lie's pessimism unwarranted?

The Thai Policy of Assimilation

Early Historical Background. Chinese economic activities in Thailand date back to 1238 under the Sukhotai dynasty (1238–1419). During the fifteenth century what the Chinese regarded as tribute-trade was conducted regularly between Thailand and China. Later, Chinese were employed as agents of taxation, trade, and foreign commerce on behalf of the Ayuthia dynasty (1350–1767). The Thai economy developed considerably under Phya Tak Sin (1767–1782), and the country's sparse population and the resultant labor shortages led to large-scale Chinese immigration.[49] Under Rama I of the Chakri dynasty (1782–1809), a Chinese commercial district was established in Sampeng Street in today's Chinatown in Bangkok, then the new capital. During the last years of the nineteenth century, Chinese economic activities gradually extended from the manufacturing and commercial sectors to agriculture and mining, and eventually spread across the entire economy.

A British-Siamese treaty of friendship and commerce was concluded[50] in 1855. Thereafter, the British, followed by the Dutch, French, and Portuguese, took over Thai foreign trade, while the commercial position of the Chinese declined. Increasing modernization on the part of the Thai elite and their growing familiarity with economic matters also increased competition for the Chinese. Nevertheless, the Chinese were able to retain their important positions as middlemen in the sale of rice and native products, and in the retail and wholesale sectors.

Size of the Ethnic-Chinese Population. Evidence of Thailand's successful assimilation policy is the overwhelming majority of Chinese in the country who have become naturalized citizens. The number of overseas Chinese (as measured by official Thai statistics) has declined steadily—from 794,000 in 1947 to 316,000 in 1975. The 1975 figure was published on July 1, 1975, following Prime Minister Kukrit Pramoj's announcement of the establishment of diplomatic relations with Peking. Since neither Thailand nor the PRC recognizes dual nationality, permission was granted at the time of Kukrit's announcement to those Chinese who were still aliens to choose freely among PRC citizenship, naturalization, and statelessness. A large proportion accepted naturalization.

Thailand's annual immigration quota for any single country has been reduced from an earlier post–World War II limit of 200 to 150 persons, so that the number of legal Chinese immigrants, other than those who are admitted under the foreign-investment regulations, is bound to be limited. This change, together with the free choice mentioned above, should reduce the number of Chinese in future official Thai statistics even further.

Different estimates of the number of ethnic Chinese—both Thai citizens and noncitizens—are available. In 1857 the number of Chinese in Thailand was estimated as 1.5 million.[51] A later, frequently cited figure is Skinner's estimate for 1955 of 2.3 million, with the Teochius accounting for 56 percent, followed by Hakkas and Hainanese.[52] Estimates provided in 1973 by ROC authorities range from 3.5 to 4 million. If Skinner's estimate for 1955 is projected to 1976 on the basis of a natural growth rate of 2.5–3 percent a year, it will also reach 3.5 million. This corresponds to the estimate put forward by United for Progress at its Manila meeting in 1974.[53]

Assimilation and Distribution of Business Ownership. More than 50 percent of the Chinese in Thailand live in the Bangkok area. They are employed in commerce or industry. Those who live in smaller towns and villages are engaged in growing rice, corn, and vegetables and in raising livestock. Chinese in southern Thailand are often coal miners; fishing is the predominant occupation on the coast. The ubiquitousness of Chinese in Thailand testifies to that nation's equal treatment of all naturalized citizens. As of 1965, the occupational distribution of ethnic Chinese was: commerce, 70 percent; industry, 16 percent; agriculture and fishing, 8 percent; and mining, 6 percent. While the larger firms continued to be Western or Japanese, as they had been prior to World War II, the medium-sized and small enterprises were almost entirely Chinese.

Official statistics on the distribution of ownership of companies formed between 1960 and 1970 show a large proportion of Thai investment, but many Thai owners are actually naturalized ethnic Chinese. For this reason, the data in Table 33 tend to understate the relative proportion of ethnic-Chinese ownership.

Commercial and Industrial Activities. Among the smaller Chinese enterprises in Thailand, dialect and district associations have retained considerable influence on occupational specialization. (This is also true elsewhere in Southeast Asia.) For example, the Teochius are engaged mostly in import and export businesses, the clothing trade, rice milling, the sale of native products and dry goods, canned food, cosmetics, hardware, jewelry, distilling, publishing, furniture, and entertainment, as well as such business services as finance, insurance, and shipping. The Cantonese-speaking group specializes in machine repair, construction, food and beverages, printing, watches and clocks, and the sugar industry. Hakkas are concentrated in leather and hides, weaving, department-store retailing, metal working, shoe manufacturing, tailoring, hairdressing,

TABLE 33

STOCK OWNERSHIP IN LIMITED COMPANIES IN THAILAND BY RACE

	1960				1970			
	Authorized Capital (Million Baht)	Percentage	Number of Firms	Percentage	Authorized Capital (Million Baht)	Percentage	Number of Firms	Percentage
Thai	684,685	67.9	1,001	67.6	3,600	90.6	3,786	90.0
Chinese	209,685	20.8	489	29.2	120	3.1	261	6.2
Foreign	114,017	11.3	54	3.2	184	6.3	155	3.8
Total	1,008,387	100.0	1,544	100.0	3,904	100.0	4.202	100.0

SOURCE: *Hua-ch'iao ching-chi kai-k'uang* [A Guide to the Economic Position of the Overseas Chinese] (Taipei: OCAC, 1974), p. 19.

truck farming, and banking. The Hainanese are in beverages, hotels, furniture making, hairdressing, and fisheries, and the Hokkiens are in the rubber and tin-mining industries, as well as foreign trade. The Yunnanese work mostly in jewelry and precious stones. Those who do not belong to the preceding speech groups, including immigrants from Kiangsu, Chekiang, and other Chinese mainland provinces, are mostly in the lumber industry, foreign trade, and modern industry. Taiwanese have specialized in the sale and distribution of imported Japanese products. As we will show later, overlapping occurs mostly in foreign trade.

The preceding list refers mostly to smaller businesses. During the past two decades, however, Chinese entrepreneurs in Thailand have moved from commerce to modern industry, including oil refining, cement, paper manufacturing, rubber tires, food additives, and textiles. These enterprises have long surpassed the traditional family and dialect-group businesses in size and extent of capitalization. The newer industrial establishments are mostly joint ventures with entrepreneurs from Singapore, Hong Kong, or Taiwan. Many have established cooperative technical arrangements with Western and Japanese businesses.

A 1964 JETRO report[54] estimated that 70 percent of the Chinese in Thailand were engaged in commercial activities, primarily imports, exports, and the wholesale and retail trades. Imports were chiefly handled by affluent Chinese; wholesale and retail firms were run by the middle and lower-income classes. The Chinese also had an important function in the export of primary products, including their collection from small producers and transportation to central markets. They had built up a domestic commercial network, at the same time maintaining close relations with business allies in Singapore, Hong Kong, and Taiwan. JETRO attributed the business success of the Chinese in Thailand to the existence of this complex distribution network.

The center of commercial organization is the Chinese Chamber of Commerce in Bangkok. Representatives of the many district associations and trade guilds in the country serve as directors of the Chamber of Commerce. Interestingly, the membership has included both Thai-Chinese and Chinese who are not citizens. Affiliated associations have similar mixed memberships. In some cases, even indigenous Thais have become members; thus these trade associations are in fact also Thai commercial organizations. Similarly, many Thai business groups have ethnic-Chinese members who are naturalized Thai citizens.[55]

Particularly worthy of note is the significant position held by Chinese in the transportation sector of the economy. Because Chinese traders have been involved in purchasing agricultural products in rural areas for a long time, they also became active in river transport. Since the 1960s they have entered ocean transportation, and more than ten Chinese-owned shipping companies have been established. Most of these work as agents for foreign steamship companies; only two actually own or lease oceangoing ships, but a beginning has still been made in a new direction. The Chinese are also active in the tourist and entertainment industries, including hotels, nightclubs, large restaurants, and the group-tour business.

The Financial Sector. In the nineteenth century, Chinese rice millers and farm-product brokers began extending loans to farmers, providing them with working capital for the purchase of seeds, farm implements, and other agricultural necessities. Some owned pawnshops that extended short-term credit. Despite its name, the Chinese-owned Yü Ch'eng-hsin Watch Company, which was also a dealer in precious stones and metals as well as a foreign-exchange broker, became the first private bank in Thailand. Following the enactment of a 1939 law,[56] all Chinese banks were required to become joint ventures with Thai citizens. The incorporators are usually ethnic-Chinese Thai citizens. Chairmen of the boards of directors are often Thai political figures, while ethnic Chinese provide administrative talent. Eleven of the larger commercial banks are owned and operated by Chinese, and three of these—the Bangkok Bank, the Bangkok Metropolitan Bank and the Thai Chinese Agricultural Bank—have branches abroad. The Bangkok Bank has overseas branches in Hong Kong, Singapore, Taipei, Tokyo, Osaka, Kuala Lumpur, Saigon, Jakarta, New York, and London. Chinese-operated banks in Hong Kong, Singapore, Malaysia, and Taipei in turn have branches in Thailand. In addition, four trust companies with large Chinese investments are active in the financial sector. (For a listing of these financial institutions, see Appendix E.)

Agriculture and Fisheries. The Chinese were responsible for introducing to the country commercial production of such crops as sugar cane, pepper, and many vegetables and fruits. The early farm workers were mostly Hakkas and Hokkiens, with the latter especially numerous in the pepper and rubber industries. More-recent immigrants who came from Yunnan through Burma after the fall of mainland China to the communist regime have settled in the Chiangmai and Chiangrai areas, cultivating rice, corn, and jute and raising poultry on the side. In addition, some twenty thousand ethnic Chinese are engaged in fishing on the coast.

Chinese Investments by Sector. The latest data on the distribution of Chinese investment in Thailand by sector (Table 34) demonstrate rather conclusively the dominant position of ethnic Chinese in the Thai economy, especially in manufacturing and commerce. Only in fishing and agriculture are indigenous-Thai interests in the majority. The estimate of $1.6 billion for Chinese investments in 1972 given in Table 34 is nearly four times Ho I-wu's estimate, which we quoted in Chapter 2. The explanation lies in the different areas covered by the two. The later estimate includes all ethnic-Chinese investments, while Ho's was limited to investments made by alien Chinese.

TABLE 34

CHINESE INVESTMENT IN THAILAND, BY SECTOR, 1972

Sector	Number of Firms	Capital ($ Million)	Ethnic-Chinese Capital as Percentage of Total in Thailand
Commerce:			
Import and export	1,000	500.0	95
Wholesale and retail	5,000	200.0	90
Restaurant	2,500	150.0	95
Service	500	100.0	80
Entertainment	150	50.0	70
Medicine	1,000	30.0	80
Transportation	10	2.0	80
Other	500	5.0	90
Banking and finance	50	300.0	50
Manufacturing	2,000	300.0	90
Agriculture	100	0.5	2
Mining	50	2.0	30
Fishery	100	1.0	20
Total	12,960	1,640.5	

SOURCE: *Hua-ch'iao ching-chi nien-chien, 1974,* p. 45.

From Restriction and Control to Assimilation. The efforts of the Thai government to restrict the economic activities of alien Chinese in Thailand began with a 1939 proclamation of *ratha niyom* ("a patriotic movement"). Following this proclamation, which urged the Thai population to take an active part in commercial and industrial enterprises and to buy Thai products, measures designed to restrict Chinese activities multiplied. The severity of the pressure varied with changing domestic and international political conditions. It was particularly severe during the first (1938–45) and second (1948—57) administrations of Lung Phibul Songkram. The same policy was continued by Marshal Sarit in 1957 and has remained essentially unchanged since that time. The series of measures listed in Appendix C was enacted in the spirit of this movement. To recapitulate, they included the 1942 royal decree reserving twenty-seven occupations to Thai nationals only, which was accompanied by new restrictions on immigration; the 1951 restriction on remittances to China by overseas Chinese; an increase in the alien registration fee in 1952; a 1956 law requiring firms employing more than ten persons to hire Thais for at least 50 percent of the positions; a 1972 law that revised the control of alien occupations; and finally, the 1974 Alien Enterprise Control Law, which made joint ventures with Thai nationals (with the latter holding 51 percent of the stock) a requirement for continued business operation by alien-owned firms not established under foreign-investment laws. About one hundred thousand applications were received within the first ninety days after the enactment of the Alien Occupation Law in 1972. Of these, 87 percent were from Chinese, 8 percent from

Vietnamese, 2 percent from Indians, and 3 percent from other foreign nationals.

In 1964 the government instructed the social-science division of the Thai National Academy to study the Chinese problem,[57] and a special commission was established for the same purpose in 1971. A preliminary report on the Thai-Chinese problem was finally submitted by the commission in 1973; the recommendations in this report deserve consideration.

The report defined three groups of ethnic Chinese in Thailand: (1) real aliens who have Chinese nationality and are of ethnic-Chinese parentage; (2) ethnic Chinese born in Thailand who have Thai citizenship and enjoy the same treatment under the law as indigenous Thais; and (3) children of the second group who are third-generation ethnic Chinese and are entirely assimilated as Thais. Members of the last group, as the report pointed out, now hold influential positions in the Thai economy and society.

The commission also indicated that ethnic-Chinese organizations are important vehicles for promoting solidarity in Chinese communities. Given the demographic background of the Chinese and the economic position they have already established, it would be impossible to alter entirely the traditional practices and ways of life of the older ethnic Chinese and to make them adopt Thai ways. At the same time, the report continued, certain Chinese commercial and economic characteristics definitely merit Thai emulation. In the circumstances, it would not be practical to try to replace the Chinese through competition on the market or to seize national economic control by political means. Therefore, the commission recommended that the government adopt the following approach in handling Thai-Chinese economic relations:

1. It should initiate cooperation with ethnic Chinese, inviting Chinese businessmen and leaders of the Chamber of Commerce to help in the development of the Thai economy in a way that would promote mutual understanding.
2. It should at the same time take positive action to aid ethnic-Thai citizens in gaining skills in finance and business management. The government should exercise control over alien occupations rather than attempt to make certain areas of the economy private reserve for Thai nationals, realizing that any threat to the Thai economy by alien economic interests would not come from the Chinese alone.
3. The government should emulate Singapore's approach—treating Chinese and other races on an entirely equal footing to promote the absorption and assimilation of ethnic Chinese who are descendants of aliens; at the same time, however, it should bar illegal immigration of Chinese into Thailand.
4. The government should encourage the indigenous Thai to become more like the Chinese with regard to such characteristics as industry, the work ethic, and a keen awareness of the rigorous demands of economic life and the free market.

These recommendations appear eminently rational since they combine positive affirmative action for the Thais with cooperation with and assimilation of the ethnic Chinese. This policy stands in sharp contrast to that of restriction and replacement advocated in Indonesia and especially Malaysia.

Chinese in the Philippines

Early History. Records of trade between China and the Philippines go back to the Chinese T'ang dynasty. During the Sung dynasty, Chinese businessmen visited Mait or the Three Islands and Chinese merchant vessels called on Sulu in the southern Philippines. By the Ming dynasty, more than ten thousand Chinese had already settled on Luzon. Writings of the mid-Ming (1521–74) dynasty contain descriptions of Chinese traders and residents in Parian near the Pasig River in present-day Manila.[58]

During the period of Spanish rule, Chinese in the Philippines were known as Sangley, an obvious transliteration from the Chinese term for businessmen. Because of their increasing numbers and commercial competitiveness, they often became targets of oppression and heavy taxation. Massacres of Chinese in 1639, 1662, 1663, 1686, and 1762 failed to deter continued immigration. The economic foundations of the Chinese community were laid during the three centuries of Spanish rule (1570–1898); their contribution to Philippine well-being was generously acknowledged by Juan de la Concepcion, who wrote, "Without trade and commerce of the Chinese, these dominions could not have subsisted."[59]

Chinese economic activities continued to expand until 1941, when the Japanese occupation ushered in the darkest period for the Chinese community. After the war and the attainment of independence by the Philippines in 1946, Chinese economic activity became the target of restriction under the country's Filipino-First policy.

For example, Philippine immigration authorities reportedly stated at one time that there was no record of the naturalization of any Chinese before 1949,[60] although following long residence and intermarriages, many second- and third-generation Chinese had in fact been naturalized. Records presumably had not been kept. The same authorities[61] list 4,880 naturalizations of Chinese between 1949 and 1957, but this figure, too, is disputed. A study by Huang Ming-teh indicated that 25,000 Chinese were naturalized before 1955. Furthermore, immigration records show 138,000 alien Chinese in 1957 versus only 125,000 in 1965. All this seems to indicate that many more ethnic Chinese had become Philippine citizens than were officially recorded as Chinese in 1965.[62] The latest estimate put the total number of ethnic Chinese, including both Philippine citizens and others, at 600,000. Of this number 85 percent were Fukienese; the remainder from Canton and other provinces.

In an effort to encourage naturalization on the eve of the diplomatic recognition of Peking by Manila, the Philippine government relaxed the rules governing that process through Presidential Letter of Instruction No. 270 dated April 22, 1975. Naturalization was to be granted fairly quickly upon application by qualified aliens—those who were of good character and over twenty-one, who had entered the country legally and stayed more than ten years, who were employed, and who could read and write Tagalog, English, or Spanish. The applicants also had to have children studying in the Philippines and Filipino friends who could vouch for them. Although the qualifications appear somewhat stringent, 20,000 families—80,000–90,000 persons—applied under this law.[63] Another special group of 1,785 Chinese came to the Philippines as visitors following the occupation of the Chinese mainland by the communists. They overstayed and became a serious source of friction between the Philippines and the Republic of China, but were finally given permanent residence on June 7, 1975. More than 300,000 of the 600,000 ethnic Chinese live in greater Manila; the rest are scattered over all the islands.

Chinese Economic Activities. A 1932 Philippine official estimate gave percentage distribution of investments by race and nationality as: Chinese, 42 percent; Filipino, 28.6 percent; American, 8.5 percent; Japanese, 7.8 percent; and other foreigners, 13.0 percent.[64] As we noted earlier, Fukuda's estimate for 1930 indicated that Chinese investment in the Philippines was heavily concentrated in the commercial and service sectors, which then accounted for 81.1 percent of the total. The primary sector accounted for only 0.1 percent of Chinese investment, while the secondary sector, manufacturing and mining, was responsible for 18.8 percent. If the two estimates are taken together, it is evident that the Chinese invested heavily in the commercial and service sectors, while Filipino investment was concentrated mostly in the primary sector. The secondary sector was shared by Chinese, Japanese, and Westerners.

The recovery of the Philippines from the devastation of World War II was fairly rapid. The first official postwar survey in 1948 put Chinese investments at 372 million pesos, or 16 percent of the total capital stock surveyed. This estimate, which presumably included only alien Chinese investments, was distributed as shown in Table 35. Approximately three fourths of Chinese investment was in commerce, and 90 percent of this was concentrated in retailing and the service industries.

A more detailed breakdown of capital distribution by industry was presented in a 1956 study (see Table 36). The Federation of Chinese Chambers of Commerce, which is the all-Philippine Chinese business organization, composed of 63 trade associations in the greater Manila area and 116 similar organizations in the provinces and other cities, plus 29 nonorganizational members, reported on thirty-five major categories of trade and two hundred subcategories in which the Chinese were active. Chinese enterprises occur in a variety of combinations. Some are run by alien Chinese; others are operated by Filipino citizens of Chinese descent; and still others are joint ventures between alien Chinese and

TABLE 35

ESTIMATE OF CHINESE INVESTMENT IN THE PHILIPPINES, 1948

Sector	Ethnic-Chinese Investment (Million Pesos)
Commerce	282.0
Manufacturing	68.5
Forestry	16.4
Transportation and communications	0.6
Mining	3.8
Electric utilities	0.4
Fisheries	0.4
Total	372.1

TABLE 36

ETHNIC-CHINESE CAPITAL INVESTMENTS IN THE PHILIPPINES, 1956

Sector	Number of Enterprises	Total Investment (Million $)
Wholesale, import and export	3,000	500.0
Retail	20,000	300.0
Manufacturing	3,000	300.0
Real estate		150.0
Rice and corn growing	400	60.0
Banking	4	50.0
Forestry	100	40.0
Tobacco growing	50	40.0
Other agriculture		20.0
Mining, fishing, transportation, and electricity		20.0
Professional services		20.0
Personal and recreation services		8.0
Insurance	18	8.0
Construction		5.0
Total	26,572	1,521.0

SOURCE: Huang Ming-teh, *Fei-lü-pin hai-wai hua-ch'iao ching-chi* [Overseas Chinese Economy in the Philippines] (Taipei: Hai-wai ch'u-pan-she, 1956), pp. 132–33.

Filipino-Chinese, between alien Chinese and indigenous Filipinos, between naturalized citizens of ethnic-Chinese origin and indigenous Filipinos, or among alien Chinese, Filipino-Chinese, and non-Chinese foreign partners. These combinations reflect the extreme complexity of the social and economic position of ethnic Chinese in the Philippines. They also reflect the mutual tolerance that prevails between indigenous Filipinos and Chinese, as well as the readiness of native Filipinos to invest in commercial enterprises.

Commercial Activities. A 1948 census listed 135,500 commercial establishments in the Philippines employing 456,500 persons. The total assets of these establishments were given as 1.2 billion pesos, of which ownership by Filipinos accounted for 46.2 percent; by Chinese, 23.3 percent; and by U.S. citizens, 12.9 percent. The balance was held by other foreign interests.[65] A 1947 report had stated that Chinese firms were responsible for 39.1 percent of total imports and 24.1 percent of exports. Their share in the total foreign trade of the country was just over one third, only a shade below that of American firms, while Filipino firms were responsible for only 22.7 percent of foreign trade.[66]

Statistics of this kind underscore the conspicuous position of Chinese businessmen, which inevitably made them the primary targets of the Filipino-First movement. The earliest discriminatory moves against Chinese business came in the area of foreign trade. Under the foreign-exchange regulations of December 1949 that were introduced by the Quirino administration, only Filipino and American citizens were allowed to register as new importers and enjoy the right to foreign-exchange allocations. While Chinese importers were permitted to continue in business, no new Chinese firms could be established. In addition, statistics on foreign-exchange allocations released by the Philippines Central Bank appear to show discrimination against Chinese, and to a lesser extent American, applicants (see Table 37).

The wide disparity between the official and market rates of exchange in this period allowed some recipients of official import quotas, which entitled them to purchase foreign exchange at the official rate, to sell their quotas at a profit. Chinese importers who received reduced allocations were handicapped in competing with United States and Filipino firms. The emergence of ghost firms and gross favoritism in allocating foreign exchange finally led to the abolition of the system under President Macapagal on January 21, 1962.

The next major restrictive order was issued by the Magsaysay administration. The Retail Trade Nationalization Law (Republic Act No. 1180), adopted on June 19, 1954, required Chinese-owned retail establishments to cease operating by a final deadline of June 1964.[67] No new alien-owned retail establishments were to

TABLE 37

Foreign-Exchange Allocations in the Philippines
(Million Pesos)

	1949	1951
Filipinos	263	354
Americans	333	275
Chinese	423	257
Total	1,019	886

be permitted after July 1955. A National Marketing Corporation (NAMARCO) was established on June 18, 1955 (Republic Act No. 1345). Armed with thirty million pesos of government funds, NAMARCO purchased goods for resale at subsidized prices to Filipino retailers. The company was also given a one-million-peso annual operating budget. By the beginning of 1967 its capital had been exhausted, and a hundred-million-peso debt to the government bank had accumulated. The company was finally phased out by President Marcos in March 1967.

Under the double-barreled attack of the Retail Trade Nationalization Law and the operations of NAMARCO, the number of alien-owned retail establishments declined from 20,268 in 1954 to 11,078 in 1964. Only 7,624 were left at the time of reregistration in 1970. The number of annual closings reached peaks of 1,865 in 1960 and 1,339 in 1961, stimulated by the enactment of a law nationalizing all rice and corn businesses on August 2, 1960, under President Garcia. This act required the winding up of alien retail and wholesale establishments in these fields within six years. Data from private Philippine sources (given in Table 38) demonstrate the restrictive effect of the last measure.

As a result of the decline in alien-owned businesses, 146,578 of the 160,030 retail establishments reported in 1961 were owned by Filipinos. Some of the additions were new Filipino rice and corn distributors. The 1960 law was abolished in May 1973 under Presidential Instruction No. 194 when grain shortages became acute.

The restrictive measures against aliens did not entirely accomplish their objectives. Chinese businessmen continued operation by using Filipino fronts, became naturalized Filipino citizens, or employed Filipinos to act on their behalf. Large numbers of Chinese workers, however, as well as native Filipinos, were unable to find employment as a result of closings. Another aspect of the

TABLE 38

ALIEN-OWNED RICE AND CORN BUSINESSES IN THE PHILIPPINES

		Rice and Corn			
	Rice Mills	Retail Establishments	Wholesale Establishments	Total Number of Alien-owned Firms	Total Alien Investment (Million Pesos)
1948	130[a]	...	...	...	...
August 1960	691[b]	3,821	1,597	6,109	22
August 1962	...	...	...	2,177	...
End of 1962	...	...	...	400	...
1963	...	...	...	80	...
1964	...	...	...	negligible	...

[a]In 1948, there were forty corn mills. Total investment in the corn and rice mills amounted to ten million pesos. There were twenty-five hundred Chinese owners and more than ten thousand employees, both Chinese and Filipino.

[b]Including warehouses.

adjustment process was the transfer of Chinese capital from retailing to wholesaling, foreign trade, and manufacturing, as the changing distribution of paid-in capital of new business establishments between 1955 and 1963 shows (see Table 39).

Industrial Activity. Following the enactment of martial law, there was a substantial improvement in the investment climate in the early 1970s. Since then both alien-Chinese and Filipino-Chinese industrial investments have prospered. In addition, ethnic-Chinese capital from Hong Kong, Taiwan, and other parts of Southeast Asia has come into the country. Within the textile industry ethnic Chinese owned 54 percent of all spindles and 67 percent of the looms, while Filipinos owned 38 percent of the spindles and 28 percent of the looms.[68] A survey of newly registered firms in the three-year period ending June 30, 1974, made by the Philippine Securities and Exchange Commission, showed that alien-Chinese-owned establishments accounted for as much as 10 percent of registered capital. Chinese-owned manufacturing firms were mostly small in scale and were scattered in a number of light-manufacturing industrial districts in

TABLE 39

ALIEN-CHINESE CAPITAL INVESTMENT IN NEWLY REGISTERED BUSINESS ORGANIZATIONS IN THE PHILIPPINES, 1955 AND 1963

	Paid-in Capital			
	1955		*1963*	
Kind of Business	Value (Thousand Pesos)	Percentage	Value (Thousand Pesos)	Percentage
Agriculture	72	0.2	55	0.1
Forestry, fishing, and livestock	424	1.4	1,193	2.7
Mining of metals	38	0.1	33	0.1
Nonmetallic mining and quarrying	...	...	...	...
Manufacturing	8,622	29.2	13,994	31.0
Construction	60	0.2	91	0.2
Electricity, gas, and water service	...	...	...	...
Wholesale and retail trade	18,401	63.0	25,535	57.0
Banking and finance	862	2.9	918	2.1
Insurance	34	0.1	115	0.3
Real estate	499	1.7	139	0.3
Transportation, storage, and communication	147	0.5	45	0.1
Community and business service	120	0.4	1,347	3.0
Recreation and personal service	250	0.8	1,166	2.6
Total	29,529	100.0*	44,631	100.0*

SOURCE: Schubert S. C. Liao, ed., *Chinese Participation in Philippine Culture and Economy,* Appendix C, table 1, p. 429–34; original data from the Bureau of Commerce, the Securities and Exchange Commission, and the Central Bank of the Philippines.

*Components may not add to 100 due to rounding.

the greater Manila area. Larger businesses established with direct foreign investment from ethnic-Chinese interests in Hong Kong, Taiwan, or elsewhere were corporate businesses under modern management producing textiles and chemicals.

Financial Investment. There were only four Chinese-owned banks in the Philippines in 1956. The China Banking Corporation and the Philippine Bank of Communications were owned by alien-Chinese interests. The Equitable Banking Corporation and the Pacific Banking Corporation, on the other hand, were owned by Filipino-Chinese. As of June 1971, there were nine important Chinese-owned banks with total assets of 3.25 billion pesos. These banks all have their head offices in Manila with branches in other cities (see Table 40).

The Equitable Bank has a branch in Hong Kong and one in San Francisco using the name Bank of the Orient, and the Metropolitan Bank has a branch in Taipei. The formerly alien-Chinese-owned Bank of Communications was taken over by ethnic-Chinese owners in participation with the Irving Trust Company of New York. There are, in addition, twenty-three insurance companies with Chinese investment that account for approximately one sixth of the total insurance industry. The Great Pacific Insurance Company is the largest. By 1975 there were also two Chinese trust companies.

Agriculture, Forestry, and Shipping. Chinese undertakings in agriculture and forestry have been subject to restrictions on land ownership and land use by aliens. The firms have had to lease land from Filipinos or be operated by Filipino-Chinese. Truck farming, mostly by ethnic Chinese from Kwangtung, is concentrated in northern Luzon and the Baguio area. A number of stock ranches and plantations are in Mindanao, and Chinese have taken a part in developing banana production for export to the Japanese market. Ethnic Chinese are also active in the export of timber, sugar, copra, and coconut oil.[69]

Other areas of Chinese activity are domestic shipping and the tourist business, which has been expanded to neighboring countries, including Hong Kong, Taipei, and others in Southeast Asia.

The Economic Condition of Chinese in Socialist Burma and Behind the Communist Wall in Indochina

Burma. During the Han dynasty, Chinese businessmen going to India took a land route between China and Burma. A Burmese embassy visited China during the T'ang dynasty in the company of a representative from the Shan kingdom of Nanchao, which is today part of Yunnan.[70] Kublai Khan's forces invaded Burma in 1284 and destroyed the city of Pagan. When the Ming dynasty came to an end in 1644, Chinese immigration to Burma rose. Burma was absorbed into India in 1886 at the end of the third British-Burmese war.

TABLE 40

CHINESE CAPITAL INVESTMENT IN COMMERCIAL BANKING IN THE PHILIPPINES, JUNE 30, 1971
(Thousand Pesos)

Bank	Total Assets	Earning Assets	Deposits	Net Worth	Number of Branches
China Banking Corporation	604.5	495.3	360.1	96.4	5
Equitable Banking Corporation	578.1	465.3	418.0	63.2	24
Consolidated Bank and Trust Corporation	507.9	360.5	323.3	42.6	...
Pacific Banking Corporation	421.9	326.6	327.5	42.7	27
Rizal Commercial Banking Corporation	384.3	331.0	212.9	28.5	24
Philippine Bank of Communications	304.3	252.6	181.4	37.4	2
Metropolitan Bank and Trust Co.	247.9	181.0	140.7	23.4	70
Bank of Asia	115.2	94.8	48.4	22.1	...
Associate Banking Corporation	87.7	68.3	36.3	21.5	25
A. Total Chinese investment	3,251.8	2,575.4	2,048.6	377.8	...
B. Total investments in all commercial banks	14,676.0	11,449.2	8,622.9	1,449.4	
A as a percentage of B	22.2	22.5	23.8	26.1	

SOURCE: *The World Chinese Financial Convention Report* (Taipei: World Chinese Trades Convention Liaison Office, 1972).

Separation from India occurred in 1937, and Burma became independent in January 1948.

There was border trade between Yunnan and Burma during the T'ang dynasty; Chinese also farmed on the Burma side of the border. Chinese emigrants from Kwangtung and Fukien arrived by sea during the Sung and Ming dynasties. Few Chinese took up long-term residence in Burma, however, until the Yüan dynasty, when Chinese business activities in Burma expanded beyond a seasonal-visit level. With the stepping-up of economic development of Burma by the British at the turn of this century, many Chinese came from Malaysia.

The Chinese in Burma, known as *Pauk Paw* ("close relatives"), numbered 193,594 in the 1931 census. In 1947, Purcell estimated the Chinese population at 300,000. Both the official 1953 Burmese estimate and an estimate by Purcell for 1960 put the Chinese population at 350,000.[71] A much higher figure, however—650,000 persons—was given by ROC sources as the total ethnic-Chinese population in Burma in 1973. This number presumably included refugees from China after 1949, but the estimate may not have allowed for the subsequent emigration of large numbers of these refugees from northern Burma to northern Thailand, or for the departure of many Chinese from Burma in response to the 1962 nationalization program of the Ne Win government. Consequently, a more conservative estimate of half a million ethnic Chinese appears reasonable.

Most Chinese in Burma came from Fukien, with lesser numbers from Kwangtung and Yunnan. Twenty percent of them live in the Rangoon area; the Shan states account for another 20 percent, Pegu and Irrawaddy for 13 percent each, and the Mandalay and Tenasserim divisions for the rest.

The Chinese in Burma have a somewhat different history from Chinese in other parts of Southeast Asia. Before World War II, there were more Indians in Burma than Chinese, but as a result of a planned withdrawal of Indians after the war, many of their retail stores, including buildings, inventories, and equipment, were acquired by the Chinese. This transition put the Chinese in first place in Burma's commercial life for a time.

Before World War II, Chinese businessmen in Burma played the role of intermediaries, as they did elsewhere in Southeast Asia, buying rice, timber, minerals, and native products for resale to the large British companies. They also sold British goods to the local population, but the greater part of the trade in this period was conducted by Indians, who numbered over a million and dominated the ranks of the civil service. The primacy of the Indians as money lenders in the rural sector also was not challenged by the Chinese, as the occupational distribution of ethnic Chinese in Burma in 1931 shows.[72]

For more than a decade after World War II the Chinese enjoyed considerable prosperity. They controlled 70 percent of the collection and transportation of rice, which accounted for 80 percent of the country's exports. Of the 1,200 rice mills in Burma, 300 were owned by Chinese.[73] The proportion of Chinese who were traders and merchants rose to 50.5 percent and those engaged in small-scale manufacturing increased to 40 percent; only 9.5 percent were found in other occupations. These figures represent a marked shift from the 1931 distribution.

A 1956 estimate of Chinese investments in Burma reported in the *Far Eastern Economic Review* put their total value at $101 million. A much lower figure of $70 million was given in 1960. Developments between 1946 and 1962 can be divided into three stages.

During the first period (1946–51) when the Anti-Fascist People's Freedom League (AFPFL) was in power, the Indians were ousted and Chinese activities were restricted. Rice export was nationalized by the U Nu government in 1949.[74] The State Agricultural Marketing Board was established, foreign trade was controlled, aliens were prevented from acquiring real estate, and consumers' cooperatives were set up in all urban centers. All these measures were taken at the expense of Chinese foreign traders and retail merchants.

During the second period (1952–61), the earlier socialist solution was abandoned, and the U Nu government adopted a more conservative policy. Foreign investment was encouraged under the 1953 economic plan, and discrimination against aliens was stopped. Small industry was again placed under private operation in 1957, and foreign exchange was allotted for the purchase of raw materials and equipment from abroad. U Nu apparently believed that only a more open policy could help begin the socialist construction of Burma. Chinese capital was now transferred into industrial investment, and many Chinese businesses prospered. This was the best postwar period for Chinese businessmen in Burma.

The third period began in 1962 when a virtual dictatorship was established by the Ne Win government. Burma embraced socialism, and private factories and commercial establishments were nationalized. The process was begun in the larger cities; by 1964 it had spread all over Burma.[75]

Ne Win established a number of government agencies to operate nationalized individual enterprises. Among them were the Agricultural Multi-product Cooperative Society, which supplied consumers through people's food shops. Imports were handled by the People's Stores Cooperative through international open bidding. The Union of Burma Agricultural Marketing Board specialized in rice export, the State Timber Board in timber sales, and the Myauma Export and Import Corporation in the sale of such items as cotton, legumes, and other agricultural products. Precious stones were exported by the Mineral and Petroleum Corporation. Under state management Burma's rice exports fell from 1,670,000 metric tons in 1961–62 to 190,000 in 1974–75. Shortages developed, the black market became quite active, and farmers refused to sell their crops to the government. Social unrest and economic hardship finally forced Ne Win to alter his isolationist policy in 1974, and a search for foreign aid and loans began. As the Far Eastern Economic Review put it, however, "it is necessary to bear in mind the historical experiences that shaped the 'socialist' decision of President Ne Win. . . . What is the scope for foreign investment in Burma? . . . How much free enterprise will be permitted?''[76]

Chinese economic activities have been severely curtailed since 1967. Limited opportunities for businessmen can be found in only four general areas, and their participation is allowed in these because qualified Burmese are not available. The first area is service industries, such as hotels, restaurants, barber shops, and photography shops. Also open but limited is the category of light manufacturing, including such businesses as cottage industries, watch and clock repair, tailoring, shoe manufacturing, and candy making.

At a lower economic level, some ethnic Chinese, primarily those holding Burmese citizenship, eke out a living in the pervasive black markets created by the corruption and poor management of the state trading companies. There is also a free market, restored in 1967, that deals in some agricultural products. Finally, a number of rice mills and textile factories have been partially denationalized; this means that Chinese can work as wage earners and participate in some profits, although the government continues to be the real owner.

Vietnam. Under the Geneva agreement of 1954, Vietnam, including prewar Cochin China, Annam, and Tongking, was divided into two parts. This division between the Republic of Vietnam in the south and the Democratic Republic of Vietnam in the north was finally ended in 1975, when Saigon fell to the communists. This was followed by the fall of Phnom Penh. Within the area of former French Indochina there were some 2,660,700 ethnic Chinese: about 2 million in South Vietnam, 175,000 in North Vietnam, 425,000 in Cambodia, and 60,700 in Laos.

Chinese relations with Indochina began in 214 B.C. during the Ch'in dynasty.[77] The Han dynasty used the Giaochi area for exiling its criminals. Since then, refugees from China during periods of dynastic change have sought shelter in Vietnam. This was the case during the Huang Ch'ao uprising in 877, toward the end of the T'ang dynasty, when many fugitive warriors of the T'ang court sought refuge in Tongking and Chenla (Chan-lap or present-day Cambodia), and again at the end of the Ming dynasty when refugees fled to Dongnai. Bienhoa and Mytho were both established by Chinese immigrants in the latter wave of immigration. Chinese émigrés who went to Cambodia in 1715 settled at Hatien.

During the sixteenth century, the king of Giaochi designated the town of Faifo as the trading port for Chinese merchants. Cholon was founded by Chinese in 1778. A Chinese was appointed as the chief (*Bang Truong*) from 1775 to 1820 to help the local government control matters of taxation and immigration involving Chinese residents.

Under French rule the Saigon-Cholon area became Vietnam's commercial center, and Chinese influence in Indochina grew. A poll tax and a special personal capital tax were imposed on the Chinese, and further Chinese immigration was restricted. At this time Chinese businessmen were engaged in pepper growing in Hatien and Kampot in Cambodia. Surface transportation, rice milling, and agricultural credit were mostly in Chinese hands. A comprehensive commercial network developed that included facilities for inland river transportation and warehousing. Chinese controlled about 80 percent of commercial activities, particularly retail business, in Saigon, Phnom Penh, and Luang Prabang in Laos. Fukuda's survey in 1930 estimated Chinese investments in the agricultural sector of Vietnam, Cambodia, and Laos at 4.9 percent of total investments; in the industrial sector at 13.1 percent; and in the commercial sector at 82 percent.

In August 1956, the South Vietnamese government declared that all Chinese born in Vietnam would henceforth be regarded as Vietnamese citizens.[78] Official statistics in 1959 gave the number of adult Chinese with Vietnamese citizenship as 546,200 excluding, however, children who were not of age. A 1961 census estimated the number of alien Chinese at 11,726. Purcell's estimate (1960) of ethnic Chinese was 800,000,[79] and in 1973 Ryūzō Okamoto put the number of Chinese in Vietnam at 1,200,000, plus another 190,000 in North Vietnam. A November 1974 report of the ROC embassy in South Vietnam gave the total for ethnic Chinese, including both Vietnamese citizens and aliens, as 1.5 million. Taipei revised this number upward in 1976, estimating the Chinese population in South Vietnam at 1,550,000 as of the end of 1975, including 1,092,400[80] who were born locally or had acquired Vietnamese citizenship. Still another figure was supplied by Vietnamese participants in a 1974 Manila conference; they put the Chinese population in South Vietnam at 2 million, and in North Vietnam at 175,000 (see Table 51).

In terms of home districts and dialect groups, Chinese in Vietnam can be divided into five categories. The Cantonese (60 percent of the total) are mostly businessmen and technical workers; the Teochius (20 percent) are largely farmers; the Hokkiens (7 percent) are in prominent industrial and business positions; the Hainanese (7 percent) are mostly laborers and workers on pepper plantations; and the Hakkas (6 percent) are retailers, tea merchants, and general workers.[81]

The Chinese population lives mostly in the Saigon-Cholon area. This concentration is explained partly by the war, but mostly by occupational distribution. A 1958 survey by Tsung-to Way, general manager of the Bank of China in Saigon, showed that nearly 89 percent of the Chinese were engaged in commercial and financial activities and services, with another 11 percent in manufacturing. The number working in agriculture, forestry, and fishery was negligible: Chinese previously employed in the farm sector had moved to urban areas for greater security.

TABLE 41

CHINESE CAPITAL INVESTMENT IN SOUTH VIETNAM, 1974

Category	Number of Firms	Capital Investments (U.S. $ Thousand)*	Percentage of Total Investment
Commerce			
Wholesale	400	8,759	30
Retail	5,000	730	30
Restaurant	25	365	50
Service	100	146	25
Amusement and recreation	170	248	20
Chinese medicine	500	730	80
Miscellaneous	5,000	7,299	40
Banking			
Chinese capital	3	44,647	7
Chinese-Vietnamese capital	11	56,937	49
Manufacturing			
Textile	5	2,920	80
Iron and steel	5	2,920	80
Paper	4	1,460	60
Chemical and allied products	9	1,460	80
Agriculture and fisheries			
Farms	10	219	. . .
Fisheries	5	73	60
Other enterprises	500	1,460	30
Total	11,747	130,373	16

SOURCE: Chung-hua Tsung-shang-hui [Chinese Chamber of Commerce] in Saigon, *Chinese Economic Statistics in Vietnam* (September 8, 1974).

*Converted into U.S. dollars at 685 piastres per dollar.

A 1974 survey of Chinese business investments showed them totaling more than $130 million (see Table 41). This figure is a gross underestimate, however, because some one thousand small manufacturing firms, as well as numerous small retail food-distribution businesses, were left out. Furthermore, most of the individual returns were based on registered capital, which tends to be understated during a period of rapid inflation.

South Vietnam also prohibited non-Vietnamese nationals from engaging in eleven occupations. According to Decree No. 53, promulgated on September 6, 1957,[82] Chinese in Vietnam, like their confreres elsewhere in Southeast Asia, were forced to transfer their investments and activities to permitted areas. This requirement led initially to the establishment of a number of textile mills with the technical and financial aid of Hong Kong and Taiwan industrialists. Success in these joint ventures further encouraged Chinese investment in other industrial sectors, so that the number of new industrial (especially manufacturing) enterprises grew rapidly between 1966 and 1970. According to the registration records of the Chinese Chamber of Commerce in Saigon, seventy-four such firms were established during this period. The list was headed by textile manufacturing, followed by plastics, iron and steel works, chemical manufacturing, electrical appliances, food additives, and vegetable-oil processing. Again the registered capital was relatively small although the real investments were considerably larger (for reasons mentioned earlier). These new investments should be allowed for in arriving at a correct estimate of Chinese investments in Vietnam. Earlier estimates include those listed in Table 42.

Chih-i Lung stated that Chinese businessmen suffered a total loss of 118 billion piastres ($172.3 million) as a result of the fall of Saigon in 1975.[83] A separate estimate by the Taipei *Hua-ch'iao Ching-chi nien-chien* (1976) put the losses of Chinese investors in Vietnam at a high of $1–2 billion. The former chairman of the Chinese Chamber of Commerce in Saigon estimated Chinese investments in all sectors before the fall of Vietnam at close to $2 billion. Additional losses incurred since the communist takeover cannot be estimated. Their magnitude is bound to be very high, however, especially in view of the large exodus of Chinese from the country in conjunction with the worsening relations in 1977–78 between communist Vietnam and its erstwhile ally in Peking.

Cambodia. Cambodia maintained a tribute-state relationship with China from the seventh to the thirteenth centuries—during the Sui, T'ang, and Sung dynasties. A detailed account of conditions experienced by Chinese in Cambodia was provided by Chou Ta-kuan, who accompanied a Yüan mission to Cambodia in 1295. Chinese emigration to Cambodia continued thereafter and expanded rapidly after 1863, when Cambodia became a French protectorate.

Wilmott estimated the number of ethnic Chinese in Cambodia in 1960 at 225,000.[84] An official ROC report at the end of 1974 put the figure at 360,000, with Teochius making up 60 percent, Cantonese 15 percent, Hainanese 6.5

TABLE 42

EARLIER ESTIMATES OF CHINESE INVESTMENT IN VIETNAM

Source	Estimate of Investments (U.S. $ Million)
Shōzō Fukuda (1930)	126.9
H. G. Callis (1937)	80.0
Singapore financial community (1940)	124.0
Uchida Naosaku (1955)	144.0
Wu Ku *(Economic Bulletin,* Hong Kong) (1956)	150.0
Yu Chung-hsün (1968)	80.0
Ho I-wu (1969)	430.0

percent, Hakkas 4.5 percent, and those from other Chinese provinces about 14 percent. Of this total, two thirds had acquired Cambodian nationality. The Hokkiens, though relatively few in number, were prominent in the important industries, including foreign trade, rice milling, and modern manufacturing. Two thirds of the Chinese resided in Phnom Penh, with the remainder scattered in such places as Oudong, Kampot, Battambang, and Kompong Chhnang.

Developments in Cambodia paralleled those in Vietnam. The Chinese were concentrated in retailing, and in April 1957 they were forced to move out of eighteen occupations from which they had been barred as aliens. Economic dislocation following this ordinance led to the establishment of a Workers Relief Committee,[85] as well as to Chinese attempts to move into small-scale manufacturing, making textiles, bleach, garments, shoes, plastics, paper, metals and machines, and wood products. In agriculture the Chinese worked primarily as laborers on the larger rubber and pepper plantations still under French ownership.

A rough estimate for the end of 1974 put Chinese investment in commercial activities at 70 percent, in industry at 20 percent, and in agriculture at 10 percent of the total.[86] Although in 1969 Ho I-Wu placed Chinese investment in Cambodia at no more than $55 million, Wilmott's much higher estimate is probably more accurate. A correct figure for 1955 should be between $200 and 400 million.[87] Investments in 1975 have been estimated at $300–600 million.

Laos. There were no more than thirty thousand Chinese in Laos before World War II, most of them Chinese immigrants from Vietnam and Thailand. Following the fall of mainland China to the communist Chinese, refugees from Yunnan substantially increased that number. The 1976 *Hua-ch'iao ching-chi nien-chien* mentions a Chinese population of a hundred thousand at Vientiane at the time of the Pathet Lao takeover in September 1975.

Chinese economic activities at Vientiane expanded considerably after 1955. In addition to local Chinese businessmen, investors came from Vietnam, Thailand, Burma, and even Hong Kong. Many of the new enterprises were joint ventures of ethnic Chinese of various nationalities including Laotian. There were also cooperative ventures involving ethnic Chinese and indigenous Laotians. Greater stability in currency and in the economy after 1958 resulted in a further increase in foreign investment. Business expansion also accelerated following the establishment of a branch of the Banque Française d'Asie in 1953 and of a joint Laotian and Thai-Chinese bank in 1956.

During the precommunist period, half the Chinese population lived in Vientiane. About 70 percent of the Chinese were reported to be Teochius, and the rest were Hakkas, Hainanese, and Yunnanese. Chinese active in wholesale trade maintained close relations with ethnic-Chinese businessmen in Thailand. Since Laos is a landlocked country, external trade was conducted via the Mekong River with the Longkai area in northeastern Thailand. Chinese retailers were found throughout the country, of course, especially in Luang Prabang, the royal capital, and the southern provinces. In July 1959 government regulations barred aliens from eleven occupations, but this move had little effect on the local Chinese since a high percentage of them had Laotian citizenship. A rough estimate has put the Chinese share in ownership of Laotian small-scale industry at 70 percent.

Following the communist takeover of Laos, firms that had been private were converted to joint ownership, with the government assuming 51 percent of the equity: this share was nominally distributed to the workers as a bonus. Because supplies of raw materials were cut off, many Chinese enterprises were forced to close their doors. These businesses were in the traditional fields of rice milling, lumber, food processing, food additives, garment manufacturing, plastics, earthenware, beverages, plywood, distilling, and leather manufacturing. Among the more unusual enterprises were electric abattoirs and the production of asbestos tiles.

Ho I-Wu estimated Chinese investment in Laos in 1969 at $40.9 million, but even a casual survey of a few Chinese manufacturing firms and public utilities shows that this figure is too low.

SOME PRELIMINARY CONCLUSIONS

Several preliminary conclusions appear warranted at this point. One is that until recently, Burma was the single country where restrictions on ethnic-Chinese economic activities seemed to have been successful. Whether the three states of Indochina will achieve the same success remains to be seen, although as of this writing (1978), communist Vietnam has already gone very far in this direction. This success was attained at the expense of all private business, however, not just ethnic-Chinese business. Nevertheless, Chinese business in Southeast Asia has demonstrated great resourcefulness in adapting to new conditions, partly because of a penchant for risk taking by Chinese entrepreneurs and partly because of the existence of persons and groups in the individual countries in which the ethnic Chinese are a minority who collaborate with the Chinese out of self-interest. Only countries with inexorably comprehensive restrictive laws that have been strictly applied have been able to frustrate Chinese enterprise: this was the case in Burma, and the experience may be repeated in Vietnam. Such countries must be quite ruthless and must possess ideologically oriented cadres in sufficient numbers. In all others, the Chinese have managed to move into less restricted areas or have survived by taking on real or nominal native partners. Some have moved out of their country of origin with both capital and personnel: many of these have returned as foreign investors when the political environment improved to testify that they would never have left voluntarily. It is possible that such flights of capital and enterprise have had an unexpected beneficial effect in that they have broadened the contacts and horizons of the businesses and persons involved and thereby contributed to future multinational interrelations.

Our second conclusion is that the futility of relentless restriction on ethnic-Chinese enterprise has become more widely recognized, if not more openly acknowledged, than seems evident at first glance. Thailand has led the parade, followed by South Vietnam under Ngo Dinh Diem, but the Philippines and Indonesia, in that order, have also moved progressively toward a policy based on citizenship. Controls are directed at alien-Chinese enterprises as foreign businesses, not as ethnic-Chinese ones. In most areas, ethnic Chinese can now acquire local citizenship more easily. All this suggests that while the creation of a national consciousness and national identity may take precedence, countries can remove the racial aspect from anti-Chinese sentiments. Although this trend has yet to be fully confirmed, and some observers warn that increasing tolerance will develop only gradually, an optimistic outlook does not seem unreasonable. After all, the new trend started in Thailand and the Philippines in the 1930s. As of this writing, Malaysia is more of a question mark than the other three ASEAN countries in which ethnic Chinese are a minority.

It appears, then, that what has been seen as a perverse phenomenon in the hitherto slower-growing Southeast Asian countries may be on the way out. If ethnic-Chinese resources can lose their alien identity, they may eventually be treated more like other domestic resources. However, a warning is needed: efforts to create a national identity and gain full national economic independence could reverse this trend. Extreme economic nationalism is detrimental to a country's economic development because it impedes the flow of foreign capital and technology. Such a policy would have an adverse impact on regional cooperation through ASEAN. In most Southeast Asian countries moderation toward the ethnic Chinese in their midst needs to be reinforced by a more international outlook. With this in mind, we can now look at the special roles of Singapore and Hong Kong.

4

The Nexus of Trade and Finance: Within and Beyond Southeast Asia

The preceding discussion has dealt with those Southeast Asian countries in which the ethnic-Chinese are numerically a minority. We turn now to the remaining ASEAN member, Singapore, which has a population that is more than three-quarters Chinese and which shares many common features with Hong Kong, another predominantly Chinese metropolis. Like these two, a third ethnic-Chinese society outside the Chinese mainland, Taiwan, has a fast-growing market economy. All three have expanded economic contacts both among themselves and with the four Southeast Asian nations with important Chinese minorities. A closer look at these economic interrelationships is important for two reasons. First, it can give us additional insight into economic conditions in Southeast Asia, as well as into the role played by the ethnic Chinese. Second, it can enable us to understand how economic development in Southeast Asia might be enhanced by taking full advantage of the Chinese connection offered by the fast-growing market economies nearby.

SINGAPORE AND HONG KONG

As their trade expanded further to the east to include both China and Southeast Asia by the nineteenth century, the British needed strategically placed natural harbors for the use of the Royal Navy and British merchant ships. Protection of the long trade route beyond India and the establishment of suitable commodity-distribution and collection centers for trade with China and Southeast Asia were two principal reasons for the acquisition of Singapore and Hong Kong as colonies under the British crown. A third important function that Hong Kong was to perform later was to assemble Chinese emigrants for shipment to other points as contract laborers. Singapore served as a transshipment area for most of those destined for Southeast Asian plantations and tin mines. Once the Chinese settlers had established themselves in their new countries, Hong Kong, because of its propinquity to their ancestral homes, became the financial center for the transfer of the emigrants' home-bound funds—overseas-Chinese remittances, to use the conventional term.

Entrepôt Trade and International Finance

Following its establishment in 1819, Singapore soon became the transshipment center for goods to and from Java, Sumatra, the Malay Peninsula, Celebes, Borneo, Bali, and the Philippines. Business connections were also rapidly established and expanded with Europe, India, and China. Tropical products from Southeast Asia were brought to Singapore by Chinese businessmen for processing, repackaging, and shipment. The same was true of Hong Kong, except that the goods in transit usually originated from or were consigned to mainland China.

Several circumstances were especially favorable to the development of entrepôt trade at Hong Kong and Singapore. Excellent facilities for docking, warehousing, ship repair, and provisioning were available at both ports.[1] No less important was the creation of a corps of skilled dock workers for loading and unloading. As free ports[2] Hong Kong and Singapore offered the international-trade community low cost and minimal bureaucratic interference. An increasing number of international banking and financial institutions were induced by these circumstances to locate their expanding regional operations in Singapore and/or Hong Kong. Free foreign-exchange markets went hand in hand with free trade.[3]

Chinese Immigration and Home-bound Remittance

From 1830 until 1874 Hong Kong served as the principal assembly point for Chinese laborers bound for Southeast Asia. Singapore was the main redistribution center, especially between 1850 and 1870, for the Southeast Asian region. Official British statistics show that more than 4 million Chinese immigrants arrived at Singapore between 1881 and 1915, although only 321,600 Chinese were left there in 1921.[4] In the absence of data on departures, we must assume that most of the arrivals during these four decades subsequently left for other parts of Southeast Asia. Many emigrants from China went to the Malay Peninsula, Borneo, and what was then the Dutch East Indies via Singapore. Others went from Singapore to Penang, and in some cases to British Burma.

During the years before World War II, funds sent home by Chinese emigrants in Southeast Asia were given to remittance brokers, usually in small amounts. These sums were combined and in normal practice transferred through Singapore and Hong Kong. The introduction of foreign-exchange controls by all Southeast Asian countries after the war made Hong Kong, which continued to have a free-exchange market, the sole center for such transfers. Amounts in excess of officially imposed limits[5] could not be remitted except through private channels; Hong Kong's free-exchange market proved immensely useful for this practice. The extreme instability of Chinese currency during the second half of the 1940s and gross discrepancies between official and black-market rates added to the importance of arbitrage and onward remittance through Hong Kong. Remittances from Southeast Asia were first converted into Hong Kong dollars and further converted into other currencies on the free market at opportune times to minimize exchange losses. Not infrequently, those in the remittance business would first use the monies they had collected to purchase goods in Singapore or Hong Kong for export to China, using the proceeds from subsequent sales to pay off the addressees of the remittances.

Structural Changes Since World War II

A major structural change in the economies of both Hong Kong and Singapore during the last three decades has resulted from the relative decline of entrepôt trade and the rise of domestic manufacturing activities. With the attainment of independence, both Indonesia and Malaysia have attempted to move toward greater national control of foreign trade, and continued use of Singapore as an entrepôt would have been contrary to the spirit of economic nationalism developing in those countries. Hostile political relations during Sukarno's confrontation with Singapore and the souring of relations between Malaysia and Singapore for some years after 1965, when Singapore left the Federation of Malaysia, have given an additional impetus to the trend. By 1975, recorded re-exports made up only 40.9 percent of Singapore's total exports (12.8 billion Singapore dollars), compared with 55.8 percent in 1971, 64.1 percent in 1968, and even higher percentages earlier.[6]

In the north, the use of Chinese ports in direct trading with the West and the establishment of state trading by Peking as the normal mode of doing business with the rest of the world have virtually eliminated Hong Kong as an entrepôt in the PRC's foreign trade. In 1970, PRC goods re-exported to the rest of the world from Hong Kong amounted to only 2 percent of that nation's total exports. The ratio dropped further—to 1.6 percent—in 1973.[7] PRC imports from the rest of the world through Hong Kong amounted to about 0.1 percent of its total imports in 1970. The corresponding ratio in 1973 was 0.2 percent. Although Hong Kong has remained a very important export market for mainland China, some three quarters of PRC sales in Hong Kong are now primarily for local consumption. Chinese purchases of goods produced in Hong Kong, on the other hand, are relatively small;[8] they constituted 11 percent of total PRC imports from Hong Kong in 1960, 25 percent in 1965, 41 percent in 1970, and 18 percent in 1975.

The greater part of PRC imports from Hong Kong are re-exports of goods produced elsewhere.

The decline of the entrepôt trade has led to a contraction of the operations of import-export agents specializing in acting as intermediaries between mainland China and Southeast Asia. The dampening effect on business had to be offset if output and employment were not to suffer. The situation has been especially serious in Hong Kong because of its large and expanding population: although the refugee flow from communist China has fluctuated, it has never stopped completely since 1949. To the south, in Indonesia and Malaysia, restrictive policies toward the ethnic Chinese have periodically encouraged those who could to emigrate to Singapore. The British withdrawal from lands east of the Suez toward the end of the 1960s and the collapse of South Vietnam in 1975, creating additional Southeast Asian refugee migrations, have also contributed to Singapore's employment problem.

In spite of these problems, both Hong Kong and Singapore have been highly viable economic entities. New manufacturing industries have more than compensated for the relative decline of entrepôt trade. As of 1972, 34.5 percent of Hong Kong's GDP was derived from manufacturing, utilities, and construction; the corresponding figure for Singapore in 1974 was 33.2 percent.[9] The same three sectors accounted for 53.6 percent of employment in Hong Kong in 1971 and for 45 percent in Singapore in March 1973.[10] In spite of their small size and lack of natural resources, Hong Kong and Singapore have been successful where other countries in Southeast Asia have failed. The transformation of their economies has been achieved through external investment and expanding foreign trade. In recent years, investors from the United States, Japan, and other nations have brought with them new products and a growing and often ready-made export market. They have also introduced new technologies, but not as fast as the local authorities would like, especially those in Singapore. In most instances these investors have concentrated on labor-intensive products. As Singapore and Hong Kong continue to develop, they will have to face the task of changing their economic structures further to accommodate more capital-intensive and high-technology-intensive products, as well as labor-intensive products of higher unit value.

The favorable conditions both Hong Kong and Singapore offer foreign investors differ in several respects. Hong Kong prides itself on giving the foreign investor no special inducements except the freedom to do virtually anything he cares to do. Its separate political existence on the fringe of communist China is based on the latter's sufferance, which in turn rests on self-interest. Singapore, as a new and small nation-state that hopes to maintain political independence on its own, does not permit total freewheeling. Accordingly, it has resorted to inducements in the form of tax benefits and various infrastructure facilities, such as the Jurong industrial estate, of a type that other developing countries offer. Singapore has enjoyed remarkable political stability in recent years, however, and economic controls are equitably applied there with minimal red tape.

An important feature shared by Hong Kong and Singapore is their standing as international financial centers. Foreign investments are important to the expansion of Hong Kong's exports and the gradual introduction of new technologies, but the colony has become a refuge for funds from all over the world, including Southeast Asia. Similarly, Singapore has benefited from its propinquity to Malaysia and Indonesia and has improved its prospects by creating an offshore Asian currency market patterned after the Eurodollar market. Consequently, there is no longer any shortage of funds in either place: instead Hong Kong and Singapore have become important conduits of funds for foreign investment as well as sources of funds themselves. In a more limited fashion, they have also helped in introducing new technologies into countries like Nigeria; they are by no means restricted to Southeast Asia in their financial and commercial dealings.

SAFE HAVENS OF CAPITAL

The ethnic Chinese have played a pivotal role in the development of Hong Kong and Singapore as financial capitals. According to one estimate quoted by Iian Buchanan, there was, toward the end of the 1960s "between $36 billion and $39 billion in U.S. currency floating around the world outside the United States and *owned mostly by overseas Chinese*" (italics added).[11] Needless to say, such estimates are conjectural, but there is ample reason to believe that over the years sizable amounts of capital owned by ethnic Chinese in Asia have been deposited in Hong Kong and that these funds have in part become commingled with monies from other sources awaiting further placement. Not only the Chinese, but also indigenous Southeast Asians have used Hong Kong as a monetary haven. More recently, Singapore's Asian dollar market has played a similar role. Both Hong Kong and Singapore benefited from foreign capital long before the stepped-up flow of foreign investment preceding the worldwide recession touched off by the 1973 oil crisis. Examples are the flow of refugee Chinese capital into Hong Kong after 1949, the retention of considerable Malaysian capital in Singapore after the separation of the two states in 1965, and the flow of Southeast Asian refugee capital from Indonesia, the Philippines, and Vietnam at different times into both Hong Kong and Singapore.

A number of estimates are available for the flow of funds into Hong Kong during the post–World War II period. The figures given in Table 43 cover only Chinese-owned funds derived mainly from China and Southeast Asia, together with some other Southeast Asian funds.

TABLE 43

FLOW OF FUNDS INTO HONG KONG, 1947–64

Year	Estimated Amount of Flow: HK $ Million, Annual Average	HK $ Million, Total	U.S. $ Million, Annual Average	U.S. $ Million, Total
1947–48	...	...	100	200
1949	300–400	300–400	...	...
1950–52	200[a]	600	...	...
1953–55	333[a]	1,000	...	...
1955	600	600	...	...
1956–58	400	1,600[a]	...	...
1959 (June–Oct.)	300	300[a]	...	...
1950–64	...	...	47[a]	700[b]
1954–63	440[a]	4,400	...	...
1964	1,000	1,000	...	...

SOURCE: Nihon bōeki shinkōkai chōsa hōkoku [A report by JETRO], *Kaigai shijō* [Overseas Market] (Tokyo, 1964).

[a]Figures are derived.

[b]Funds from Southeast Asia only.

TABLE 44

JAPANESE ESTIMATE OF CAPITAL FLOW INTO HONG KONG BY SOURCE, 1954–63

	Amount of Flow (HK $ Million)
Malaysia (East and West) and Singapore	1,200
Indonesia	1,000
The Philippines	800
Thailand	800
South Vietnam, Cambodia, and Laos	600
Total	4,400

SOURCE: JETRO, *Kaigai shijō*.

These figures indicate that funds flowed into Hong Kong during 1947–64 at the rate of about 430 million Hong Kong dollars (U.S. $80 million) a year. Hong Kong financial authorities have estimated the annual inflow of Chinese funds from Southeast Asia since 1964 at HK $1 billion (nearly U.S. $200 million).[12] As was to be expected, much of this inflow of money was the result of capital flight. This was the case with funds from mainland China in 1947–49, from Indonesia under Sukarno, from the Philippines in 1953–55 following the naturalization of retail trade, from Malaysia and Singapore during the first years of their independence, from Thailand under the Sarit government, and so on. More recently, in 1973 and 1974 before the fall of Vietnam, half the gold inflow to the Hong Kong bullion market reportedly originated in Indochina. In the first month after the collapse of Vietnam in 1975, five hundred thousand dollars worth of gold from Indochina reportedly found its way to the Hong Kong market every day.[13]

A minor portion of the Chinese funds entering Hong Kong has been transferred onward to China in traditional overseas-Chinese remittances. Some has been invested outside Hong Kong, but a major share has remained there.[14] By far the largest part (estimated by some at 67.3 percent) has been invested in real estate, with industrial and commercial investments accounting for 17.7 percent, and portfolio investments for another 15 percent.

Thus funds from Southeast Asia actually owned by ethnic Chinese or transferred by indigenous real owners via Chinese intermediaries have constituted an important source of capital flowing into Hong Kong. Other major sources of foreign capital are Japan, the United States, and Western Europe. Data on foreign direct investment as of 1974 for Hong Kong and 1975 for Singapore are given in Table 45.

INTERLOCKING BANKING CONNECTIONS AND SOURCES OF FUNDS

We should emphasize the role of Hong Kong as a source of funds rather than just a refuge for capital in flight. Singapore plays a similar role through its Asian dollar market. As of May 1976, interbank deposits in Asian currency units in Singapore had reached U.S. \$11.7 billion. Another \$2 billion was held by nonbank customers.[15] These amounts probably exceeded what the Chinese alone could muster in loanable funds. Nevertheless, some funds that are beneficially owned by ethnic Chinese may be disguised as non-Chinese, and the real Chinese share could well be larger than it appears. It is probably safe to say that Chinese funds have been a primary factor in making Singapore and Hong Kong the principal financial markets serving Southeast Asia. Owners of funds who consider their money unsafe in their own countries often invest it in more secure environments. For example, the restrictive policies applied to Chinese capital in some Southeast Asian countries have led many Chinese to pass funds through a place like Hong Kong to alter the ownership identity. (In contemporary American vernacular, this is a form of laundering funds.) This procedure can increase investment security, sometimes in the same country in which the funds originated.

Many banks in Southeast Asia are wholly or partially owned by ethnic Chinese. In the ASEAN member countries the number varies from twelve in Thailand and eleven in the Philippines to forty-four in Indonesia. There are twenty-four such banks in Hong Kong and fourteen in Singapore. As vehicles to channel funds from depositors or lenders to borrowers with connections with

TABLE 45

FOREIGN CAPITAL IN HONG KONG AND SINGAPORE
(Percentages)

Country of Origin	Hong Kong 1975	Singapore 1974	Industry	Hong Kong 1975	Singapore 1974
United States	47.2	35.4	Electric products and parts	40.4	10.4
Japan	15.4	11.6	Metals	2.9	13.9
United Kingdom	9.4	13.8	Textiles	15.0	7.0
Holland	1.3	13.8	Watches and clocks	11.1	- - -
West Germany	1.2	3.5	Petroleum and petroleum products	- - -	43.8
Others	25.5	21.9	Wood and wood products	3.1	5.3
			Food and beverages	3.5	3.7
			Other	24.0	15.9
Total	100.0	100.0		100.0	100.0

SOURCE: *Ching-chi tao-pao* [Economic Bulletin] (Hong Kong, 1976).

national financial markets in many countries, these banks are significant both within Southeast Asia and internationally.

Table 46 shows the network formed by these Chinese-owned and -managed banks in the individual countries of Southeast Asia and Hong Kong together with their foreign branches and subsidiaries in Hong Kong, Taiwan, Japan, Southeast Asia, the United States, and other countries. Although these data may not be comprehensive, we can count 143 such branches, including a few subsidiaries and affiliates. Singapore, Malaysia, and Hong Kong have the most branch banks and subsidiaries in foreign countries. The first two are in this leading position because they constituted a single economic system before their separation in 1965. Indonesian banks have no foreign branches because of laws prohibiting them. No ethnic-Chinese banks outside the Philippines have branches there because of their inability to compete with domestic Philippine banks.

Furthermore, Japanese, American, and British investors are stockholders in some Chinese-managed, if no longer wholly Chinese-owned, banks in the area. At the same time, some of the Chinese-owned banks have branches in the United States, Britain, or Japan. To a considerable extent, then, Chinese banks have direct access to financial resources in the developed countries. Furthermore, banks based in the developed countries can tap directly funds in Southeast Asian countries through their own branches in those states, and flows in the reverse direction can also take place through these branches. Even the Soviet Union reportedly has ownership interests in two Chinese banks in Hong Kong, and a subsidiary of the Moscow Narodny Bank of London operates in Singapore.

It is important to realize that the kind of network portrayed here is only one of the many types of complex financial interrelations in existence. For example, banks in one country may own finance companies, instead of banks, in another country. Finance companies, trusts, and insurance companies in different Southeast Asian countries and Hong Kong have comparable interrelations. Legal considerations, such as local regulations governing branch banking or financial holding companies, vary from country to country. Some countries may frown upon banking or, for that matter, other investment from particular foreign countries: in that case, real ownership can be camouflaged. The owners of a domestic bank, like proprietors of other businesses, may actually represent the interests of residents of another country, just as an approved foreign investment may in fact be owned by domestic residents who have brought back as foreign capital some of their own funds that had been transferred abroad earlier. Concrete examples of such transactions are readily available for some of the Southeast Asian countries. Thus the absence of branches of alien-Chinese-owned banks in the Philippines or of foreign branches of Chinese-owned banks in Indonesia should not be considered evidence of a lack of financial connections. Finally, credit relations can be established through nonbanking intermediaries. A

TABLE 46

ETHNIC-CHINESE BANKS IN HONG KONG AND ASEAN

Location of Head Office	Total Number	Banks with Foreign Branches (Based on Location of Head Office)	Private and Commercial Banks Wholly or Partially Owned by Ethnic Chinese — Location of Overseas Branches											Total
			Singapore	Hong Kong	Malaysia	Indonesia	Philippines	Thailand	Taiwan	U.S.	U.K.	Japan	Other	
Singapore	14	6	–	7	64	–	–	1	–	–	3	3	1	79
Hong Kong	24*	16	1	–	1	–	–	2	–	9	3	3	1	20
Malaysia	19	4	31	–	–	–	–	1	–	–	–	–	–	32
Indonesia	44	–	–	–	–	–	–	–	–	–	–	–	–	–
Thailand	12	2	1	2	1	1	–	–	1	1	1	2	–	10
The Philippines	11	2	–	–	–	–	–	–	1	1	–	–	–	2
Total	124	30	33	9	66	1	–	4	2	11	7	8	2	143

SOURCE: Original data supplied by local banking circles. See Appendix E for the list of banks.

*Excluding thirteen PRC-controlled banks.

firm in one country may receive from a branch or subsidiary in another country funds that the latter has borrowed locally. Such an arrangement bypasses the first country's controls over foreign investment.

An interesting recent development is the emergence of syndicates formed by Chinese capitalists and entrepreneurs in different countries who, sometimes in association with Western investors, invest funds in enterprises in Southeast Asia. One example is a holding company in Hong Kong formed by ethnic Chinese from Hong Kong, Singapore, the Philippines, Indonesia, and Malaysia. With the participation of additional Thai and Western funds, the company reportedly has already made investments in Thailand, Malaysia, and Indonesia. Another is the formation of separate corporations in different countries that share the same directors. The United Malaysian Banking Corporation and the International Consolidated Investment Company of Hong Kong are good examples of this type. The latter is a joint venture of Chan Ming Thien and his syndicate in Singapore, Johnny Cheng of the Philippines, Chian Kok Sen of Malaysia, Ong Tsiu Tsio of Indonesia, Johnny Ma of Bangkok, and Pang Kowk Chan of Hong Kong. Each of these stockholders has his own local financial backing. Their joint venture thus constitutes an alliance between Hong Kong and ASEAN. Many other financial and nonfinancial business concerns in Singapore and Indonesia or Singapore and Malaysia have interlocking directorates.

A few other widely known and successful ethnic-Chinese business figures can be cited. Their national as well as transnational interests illustrate the network of interrelationships that extends beyond Southeast Asia. Among these are Singapore financial groups represented by the Lee Rubber Company group (formerly headed by the late Lee Kuang Chin), the Shaw Brothers Company, the Hong Leong Company, and the Overseas Chinese Banking Corporation of Tan Chin Tuan. In Indonesia a powerful financial group is headed by Lim Shao-liang and his brother, who reputedly have close ties with major figures in the Indonesian government. In the Philippines, the three principal companies in the tobacco industry are all ethnic Chinese—La Perla Industries, Inc., of Johnny Cheng, Columbia Tobacco, Inc., of Yao Shiong Shio, and La Suerte Cigar and Cigarette Factory of Ching Tan. In addition, the late Antonio Roxas Chua, head of the Pacific Banking Corporation, was an important figure in the sugar industry. Cojuangco, a local-born ethnic Chinese who has the reputation of being the wealthiest Chinese businessman in the Philippines, is another prominent entrepreneur. In Thailand, the chairman of the board of directors of the Metropolitan Bank is an ethnic Chinese, as is the head of the Bangkok Bank. In spite of the collapse of Vietnam in 1975, some Chinese industrialists from Saigon are continuing their business operations overseas—testimony to their resilience and prior diversification of interests. Financial groups such as these have gone a long way toward modernizing their operations and expanding investment through joint ventures with Western firms. One recent example of such activity is the acquisition of an 8 percent interest in Sime Darby by Singapore's Overseas Chinese Banking Corporation group.[16]

Traditionally, multilateral cooperative efforts by ethnic-Chinese interests have tended to fall into two groups: a northern tier composed of Thailand, the Philippines, and Hong Kong and a southern tier made up of Indonesia, Malaysia, and Singapore. Geographical propinquity is a more important inducement in the case of Singapore. As for Hong Kong, its free-exchange market and a tradition of business privacy that keeps business from the prying eyes of governments are highly prized attractions.

In the new multinational groupings, both racial and national boundaries have become increasingly blurred. One important characteristic of these efforts is frequent involvement of ethnic Chinese with non-Chinese indigenous interests in certain Southeast Asian countries. The traditional linkages among ethnic Chinese provided by membership in the same district or dialect associations have by now transcended regional or national bounds. Further extension of regional and multinational investments and joint ventures has already become a principal objective of ethnic-Chinese business activities in Southeast Asia. For this reason, their operations are frequently based in Hong Kong, where syndication and cooperation with Western or Japanese financial interests can take place relatively easily.

Finally, organized efforts have been made by Chinese Chambers of Commerce and similar associations in the different countries to explore possible joint ventures involving their respective memberships. The Singapore Chamber of Commerce, for example, sent special economic delegations to the Philippines in 1973 and to Indonesia in 1975. Some joint ventures have resulted, but so far these undertakings have tended to be quite small.

THE TAIWAN–HONG KONG–SINGAPORE TRIANGLE

The flow of funds between Hong Kong and Singapore on the one hand and the other four ASEAN countries on the other has often involved Taiwan. Direct investors based in Hong Kong and Singapore are the most active in Indonesia, Malaysia, Thailand, and the Philippines, but they also frequently embark upon joint ventures with investors from Taiwan. Since Taiwan is more advanced in certain aspects of manufacturing, construction, and agricultural production and processing, its representatives frequently provide both investment funds and an introduction to new technologies.

In Thailand and the Philippines, investments from Taiwan have been substantial. They reached 17.0 percent of total foreign investments between 1968 and 1975 in the Philippines and 11.4 percent between 1960 and 1976 in Thailand. In Indonesia, investments from both Taiwan and Singapore are sometimes made through Hong Kong because of political sensitivities. Table 47 shows that a total of $16 million was reportedly invested in Indonesia by Taiwan-based interests from 1972 through 1974.

The capital-importing Southeast Asian countries gave a higher figure for these investments than Taiwan sources reported: according to ROC statistics, total investments in four Southeast Asian countries and Hong Kong for the period 1959–75 came to only $13.54 million, compared with $26.4 million for

TABLE 47

FOREIGN INVESTMENTS IN SELECTED SOUTHEAST ASIAN COUNTRIES BY INVESTORS IN HONG KONG, SINGAPORE, AND TAIWAN
(U.S. $ Million)

		Total from all Countries	Hong Kong	Singapore	Taiwan
Indonesia					
Approved investment projects	1967	179.2	0.3	–	---
	1968	245.1	8.0	6.7	---
	1969	742.7	15.5	28.0	---
	1970	265.8	19.4	29.7	---
	1971	376.1	72.3	8.2	---
	1972	497.8	50.9	25.6	---
	1973	521.6	101.0	2.3	16.0[a]
Total		2,828.3	267.4	100.5	
Philippines					
Investments by BOI[b] Approved firms	1968	24.8	...	...	0.3
	1969	29.5	---	---	2.6
	1970	14.8	---	---	1.1
	1971	80.8	---	---	57.0
	1972	47.1	---	---	1.8
	1973	79.9	---	---	5.7
	1974	216.3	---	---	9.1
	1975	7.5	---	---	7.5
Total		500.7			85.1
Thailand					
Total registered capital	1960–May 31, 1975	197.1	11.2	2.3	22.6
Malaysia					
Total approved investments	1974	263.2	26.7	70.8	1.4
	1975	272.3	29.3	73.7	1.4
Total		535.5	56.0	144.5	2.8

SOURCES: Data from the Board of Investment, Bangkok, Thailand; the Board of Investment, Manila, The Philippines; the Investment Coordinating Board, Indonesia (BKPM); and the Federal Industrial Development Authority, Malaysia.

[a]Cumulative to 1975.

[b]Board of Investment.

investments in all countries during those same years.[17] This discrepancy supports a belief that some investments credited to Taiwan investors have been made from outside Taiwan, probably from Hong Kong or Singapore. Like Japan, Taiwan must eventually expand its foreign investments to enlarge its sources of supply of raw materials as well as its foreign markets. Thus far it has made a small but determined start.

In the reverse direction, investments in Taiwan by ethnic Chinese from Hong Kong from 1952 to May 1976 amounted to $182.1 million; corresponding investments from Japan and other Asian countries were $27.4 million and $163.6 million, respectively. Most of the investments from other Asian countries, as well as some from Hong Kong, clearly originated in Southeast Asia.[18] The growth of these investments has increased sharply since 1967.

In 1974 and 1975 annual exports from ASEAN countries to Hong Kong, Taiwan, and Singapore averaged, respectively, $701 million, $327 million, and $1,597 million, for a total of $2,625 million. Exports to Hong Kong and Singapore still included some entrepôt trade, but the dollar total for these three markets came to one tenth of the total value of the region's exports to the world, nearly equaling the value of its direct exports to the EEC. If we add Japan to the three communities with ethnic-Chinese majorities, then the combined total value of ASEAN's exports to them exceeds the total for the United States, the EEC, and the oil-exporting countries (excluding Indonesia).

Alternatively, we can add the value of ASEAN's intraregional exports to that of ASEAN exports to Hong Kong and Taiwan. This total would be about the same as the dollar value of ASEAN direct exports to the United States. Table 48 makes these comparisons clear. ASEAN imports from Singapore, Hong Kong, Taiwan, and Japan in 1974 and 1975 exceeded in value direct imports from the EEC and the United States combined, while ASEAN intraregional imports, plus those from Taiwan and Hong Kong, were greater in value than direct imports from either the United States or the EEC.

Little more needs to be said, therefore, about the possibilities that closer ties with Hong Kong, Singapore, and Taiwan open up for the four ASEAN countries. Hong Kong and Singapore, which have served as a haven for refugee capital of ethnic Chinese from all parts of mainland and insular Asia, are now in a position to provide much of the necessary financing Southeast Asia needs for economic development. Furthermore, the continued rapid economic growth of Hong Kong, Singapore, and Taiwan will provide additional markets for the products of Southeast Asia if economic development in the latter area can be accelerated.[19] These expanding markets will be a welcome addition to the indispensable Japanese, U.S., and EEC markets. Finally, much of the acceleration in Southeast Asian development could come about through aid in technology and training provided ethnic Chinese from Southeast Asia by their cousins in Taiwan, Hong Kong, and Singapore.

TABLE 48

DIRECTION OF ASEAN EXPORTS AND IMPORTS BY COUNTRY AND GROUP

	Annual Average	
	1974–75 ($ Million)	Percentage of Total
Exports		
Total ASEAN exports to the world	22,036	100.0
Sum of ASEAN exports to Singapore, Hong Kong, and Taiwan	2,625	11.9
Sum of ASEAN exports to Singapore, Hong Kong, Taiwan, and Japan	8,808	40.0
Sum of ASEAN intraregional exports and exports to Taiwan and Hong Kong	4,525	20.5
ASEAN exports to the EEC	2,753	12.5
ASEAN exports to the United States	4,293	19.5
ASEAN exports to the United States and the EEC	7,046	32.0
Imports		
Total ASEAN imports from the world	24,042	100.0
Sum of ASEAN imports from Singapore, Hong Kong, and Taiwan	1,672	7.0
Sum of ASEAN imports from Singapore, Hong Kong, Taiwan, and Japan	7,349	30.6
Sum of ASEAN intraregional imports and imports from Taiwan and Hong Kong	4,040	16.8
ASEAN imports from the EEC	3,724	15.5
ASEAN imports from the United States	3,544	14.7
ASEAN imports from the United States and the EEC	7,268	30.2

SOURCE: Appendix A.

For a number of years Taiwan has been active in educating and training ethnic-Chinese students from outside the island, mostly from Southeast Asia, especially in technical and business subjects. Upon their return to their own countries, these young men and women will be potential promoters of trade and joint ventures with Taiwan. The data given in Table 49 deal with enrollees in summer training courses only, over and above the year-round student body. Some of the summer trainees are probably active workers in business and industry. This distribution by field of interest, based on the cumulative enrollment figures, is therefore especially illuminating from the point of view of future impact.

IMPLICATIONS OF THE INTERNATIONAL DIMENSION

The changes in the economic roles of Hong Kong and Singapore over the years constitute an interesting example of economic evolution. The same may be

TABLE 49

DISTRIBUTION OF ETHNIC-CHINESE STUDENTS (GRADUATING CLASS) FROM OUTSIDE TAIWAN IN SUMMER TRAINING COURSES BY FIELD OF INTEREST, 1961–75

Field of Interest	Year Field Introduced	Cumulative Total Number of Students
Engineering and technology		
Electrical engineering	1961	388
Mechanical engineering	1961	538
Chemical engineering	1961	464
Agricultural engineering	1963	25
Textile engineering	1963	6
Mining	1963	32
Civil engineering	1963	310
Hydraulic engineering	1964	12
Architecture	1964	41
Marine-products manufacturing	1965	4
Metallurgy	1968	3
Industrial engineering	1968	2
Agricultural machinery	1968	5
Electronics	1970	36
Computers	1972	9
Physics	1972	4
Navigation	1972	1
Marine mechanics	1972	8
Urban planning	1972	1
Shipbuilding	1972	10
Food technology	1972	7
River and ocean engineering	1974	1
Mining and petroleum industry	1975	3
Engineering science	1975	1
Total engineering and technology		1,911
Life, agricultural, and medical sciences		
Horticulture	1963	71
Forestry	1963	44
Agricultural chemistry	1963	93
Animal husbandry	1963	53
Agronomy	1963	50
Veterinary medicine	1963	18
Agricultural extension	1964	6
Plant pathology	1964	40
Fishing industry	1965	2
Entomology	1968	5
Botany	1970	3
Soil conservation	1971	4
Agricultural-products processing	1974	5
Afforestation	1974	1
Total life, agricultural, and medical sciences		395

TABLE 49 (Cont.)

Field of Interest	Year Field Introduced	Cumulative total Number of Students
Business and economics		
Economics	1962	111
Industrial and business management	1962	49
International trade	1962	107
Business administration	1963	23
Agricultural economics	1963	33
Banking	1963	94
Accounting	1963	132
Maritime management	1964	7
Finance and taxation	1964	6
Enterprise management	1965	85
Cooperatives	1968	4
Customs administration	1968	1
Transportation management	1968	3
Banking and insurance	1972	3
Statistics	1972	2
Tourist business	1974	1
Total business and economics		661
Psychology	1972	4
Art	1972	1
Home Economics	1976	1
Total other		6
Total all fields		2,973

SOURCE: *Hua-ch'iao ching-chi nien-chien,* 1976, pp. 589–593.

said of their relationships with other Southeast Asian countries and with Taiwan. Formerly entrepôts serving intraregional trade and points of entry between adjacent countries and the outside world, they have become financial and manufacturing centers in their own right. The characteristics that made them highly prized international financial centers have enabled them to serve as repositories for refugee capital and short-term funds awaiting placement. The latter roles, as well as the opportunities they offer for international trade, have further enabled them to provide financial and other business services that ethnic Chinese elsewhere in Southeast Asia have demanded during recent decades. Their ability to perform these services for their Chinese customers has in turn attracted non-Chinese clients from the region. All these qualities have made them eagerly sought partners by financial and trading institutions in the United States, Japan, and Europe. Not the least of these partners is Taiwan, whose rapid economic development in recent years has greatly added to its own capacity for making international business commitments and to its need for external financial ties. At the same time, because its domestic market is larger than those in

Singapore and Hong Kong and because it has made greater advances in certain technological fields, Taiwan has expanded the capacity of the two international financial and trade centers.

We wish to stress the international as well as the ethnic-Chinese dimension of the agglomeration process we have just recapitulated. Partly through their strenuous struggle for survival, Chinese entrepreneurs in Southeast Asia outside Singapore have greatly expanded their international connections in Hong Kong, Singapore, and Taiwan as well as with Japanese, American, and European markets and financial institutions. These linkages have made the Chinese even more useful than before to their countries of domicile. Any Southeast Asian country concerned about foreign economic aggression—domination by Western or Japanese interests—now has multinational business institutions available locally. Since Singapore is a members of ASEAN, this international dimension can become a reinforcing factor in ASEAN's economic development without excluding business interests in non-ASEAN countries. From the point of view of the United States, Japan, or the EEC, the international dimension that the ethnic Chinese have developed can be extremely useful in combating excesses of economic nationalism. These potential advantages should be recognized.

5

Prospects and Recommendations

The principal points we have advanced in this volume can be briefly recapitulated as follows. First, in spite of their natural resources, Thailand, Malaysia, Indonesia, and the Philippines have not done as well since the 1960s as resource-poor countries like Singapore, Hong Kong, Taiwan, and South Korea.

Second, one principal reason for their relatively indifferent performance has been their failure to make the most of their domestic resources, particularly ethnic-Chinese resources.

Third, the ethnic-Chinese material, financial, and human resources in these countries, impressive in magnitude, are critically needed. Failure to use them at a time when foreign capital and technology are being eagerly sought is irrational, if not perverse. This behavior is a manifestation of nationalism, however, and its roots are to be found in the histories of these countries.

Fourth, the various restrictive policies adopted to limit ethnic-Chinese economic activities and to replace them with indigenous substitutes have not accomplished their original objectives. They have been disruptive and futile, and this fact is now recognized in at least three of the four countries in question.

Finally, in the course of efforts to survive policies directed against it, Chinese business in Southeast Asia has increased its linkages with other countries in the Western Pacific and with extraregional powers such as the United States. This development has increased its potential usefulness to the countries of domicile.

It follows, therefore, that the future prospects of ethnic-Chinese business activities in Southeast Asia should be hopeful provided that all parties involved *continue* to move in the right direction. What will it take to bring this about? Will the necessary conditions actually obtain?

It is important that Southeast Asian countries with ethnic-Chinese minorities be willing to treat their Chinese citizens as they do their other citizens. Experience has made it clear that to do otherwise disrupts the economy. This knowledge should eliminate the self-defeating policies we have described.

Other conditions, however, are also necessary. The Chinese themselves should demonstrate unambiguous support for national-development policies of the countries in question if these policies are nondiscriminatory. Extraregional foreign countries where Chinese are in the majority should make their own hands-off positions clearer. The relevant Southeast Asian governments need to feel secure enough politically to be able to take a more relaxed attitude toward the ethnic Chinese. Other nations can provide incentives for adoption of nondiscriminatory policies.

ETHNIC-CHINESE INITIATIVES

While much more needs to be done, ethnic-Chinese entrepreneurs and capitalists in the ASEAN region have tried in recent years to meet the governments of their countries halfway. For instance, both the Chinese Chamber of Commerce and the Association of Chinese (Chung-hua Hui-kuan) in Bangkok are now headed by ethnic Chinese who are Thai citizens. As we mentioned earlier, many indigenous Thai businessmen are members of the Thai chamber. During several recent changes in government in Thailand, the two organizations have always pledged their support to the incoming government. The Federation of Chinese Chambers of Commerce in the Philippines is now known as the Federation of Filipino-Chinese Chambers of Commerce—a symbolic gesture to mark a break with the past. Eighty percent of the federation's members are now Filipino citizens. The president of the federation follows closely the direction of the president, and the organization has pledged its support to Marcos's New Society. Ethnic-Chinese businessmen have been in the forefront of fund-raising campaigns on behalf of the government and have formed many genuine joint ventures with indigenous Filipinos—as distinct from the Ali-Baba-type arrangements in Malaysia.

In June 1968 Chinese businessmen in Jakarta formed an Indonesian Business Center (IBC) to assist in carrying out Indonesia's national economic plan. Two fifths of the organization's leadership are ethnic-Chinese entrepreneurs who are Indonesian citizens. They have been actively trying to steer Suharto's policies in a moderate direction and to demonstrate that moderation can be both successful and beneficial to all.

In Malaysia the trend toward a harmonious outcome is less discernible. There are still three groups of ethnic Chinese in Malaysia, those who are China-oriented, those who are interested only in making money, and those who are Western-educated and aspire to be (and are) Malaysians.[1] The first group will decrease in number if the call of China becomes fainter and if discrimination against its members is reduced. Obviously, these two factors are inseparable.

PRC AND ROC POLICIES

The call of China is greatly affected by the attitudes of authorities on the China mainland and in Taiwan. Peking's former foreign minister, Chiao Kuan-hua, has said, "We must properly educate overseas Chinese returnees and dependents so that, once back in their communities abroad, they can form a single body with the indigenous peoples . . . continue to love the fatherland, study Marxism-Leninism, spread Chairman Mao's thinking, and indomitably live on. . . ."[2] Earlier, in 1957, Chou En-lai told Chinese in Burma that those who were still citizens of China should strive to be "model aliens."[3] By implication, this meant that those who were citizens of other nations were no longer the PRC's concern. It may be that to be a model citizen and to be revolutionary were the same thing in the eyes of Chou and Chiao. Even this would not pose a problem for the countries concerned, however, unless their residents were "ripe for revolution," to borrow a Chinese communist expression. As long as Peking is in no position to pursue real military ventures outside the immediately adjacent area, its influence on the ethnic Chinese of Southeast Asia should not be critical. Indirect intervention through limited support of local insurgents can be effective only as long as local reasons for insurgency persist, but these are amenable to the corrective influence of appropriate domestic policies.

Furthermore, under the Teng-Hua coalition, which came into power in 1976 after Mao's death and a successful coup by a coalition of old party cadres and elements of the military against the radicals. Chinese communities outside China (those in Indochina obviously excepted) are apparently looked upon as potential sources of assistance in the PRC's modernization program. From Peking's point of view, ethnic-Chinese scientists and engineers could become a source of technological transfer and Chinese-owned capital could become a source of investment. While Southeast Asia may have less to offer in the first category than the developed Western countries, especially the United States, it is potentially important in the second category. Hong Kong Chinese entrepreneurs, in particular, may seem to the PRC to be a potential source of expertise and capital for enterprises devoted to the export market. Development of tourist business, encouragement of overseas Chinese investment in mainland China, organization of coproduction joint ventures in border areas resembling the export-processing zones of other countries, encouragement of inward remittances to China, and a more liberal policy to maximize profit on the part of the thirteen communist-owned banks and other enterprises in Hong Kong—all these are part of the PRC's current policy emphasis in dealing with ethnic Chinese abroad. This emphasis became apparent in a series of statements and editorials in January 1978 following a reexamination of policy at the end of 1977. Its pragmatic economic overtone is entirely consistent with the PRC's limited military capacity to expand its influence in the area.

As for Taipei, where the authorities are anxious to strengthen economic relations with Southeast Asia, the late Chiang Kai-shek's advice to participants in an overseas Chinese economic conference on October 28, 1956, was (1) to shift their interests from commerce to industry; (2) to aid and participate in local industrial development; (3) to reduce conflicts between commercial interests and indigenous business; and (4) to expand economic relations with Taiwan. Chiang's heirs have followed the same approach. These happen precisely to be the goals local Chinese have pursued *on their own*. It seems clear, therefore, that Taiwan's policies do not include any intention of causing discord between ethnic Chinese and their home governments in the ASEAN area.

MUTUAL TRUST AND SELF-RESTRAINT

Several operating principles ethnic-Chinese businessmen have adopted in the Philippines, Thailand, and Indonesia parallel those of foreign investors who have attempted to develop codes of conduct for themselves. A number of recent documents, for example, the 1972 Guidelines for International Investment of the International Chamber of Commerce, the Pacific Basin Charter of the same year, the Stikker Report based on the United Nations Conference on Trade and Development of 1968, and the Guidelines for Japanese Investors prepared by Keidanren and other Japanese organizations, reflect a common theme; the establishment of mutual trust and self-restraint.[4] Trust can be established between foreign investors and the national authorities of the host countries if each side can (1) show its understanding of the other side's concerns; (2) be restrained in the pursuit of its own self-interest; and (3) regard helping to promote the objectives of the other side as a part of its own responsibility. This means that foreign investors should promote participation by local capital, train local technical and managerial personnel, and safeguard local interests of a social nature. This is an expansion of the concept of social responsibility for business. For a host government, it means refraining from capricious decisions that will affect investors' profit expectations, managerial plans, or property rights. These points apply equally to the relationship between governments in Southeast Asia and their ethnic-Chinese citizens. Ethnic-Chinese could do more to promote some of the positive aspects of affirmative action mentioned in Chapter 2; for example, they need to demonstrate their readiness to help modernize the countries in which they live. On the other hand, some of the governments could also do more to show that they will not discriminate against the ethnic Chinese. Mutual trust can be cultivated only on a reciprocal basis.

In the many interviews the authors have had with ethnic-Chinese business and community leaders in Southeast Asia, several significant points have become evident.

The previous overseas-Chinese identity has been replaced by an ethnic-Chinese one, and the orientation toward China has been modified to a cultural identification with Chinese traditions and heritage. Ethnic Chinese no longer anticipate returning to China in their old age. Their home is where they are. They are prepared to adjust to the new nation-states of which many have become citizens just as they were able to adjust to the demands of the colonial governments that once ruled Southeast Asia.

Within the ethnic-Chinese communities, the old ties based on speech groups and district associations have loosened. International and multiracial connections going far beyond familial relationships have been formed. Near parity of the sex ratio in the ethnic-Chinese community has made family formation and growth within the countries of residence possible. The wandering Chinese have been replaced by long-term residents whose roots are sunk in the local community and country. The younger generation is well equipped to compete locally. Even the generation gap has become a stimulus to modernization. These social and demographic changes have reduced remittances to China for family support and increased investments in a variety of economic activities outside China. In our view, and in the views of our informants, the ethnic Chinese do not aspire to dominate the countries of Southeast Asia either economically or even culturally. They have even less political ambition, but their future is inextricably bound to the fate of Southeast Asia. Given a reasonable chance of sharing in a future prosperity to which they can contribute materially, few will not opt to stay.

INTERACTION WITH DOMESTIC POLITICS

It is more difficult to predict the political future of some Southeast Asian countries. Suharto's administration seems to have gained more self-confidence since its return to power after the last election. Large numbers of long-term internees who were arrested in retaliation for the 1965 abortive coup have been set free. The Marcos government has successfully defied both insurgency—on the part of Moslems in the south and the New People's Army in the north—and political opposition for a number of years and may continue to do so for the foreseeable future. While Thailand has seen several changes of government in the 1970s, there have been few radical changes and few are likely to occur as long as the communist insurgents can be contained. There is little need to worry about the internal stability of Singapore as long as Prime Minister Lee Kuan Yew's astute policies are maintained. How the Malaysian political scene might change is, perhaps, the principal puzzle.

The future attitudes of Southeast Asian governments toward their ethnic-Chinese minorities will also have a strong effect on internal political stability. Demonstrably nondiscriminatory treatment of all the races will create greater cohesiveness. This is the policy that the Thai National Academy study group found in Singapore and recommended to its own government as appropriate for dealing with Thai Chinese. An enlightened and moderate leadership in Malaysia might share the same outlook.

GROWTH, EQUITY, AND AN OPEN ECONOMY

Although this study has dealt principally with the role of ethnic Chinese in Southeast Asia's economic development and the relationship between economic growth and a given country's policy toward its Chinese minority, we should not ignore other essential factors in this growth. Only two such factors, however, are directly relevant to our major topic.

First, ethnic Chinese in Southeast Asia are by no means all well-to-do. It is wrong to identify the non-Pribumi or the non-Bumiputra with the rich and the Pribumi or Bumiputra with the poor. Unequal distribution of income and wealth in Southeast Asia is not determined by race. Nevertheless, the process of economic growth does have a distributive aspect. Growth cannot be maintained over any length of time without a reasonable degree of political consensus, but this is hard to come by without a degree of equality in income distribution that is acceptable to a large segment of the population. It behooves the ethnic-Chinese minority no less than the majority races of Southeast Asia to work toward achieving the goal of more equal distribution.

Second, it is politically easier to try to share the national product more evenly if the total product is increasing rapidly; an economic policy likely to generate faster growth has this point in its favor. As we have pointed out, it is apparently much easier to achieve fast economic growth in an open, externally oriented economy. This is certainly clear at the initial stages of growth, as such examples as Hong Kong, Singapore, South Korea, and Taiwan show.

The ethnic Chinese in Southeast Asia, our Chinese dimension, may well be the key determinants for the area's future economic and even political well-being. Until recently, local governments have been inclined to view them as unwelcome visitors and potential threats to national security. In actuality, the reverse is true. The Chinese, who are no longer truly alien, offer these governments opportunities unobtainable from any other source. It still remains to be seen whether the governments, the investor countries, the native peoples, and the ethnic Chinese themselves can work together to make the most of their opportunities.

2

A Historical Supplement

6

Chinese Immigration and Business Development in Southeast Asia

Restrictions on Chinese business have been an outcome of confrontation between past, and frequently successful, Chinese economic activities and the nationalist sentiments of the new nations, and the tendency of those nations to regard ethnic Chinese, citizens or not, as aliens in their midst. The following historical review will bring out certain relevant facts. First, the Chinese are not newcomers to the region and therefore not truly aliens. Second, unlike the Westerners who came later, the Chinese have never seriously tried to establish political colonies in Southeast Asia. They have been a part of the Southeast Asian scene for a long, long time, but primarily in an economic capacity.

THE ETHNIC CHINESE DEFINED

Some Alternative Definitions

The most commonly used term for Chinese in Southeast Asia is *hua-ch'iao,* or overseas Chinese. It was used by Chinese revolutionaries in publications outside China during the late Ch'ing dynasty. The customary terms employed in government documents of the same period were Chinese citizens, Chinese people, Chinese merchants, and Chinese laborers, all with the word Chinese expressed by the character hua. The word ch'iao was not used officially. Hua-ch'iao as a single term appeared in print for the first time in 1898 as the name of the Overseas (or hua-ch'iao) School in Yokohama, Japan.[1] It was later used by Hu Han-min in 1907 in the Singapore newspaper *Chung Hsing Daily*, which he edited. As Hu used it, the term included all Chinese migrants living abroad. Since then its use has become commonplace. For overseas Chinese in Southeast Asia the phrase *Nan-yang hua-ch'iao* is often used. The term Nan-yang, which stands for South Seas, first appeared in Chen Lun-ch'iung *Hai-kuo wen-chien lu* [A Record of Personal Experiences in Maritime Countries].[2] Nan-yang or *Nan-yang-ch'ün-tao* (the South Seas Archipelago) has come to be employed by Chinese to mean all the subcontinental and island countries of Southeast Asia and the surrounding seas.

Exactly who should be considered a hua-ch'iao is a point on which there are four different views. The first rests on the literal meaning of the two words: *hua* means a Chinese, whereas *ch'iao* means a short stay as a visitor. By this definition, all Chinese living outside China on a short-term basis should be regarded as overseas Chinese.

A second interpretation is based on the simple fact of overseas residence and refers to persons of Chinese citizenship. Both those who have emigrated from China to foreign countries and their offspring born and brought up in those countries qualify.

A third definition reflects a legal point of view. There are two versions. In the first, all Chinese who have emigrated to, or are residents of, foreign countries and who have not lost their Chinese citizenship are regarded as overseas Chinese. In the second version, all persons who have emigrated from China and their offspring are considered overseas Chinese even if they have acquired foreign citizenship.

The fourth interpretation uses as its first criterion the maintenance of some kind of organic relationship with China. According to Wu Chu-hui, a person's nationality implies an absolute relationship with that country, but social or economic relations are no less important.[3] If this view is accepted, then whether or not they have kept their Chinese nationality, all Chinese who continue to maintain an economic relationship with China or who maintain relations with their families or clans in China should be regarded as overseas Chinese. Even their children who maintain relations with other Chinese only through local social or dialect organizations qualify. A second criterion is the outlook of the person in question and his perception of himself. From this point of view, the term ethnic Chinese is more appropriate and descriptive than overseas Chinese for "those persons who regard themselves as being Chinese irrespective of their national status or their ability to speak the Chinese language."[4]

Given the differing circumstances faced by Chinese communities in Southeast Asia, it is difficult to find the most appropriate definition for overseas Chinese, Chinese, or ethnic Chinese. Nationality laws applied to Chinese differ considerably from country to country, as do the degree and nature of national consciousness among persons of Chinese descent.

To use nationality or citizenship as a criterion poses difficulties. Many Chinese emigrated from China long before the promulgation in 1909 of the Manchu government's statute on the acquisition and loss of citizenship. Others emigrated before the revision of the nationality law in 1929, and still more left before the Chinese Household Registration Act was enacted and thus had no opportunity to be included in the register of Chinese households. None of these persons, therefore, could have maintained a legal relationship with China. To regard the possession of Chinese nationality as an important criterion for overseas-Chinese status would exclude these older emigrants and their descendants. Furthermore, in the post–World War II period, many Chinese in Southeast Asia either have voluntarily acquired citizenship in the countries of their residence or have been compelled to do so by circumstances.

The Southeast Asian countries have five basic—and very different—types of naturalization policies that apply to the Chinese. First, some countries, such as the Philippines, require aliens to complete a special application for naturalization before citizenship can be granted. Second, in some cases citizenship is granted only if the applicant meets certain conditions, such as length of residence or competence in the national language. This is true in Malaysia as well as the Philippines. Third, in contrast to the first two types, naturalization can be compulsory, as in the case of Vietnam under Ngo Dinh Diem.[5] Fourth, in some cases residents are given the right to choose between Chinese citizenship and local citizenship through naturalization. Following the November 1963 coup, the Saigon government allowed Chinese immigrants, as well as native-born Chinese, to choose between Vietnamese and ROC citizenship. This is also the case in Indonesia under its new citizenship act, although three choices are offered: Indonesian citizenship, PRC citizenship, and statelessness—the last for those who opt for ROC citizenship.[6] Fifth and last, assimilation of the Chinese minority may be actively promoted, as in Thailand.

It should be noted that until recently the views of the Nationalist Chinese and PRC governments differed considerably on this subject. Traditionally, the ROC government had regarded all Chinese living abroad as overseas Chinese whether or not they had given up their Chinese citizenship and become naturalized citizens of other countries. The Nationality Law of 1929 combined jus sanguinas with jus soli, thus recognizing the existence of dual nationality. The PRC, however, took a different approach.

At his October 1956[7] meeting with David Marshall, then Singapore's chief minister, Chou En-lai stated, first, that Chinese living in Singapore should, if they wished, be able to surrender their Chinese nationality and assume Singapore citizenship once Singapore became an independent nation. He also made it clear that any Chinese residing in Singapore who voluntarily adopted Singapore citizenship would immediately cease to be Chinese citizens in spite of the racial and cultural affinity that would remain. Next Chou said that any Chinese who, having acquired Singapore citizenship, later wished to adopt Chinese citizenship again might do so in accordance with the law of Singapore. Finally, he stated that Chinese citizens living in Singapore should be protected against any discriminatory treatment, but that they should also respect local laws.

Both in his 1955 negotiations with Indonesia on the nationality issue and in a February 1957 speech in Rangoon,[8] Chou En-lai was consistent in maintaining that the dual nationality of overseas Chinese should cease and that they should be able to choose freely between Chinese citizenship and that of their country of residence. Peking maintained the same attitude in its negotiations with Razak of Malaysia in 1974 and with President Marcos of the Philippines in 1975. In Indonesia, those Chinese who are not citizens and who do not wish to become citizens of the People's Republic have become stateless persons. As of 1973, there were approximately 79,400 such stateless ethnic Chinese.[9]

Although the govenment of the ROC still recognizes dual nationality, its present policy is to let Chinese in foreign countries freely choose their own citizenship and to acquiesce in their choice.[10] Persons who continue to hold ROC passports are called overseas Chinese; those who travel under foreign passports are called persons of Chinese descent. The official policy in Taiwan is to treat the latter as visiting relatives.

Persons of Mixed Parentage

In Southeast Asia, Chinese who came from China or from such places as Hong Kong or Macao where Chinese are a majority are known as newcomers or *Shin-keh*. The ethnic-Chinese population, however, includes a much wider variety of racial mixtures. Some Chinese, of course, have two Chinese parents, but others have one parent, usually the mother, who is non-Chinese. In the third generation, the range of possible combinations increases. While it is arguable that the Chinese element in these racial mixtures tends to dominate—that is, that the children of mixed marriages have been more inclined to consider themselves Chinese than natives of their countries of residence—their habits, language, and life-styles become more and more indistinguishable from those of the native population.[11] Those differences that remain are recognized; all the Southeast Asian countries have special terms to describe these *métis*, such as *Luk-chin* (children of Chinese) in Thailand, peranakans in Indonesia, or *mestizøs* in the Philippines. Broadly speaking, individuals in this group have been granted local citizenship routinely; but as we have seen, in recent years most Southeast Asian nations have also permitted naturalization of residents of pure Chinese parentage.

In Singapore, the nationality law stipulates that citizenship can be acquired by birth, inheritance, registration, or naturalization. Those who acquire Singapore citizenship by birth do not have to be registered as citizens. The same is true in Malaysia.[12] Thai citizenship law stipulates that all children born in Thailand are automatically citizens unless their alien parents have registered them in foreign diplomatic missions in Thailand as non-Thai citizens. Because of the absence of Chinese diplomatic representation in Thailand during World War II, however, ethnic Chinese born there before 1946, whether of pure Chinese or mixed parentage, were all registered as Thai citizens.

Before World War II in Indochina, nineteen out of every thousand persons were of pure Chinese blood, and six were classed as *Ming-houng* (of mixed parentage). The latter, therefore, made up approximately one quarter of the ethnic Chinese community.[13] On August 21, 1956, Decree No. 48 gave all Chinese born in Vietnam local citizenship without choice, but an option was subsequently restored.

In the Philippines, both pure Chinese and mestizos are accepted in society. This is especially true for the mestizos: many of the Philippine elite have Chinese ancestry. Thus the situation parallels that in Thailand. Until recently, the cost of naturalization in the Philippines was often high for a pure Chinese. Restrictions have been progressively relaxed since a presidential instruction in 1975. At the end of 1976, President Marcos stated in an address to the Federation of Filipino-Chinese Chambers of Commerce that additional facility would be given to Chinese applying for naturalization, implying thereby greater latitude and a less time-consuming and costly process for the applicants.[14]

In Indonesia, persons of Chinese descent are either peranakans or *totoks*. Those who speak Indonesian and regard themselves as Indonesians are peranakans, which means Indonesian-speaking persons who look upon Indonesia as their home. The totoks speak Chinese and are more China-oriented. Under the nationality law, citizens of Chinese descent are treated just like other citizens. Neither the 1961 nor the 1971 census retained distinction by race, but citizens (WNI) and noncitizens (WNA) were listed separately. In October 1971, Indonesia's bureau of immigration reported 1.5 million aliens in Indonesia, of whom 95 percent were Chinese.[15]

In recent years, as a result of the increasing economic interrelations among Southeast Asian countries—and for political reasons as well—Chinese living in Southeast Asia have greatly increased their mobility. Some have moved from one Southeast Asian country to another or have acquired new residences or citizenships. For instance, many Chinese from Vietnam have taken refuge in Thailand. Others have moved from Indonesia to Malaysia and Singapore, and still others have acquired either citizenship or right of residence in countries in which they have investments. For a time, alien investors in Singapore could apply for residence there, and following a stipulated period, even citizenship. Recently these rights have apparently been curtailed. Under these conditions, some Chinese who are citizens of one country either by birth or through naturalization may be regarded as aliens from that country in the country of their residence. In some Southeast Asian countries, Chinese from third countries may be treated as nationals of those nations rather than alien Chinese. On the other hand, Chinese from Hong Kong and Macao are usually treated as alien Chinese.

The Ethnic Chinese

The foregoing discussion should demonstrate the complexity surrounding the status of Chinese in Southeast Asia. It is both difficult and unnecessary to find a single definition that covers every important variation.

In this study, which focuses on the economic role of Chinese in Southeast

Asia, we have adhered to the term ethnic Chinese. Our view is that all Chinese in the region should be regarded as members of the ethnic-Chinese community if they maintain a degree of Chinese cultural identity and think of themselves as Chinese, and if both the countries of their residence and third parties, including persons of other nationalities, regard them as Chinese.[16] Figure 1 illustrates the composition of this ethnic-Chinese community.

FIGURE 1

COMPOSITION OF THE ETHNIC-CHINESE COMMUNITY IN SOUTHEAST ASIA

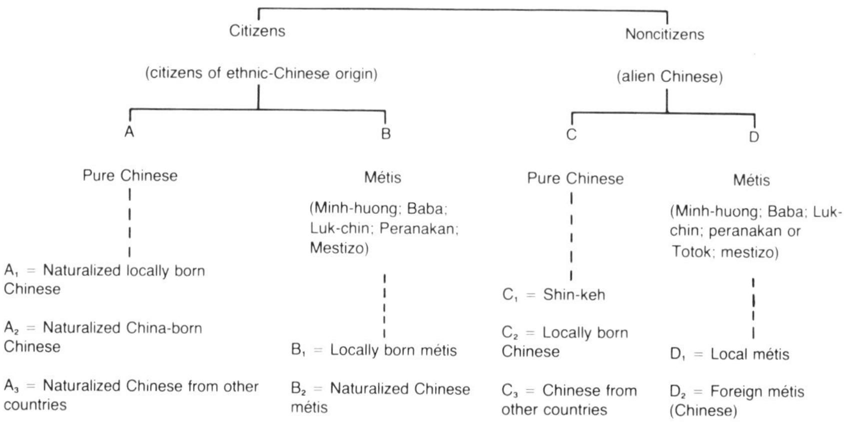

AN OVERVIEW

A Chronicle of Early Contacts and Records

Chinese contacts with the Indochina peninsula began in 1110 B.C., during the sixth year of the reign of King Cheng, the second ruler of the Chou dynasty.[17] During the third century B.C., the first emperor of the Ch'in dynasty (221–205 B.C.), Shih Huang Ti, conquered the area that is Vietnam today. The exploits of the emperor's soldiers who went overland marked one of the few known occasions before our time when Chinese armed forces were employed in Southeast Asia in large numbers either to attempt conquest or to spearhead trade and influence. According to Olov R. T. Janes, Chinese pioneers very possibly were in Vietnam during the third century B.C. Evidence of Chinese artisanship and customs have been found dating back to that time.[18]

Use of sea transportation by the Chinese to reach Southeast Asia can be traced to the reign of Emperor Wu (140–87 B.C.) of the Han dynasty.[19] Judging from earthenware excavated in Sumatra, Java, and Borneo, De Flines believed that traders and immigrants from China had already settled on these islands during the Han period (206 B.C.–A.D. 221).[20]

During the period of the Three Kingdoms (A.D. 226–231), two envoys were dispatched to the South Sea countries by Sun Ch'üan shortly after Sun proclaimed himself in 229 first emperor of the Wu dynasty.[21] One hundred and seventy years later, toward the end of the Chin dynasty, a Chinese Buddhist monk named Fa Hsien set out for India to secure a complete set of the Buddhist sutras in the original language. He returned by sea, traveling via Ceylon and the Strait of Malacca, and was, in the year 413, as far south as Java (referred to as Ye Po Ti) and the Malay Peninsula. Fa Hsien's accounts of incidents during his long journey were published in what is now known as the *Fu-Kuo-Chi* [An Account of the Buddhist Countries].[22]

Beginning in the Liang dynasty (502–557), envoys from the South Seas bearing tributes—a form of barter in effect—regularly visited Nanking, the capital of the southern regime in a time when China was divided into two parts.[23] Emperor Yang of the Sui dynasty (589–618), who reunited the empire, dispatched envoy Chang Chun to Ch'ih-t'u (literally, the red earth)—present-day Songkla in southern Thailand—to establish trade relations.[24]

Because of the mountainous terrain on the southwestern border of China, early travelers from China usually went to Southeast Asia by sea. Basing his studies on the "Ti-li-chih" in the *Hou-han shu* [Annals of Geography of *The Book of Later Han*]. Feng Ch'eng-chün has suggested that during these voyages boats from Han China went only as far as Cambodia—perhaps up to the Malay Peninsula occasionally—and that transportation farther afield was probably continued on boats sailed by native traders.[25] Until the seventh century, Chinese boats were not designed to survive the open sea; they usually hugged the coastline. Only during the T'ang dynasty (618–907) did they venture onto the high seas, going as far as Persia. The boats carrying T'ang Buddhist priests often left from Canton or Ch'ao-chou (Teochiu). They stopped at Sri Vijaya in Sumatra and went as far as Ceylon, then known to the Chinese as Lion Country (Shih-tzu-kuo).

Among notable early cultural contacts between China and the rest of Asia was the pilgrimage (629–645) of the Buddhist priest Hsüan Tsang, better known as San Tsang, to India.[26] In 671, seven years after San Tsang's death, another Buddhist priest, I Ching, set out for India by sea.[27] After spending six months at Palembang in Sumatra to study Sanskrit, he sailed to Tamralipti, also in Sumatra, and then went to Nalanda, where he stayed for the next ten years. In 692 I Ching was in Langkasuka (present-day Trengganu in Malaysia). He returned to China three years later and was received with great honor.

In *Chu Fan Chi* [A Record of Foreign Lands], two volumes of detailed description of Chinese trade with parts of the Malay Archipelago during the Sung dynasty (960–1280), Ju-kua Chau used information supplied by merchants from

India, Arabia, Persia, Portugal, and other countries that he had collected during his tenure (1209–14) as superintendent of customs at Ch'üan-chou (in Fukien province).[28]

In 1280, Kublai Khan, grandson of Genghis Khan, became the emperor of China. Twelve years later, a fleet with twenty thousand men recruited from Kwangtung, Fukien, Hunan, and Kiangsi was dispatched to parts as far south as Java.[29] The expedition was unsuccessful, and many soldiers stayed behind as settlers on the islands they had invaded. Kublai Khan's expedition was the second major military effort mounted from China against Southeast Asia. The first was the conquest of Vietnam by Shih Huang Ti some fifteen hundred years earlier.

Three years after the start of the expedition, in 1295, a mission from the Yüan court was sent to the Khmer kingdom, then known to the Chinese as Chenla (Chan-lap in Vietnamese). The *Chin La Feng Tu Chi* [Local Manners and Customs of Cambodia], written by Chou Ta-kuan, who accompanied the mission, contains a vivid account of Cambodia.[30] Again in 1349, late in the Yüan dynasty (1280–1368), a Chinese businessman named Wang Ta-yüan wrote an account of his own tour of the South Seas islands.[31] Wang's book, entitled *Tao I Chih Lu* [A Summary Report on Island Tribes], included a description of the Chinese quarters of Tumasik (present-day Singapore).

Chinese writings up to the Yüan dynasty referred to present-day Southeast Asia either as *Nan-hai* (the South Sea) or as *Hsi-nan-hai* (the Southwestern Sea). Chang Hsieh, who lived during the Ming dynasty (1368–1644) and wrote the *Tung Hsi Yang K'ao* [A Study of the Eastern and Western Oceans], thought of Brunei as the meeting point of two oceans.[32] He treated Brunei and lands to its east as part of the Eastern Ocean (*Tung-yang*).

Early in the fifteenth century, seven naval expeditions to Nanyang were undertaken by Cheng Ho, a renowned officer from Yunnan province.[33] These expeditions of the Ming dynasty were the last major Chinese effort to reach Southeast Asia with armed forces. The first of Cheng's voyages involved sixty-two ships, which carried 27,800 troops from Woosung, near Shanghai, to the coast of Cambodia and Siam. Later voyages reached Sumatra, Ceylon, and even Persia and Africa. While Cheng's troops were in Malacca, they helped the Malays defend themselves against Siamese invaders, and a temple was built in Malacca to commemorate this event. More than thirty states were visited by Cheng's men, whose voyages were examples of trade promotion and of the use of port calls to show the flag. While Cheng's undertaking appeared to menace the South Seas states, the Ming court was probably more anxious for economic gains than for military conquest. The Mings had been plagued for a long time by Mongols in the north and Japanese pirates in the east, as well as unrest in the southwestern border areas. External trade was regarded as one way of replenishing national coffers depleted by heavy defense costs.[34]

Stages of Chinese Emigration

According to Li Ch'ang-fu,[35] Chinese emigration to Southeast Asia can be divided into four periods. The first dates from the middle of the thirteenth century, when the declining Sung dynasty was about to be replaced by Mongol rule. China's external contacts by sea were beginning to expand, making migration relatively easy. The second period spanned two and a half centuries, beginning with the Yüan dynasty under the Mongols and ending at about the midpoint of the Ming dynasty. The states of Southeast Asia were then in control of their surrounding waters, and Chinese immigration into the area rose. During the third stage, from the sixteenth century to the middle of the nineteenth century, European influence was increasing in Southeast Asia, and Chinese settlers in the area suffered repeated setbacks. The fourth period, from the mid-nineteenth century to the outbreak of the Pacific War, saw almost all Southeast Asia under the colonial rule of Western powers. Large numbers of Chinese immigrants were recruited during this period because of increasing manpower needs for economic development.

During the first two stages and for several centuries earlier, trade with Southeast Asia had been controlled almost exclusively by Arabs. Such places as Cambodia, Sumatra, and Java boasted highly developed civilizations, and Chinese merchants visiting the South Seas could readily appreciate the economic and geographical importance of the area. These businessmen sought to develop trade not only with the residents of the area, but also with traders from beyond the Indian Ocean. On the southeast Chinese coast itself, trading ports sprang up one after another. Canton and Ch'üan-chou were among the major ports designated by the authorities of the T'ang and Sung governments for trade with foreigners, and superintendents of customs were appointed to levy duties and to administer external commerce. The two southeast coastal provinces, Kwangtung and Fukien, which were the first to have external contacts with the outside world by sea, naturally sent by far the largest numbers of Chinese emigrants to Southeast Asia and beyond.

Trade, then, was the primary motive for early Chinese contacts with Southeast Asia. Besides traders, Chinese travelers to Southeast Asia were pilgrims or government envoys, but the latter were also economic emissaries interested in trade. Almost none, however, were settlers. Few Chinese who went to the South Seas in these early times had any intention of establishing residence; the need to do so evolved gradually as trade expanded.

In his book *Golden Pasture,*[36] Abu-'l Hasan Ali Elmasudi wrote that quite a few Chinese settlers were found tilling the land in Sumatra in the year 943. Many Chinese had fled South China in the late 870s, during the Huang Ch'ao rebellion near the end of the T'ang dynasty, and these were probably refugees or their descendants. Refugees from T'ang China have also been reported on other islands in the South Seas; Chinese in the area have since been called the T'ang people.

As we mentioned earlier, many of the twenty thousand men from Kublai Khan's expedition to Java in 1292 elected to settle in the South Seas. Following the restoration of Han-Chinese rule in China under the Ming dynasty late in the fourteenth century, the seven voyages of Cheng Ho further expanded Chinese contacts in the area. Ch'eng-tsu (also renowned as Yung-lo), the third emperor of the Ming, reversed the policy of passive seclusion pursued by the founder of the dynasty, who had been preoccupied with defense against the Mongols in the north. The Ming court under Ch'eng-tsu was more interested in the economic gains that contact with the South Seas appeared to promise. This change in court policy also meant a relaxation of the ban on overseas travel by Chinese. External trade relations were pursued more vigorously both under the Mongols and during the Ming dynasty, and Chinese traders went as far as the Spice Islands (Moluccas) and Timor.

For thirteen centuries, however—from the T'ang period to the mid-Ch'ing dynasty—China's court paid little attention to the well-being of Chinese who had settled abroad. No offer of assistance was made to emigrants; on the contrary, restrictions of varying degrees of strictness were imposed on emigration by different rulers. This negative policy, which is generally referred to in discussions on overseas-Chinese matters as the sea ban, reflected the Chinese governments' Sinocentric view. Since China was regarded as superior to the rest of the world, all Chinese were supposed to be content in the Middle Kingdom. Persons who sought to leave the country were regarded as a cause of national disgrace who should be punished.

The T'ang court stipulated that people should not remain abroad too long; even brief trips without a valid purpose were not allowed. On the other hand, traders, envoys, and priests were permitted to travel overseas as long as appropriate taxes and levies in the form of service were paid. In 976, during the reign of the second Sung emperor, the Sung court decreed that all persons caught trying to put out to sea without permission would be banished to desolate islands. Toward the end of his reign in 995, the emperor reiterated the ban. Businessmen were allowed to go abroad, however, after securing official permits. Granting of the permit was a means of assuring the state of tax revenue and of preventing self-exile from the Middle Kingdom, which would be a disgrace. Between 1284 and 1322, under the Mongols, external trade was at times under state control and at times under private management. While the administration of trade was not always consistent, the ban on emigration for permanent settlement abroad was maintained throughout eighty-eight years of Mongol rule. The same policy prevailed during the first years of the Ming dynasty. A decree issued in 1381, the fourteenth year of the reign of the first Ming emperor, strictly banned all unauthorized exit from China by land or sea. Later, discretionary control was substituted for the outright ban. Only when Cheng Ho's fleet began its expeditions to the South Seas did emigration from China become relatively free.

After pirates became active in Chinese waters a century later, a strict sea ban was again imposed in 1523 to prevent the people from colluding with outlaws and barbarians. Another century later, under the statutes and laws of the Great Ch'ing dynasty[37] proclaimed in 1648, the fourth year of the new Manchu regime, no one was allowed to leave China for either trade or settlement. Violators of the rule were to be beheaded as traitors, and local officials found negligent in enforcing the ban were to be punished accordingly. The severity of the law reflected the government's fear inspired by the exploits of Cheng Ch'en-kung (Koxinga), who was trying to re-establish Ming rule using Quemoy and later Taiwan as his bases of operation. His war vessels and troops were so successful that the Manchus ordered the evacuation of the southeast coastal zone to form an unpopulated belt that would be easier to defend against enemy landings. The sea ban was an integral part of this defensive tactic.

The ban was not always successful, however, and Manchu policy toward Chinese settlers abroad shifted from time to time. In 1712, the K'ang-hsi emperor ordered all Chinese settlers abroad to return to China within certain time limits. This order was reversed in 1727, when the Yung-cheng emperor decided that those who had settled in foreign countries should not be called back because they were not law-abiding people, but the sea ban remained on the books.

Article 5 of the 1860 Sino-British Treaty of Peking and Article 9 of the Sino-French Treaty, also signed in Peking, of the same year provided that persons who sought to make a living abroad might do so. Although the Manchu court was forced to sign the two treaties it was not yet willing to lift the sea ban. Not until 1893, when the court accepted the recommendation of Hsüeh Fu-ch'eng, the Chinese envoy to Great Britain,[38] were restrictions on foreign travel and emigration ended.

Attitudes of the Chinese Immigrants and Their Treatment in the Colonial Period

Colonial rule in most of Southeast Asia began when Portuguese seafarers first reached the Pacific and lasted until the outbreak of the Pacific War.[39] The development of capitalism in the West during this period greatly increased the demand for industrial raw materials and tropical consumer products. It also necessitated an expansion of the market for Western manufacturers. Colonies in Southeast Asia supplied both these needs, and the expanding economies of the colonies in turn created an increasing demand for labor that the Chinese immigrants were to supply.

In addition to Chinese who came to the South Seas voluntarily, others were forcibly recruited. When the Dutch came to Indonesia as colonizers early in the seventeenth century, they were dependent upon Chinese labor. Armed Dutch boats plying the South China Sea intercepted Chinese boats and took the passengers and crews off to serve as laborers. When the demand for labor increased sharply in the nineteenth century, new tactics were introduced. Lured by promises of high wages and good working conditions, able-bodied men were signed on in the coastal ports of Fukien and Kwangtung. Barracks, known as barracoons, were set up in Macao and Hong Kong, and served as virtual places of detention for Chinese workers awaiting transportation. Hong Kong, Macao, Canton, and Amoy became bases for such operations by European recruiters for the overseas labor market, which by the nineteenth century included both Southeast Asia and the west coast of the United States. Underground organizations were set in motion for what the Chinese called the piggie trade. Between 1830 and 1874, Singapore became the major transshipment point for the redistribution of Chinese workers in Southeast Asia.[40]

After the Treaty of Nanking (1842) forced the Manchu court to cede Hong Kong to the British and open five treaty ports in China, the sea ban was no longer enforceable, and China became an increasingly stable source of labor supply to Western colonies in Southeast Asia. As we noted earlier, the Treaties of Peking (1860) further compelled the Manchu authorities to recognize the right of Chinese workers to seek a livelihood abroad under contracts they themselves freely entered into.[41] Nevertheless, the transition to regulated migration under contract was a slow process.[42]

The colonial rulers did not treat the immigrant Chinese the same as the indigenous peoples. In direct dealings with the latter, high-handed methods alternated with attempts at pacification. Toward the Chinese, however, the usual policy was to let them control both themselves and—indirectly—the indigenous population. Leaders selected from among the Chinese were made responsible for the dissemination and execution of government orders within the Chinese community. They came to be known as *kapitans* in Java, Malaya, and the Philippines, and *bang truong* (chief assistants) in Indochina.

Unfortunately for the ethnic Chinese, the colonial powers soon discovered that the Manchu court regarded emigrant workers as *hua-wai-chih-min* (unreformed persons beyond the pale). Since the authorities in China showed no particular interest in their welfare, the Chinese in Southeast Asia were often treated more than a little harshly by the local colonial authorities. Among their misfortunes were five massacres in the Philippines during the period 1603–1762 and the Red River incident of 1740 in Batavia (now Jakarta). Some sixty thousand Chinese lives were reportedly lost in the Philippines massacres and nine thousand in Batavia.[43]

For the Chinese immigrants, the desire to earn a living and to escape from hardships in China were the principal motives for emigration. Nevertheless, most of them held firm to the Chinese idea that "fallen leaves always return to the roots." They looked upon the countries where they earned their living or, in some cases, made their fortunes, as places of residence that they would eventually leave so that their souls could dwell in their native lands. This attitude was encouraged by the treatment they received from both the colonial rulers and, later, the indigenous peoples among whom they lived.

While Li Ch'ang-fu limited himself to denoting four major waves of emigration, each of which involved persons who were opposed to a new political regime or were simply refugees from the general turmoil, two additional waves of Chinese emigration occurred in more recent times. During the 1930s the populations of Fukien, Kwangtung, and Kiangsi were plagued by Chinese communist and counterinsurgent military activities. The ravages of the civil war were followed by the Japanese invasion of China in 1937 and the subsequent outbreak of the Pacific War in 1941. A sizable movement of persons to Southeast Asia during these years constituted a fifth exodus.

The fall of the Chinese mainland to the communists in 1949 started a sixth exodus that has not yet ended. The number of escapees to Hong Kong alone before 1964 exceeded one million.[44] Following the U.S.-PRC rapprochement in 1971, some persons were permitted by the PRC authorities to leave China. Among them were former residents of Southeast Asia who had returned to China. According to Hong Kong statistics, the number of such immigrants and escapees into Hong Kong totaled 55,658 in 1973, 32,918 in 1974, and 25,649 in 1975,[45] exceeding the unofficial quota of 50 persons a day, or 18,250 a year, by a wide margin.

A survey by Ta Chen of 905 families in the Swatow area of Kwangtung from September 1934 to April 1935 produced the percentage distribution illustrated in Table 50 of the principal causes of emigration at that time.

TABLE 50

PRINCIPAL REASONS FOR EMIGRATION FROM THE EMIGRANT COMMUNITY NEAR SWATOW, 1934

Reason Given	Number of Families	Percentage of Emigrants
Economic pressure	633	69.95
Previous connection with Nanyang	176	19.45
Losses from natural calamities	31	3.43
Plan to expand specific enterprise	26	2.87
Bad conduct	17	1.88
Local disturbance	7	0.77
Family quarrel	7	0.77
Other	8	0.88
Total	905	100.00

SOURCE: Ta Chen, *Nan-yang hua-ch'iao yü min-yüeh she-hui* [Relations of Southeast Asian Chinese with Fukien and Kwangtung Communities] (Ch'ang-sha: The Commercial Press, 1937), p. 48.

For emigrants from this area, who were probably typical, economic pressure and previous connections with Nanyang accounted for nearly 90 percent of the total. (Strictly speaking, previous connections with Nanyang was more a factor in choosing a destination than a reason for emigration.) Of the first group of 633 families that listed economic pressure as their reason, 353—nearly 40 percent—gave individual unemployment as the specific cause. Nearly 30 percent—280 families—listed such economic reasons as lack of assets, limited income, overcrowded households, and so on.

An earlier survey Chen undertook in 1920 gave an estimate of 13,158,000 persons in an area of 46,332 square miles in Fukien province.[46] He estimated that there were 37,168,000 persons in an area of 100,000 square miles in Kwangtung. The high population density, the uneven distribution of farmland, and the prevalence of tenant farming in both Kwangtung and Fukien contributed to low farm income. Under these conditions, food shortages developed whenever natural calamities struck. According to one source,[47] there were twenty-nine serious droughts and twenty major floods in Fukien from the mid-fourteenth to the mid-seventeenth centuries, or approximately one large disaster every six years. Kwangtung, which was slightly more fortunate, suffered eight droughts and seventeen floods of major proportions during the same period. For China as a whole, no fewer than 23.4 million lives were lost during the three major famines of 1846, 1849, and 1877.[48] Whenever natural or man-made disasters occurred in North China, the population affected was likely to move south. Those in South China, especially the coastal provinces, emigrated to Southeast Asia.

Such population movements were facilitated by the demand for labor in Southeast Asia. During the nineteenth century, no fewer than three million Chinese from Fukien and Kwangtung answered this rising demand. Later emigrants from China, as Chen's 1934 survey shows, were drawn to places where they had relatives and friends who had emigrated earlier.

Evolution of Chinese Economic Activities before World War II

Chinese economic activities evolved through several stages. Before the sixteenth century Chinese businessmen visited Southeast Asia on a nonpermanent—frequently seasonal—basis. Because of the mountainous terrain of continental Southeast Asia and the adjacent provinces of southwest China, much of this trade was conducted by merchants who traveled by sea. Contacts were made with the Arab traders and through them with markets farther afield. However, it was only during the period between the mid-thirteenth and the fifteenth centuries that Chinese began to establish settlements in Southeast Asia. These settlements were populated by Chinese immigrants who had left their homeland in spite of the periodic official discouragements already noted. The Chinese communities became entrenched in commerce, as well as simple manufacturing and agriculture, during the period between 1500 and the first part of the eighteenth century: this could be regarded as the second phase in the development of Chinese economic activities in the area.

From the mid-eighteenth century to the 1930s, as colonial regimes became firmly established in Southeast Asia, Chinese immigration into the region increased in scale. These settlers supplied labor for economic development and acted as intermediaries between producers and consumers in internal as well as external commerce. Chinese businessmen came to dominate retail trade, but their activities also extended to plantation agriculture, mining, finance, transportation, and modern manufacturing, although generally on a smaller scale than European enterprises in the area.

For simplicity, Figure 2 presents this historical development in schematic form.

FIGURE 2

EVOLUTION OF ETHNIC-CHINESE ECONOMIC ACTIVITIES IN SOUTHEAST ASIA

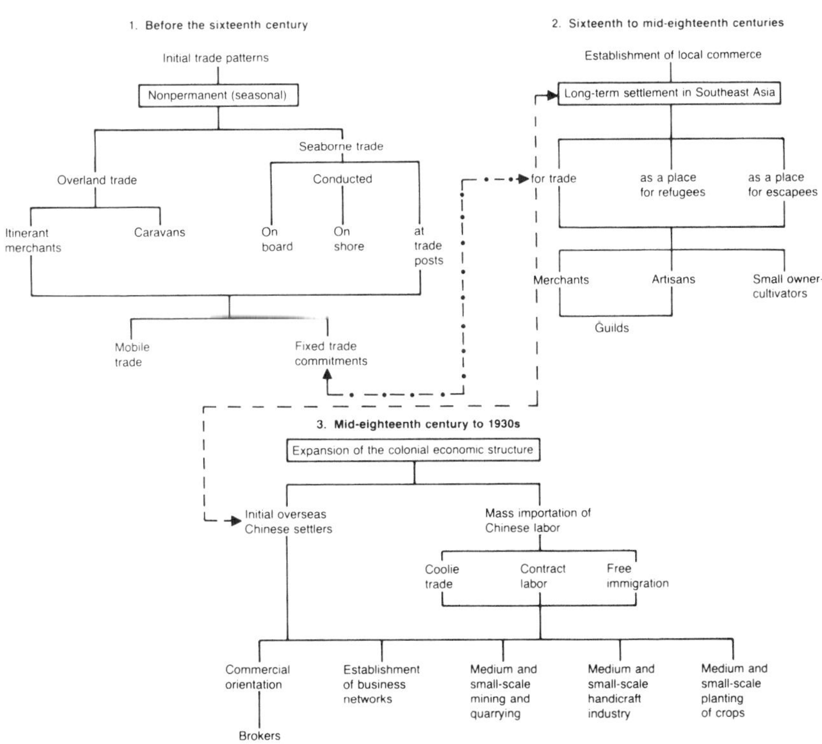

NUMBERS AND DISTRIBUTION OF ETHNIC CHINESE IN SOUTHEAST ASIA

The proportion of ethnic Chinese in Southeast Asia varies from less than 1 percent of the total population in North Vietnam to more than 76 percent in Singapore. Among the ASEAN nations, the lowest proportion of ethnic Chinese is 1.5 percent in the Philippines.

Victor Purcell estimated that there were 8.5 million ethnic Chinese out of a 1947 population of 157 million in Southeast Asia.[49] (By Southeast Asia he meant Burma, Thailand, Malaya, British Borneo, Indonesia, the Philippines, and the Indochinese nations.) This number was subsequently projected forward to 1960, using two alternative annual growth rates, 2.5 percent and 3 percent. The 3-percent growth rate was based on P. E. Smith's estimate for the period 1950 to 1960.[50] These projections yielded estimates of a 1960 ethnic-Chinese population of 12–12.5 million. If the projections were extended to the period 1961 to 1974, the estimates for 1974 would be 17.1 million at an annual growth rate of 3 percent or 16.1 million at a growth rate of 2.5 percent. These figures may be compared with the estimate of the Overseas Chinese Affairs Commission (OCAC) of the Republic of China—a total of 15.5 million by the end of 1973.[51] (No sources, however, are given for the OCAC's estimates.)

A set of more detailed estimates, however, is available from United for Progress, an organization of ethnic Chinese in the Philippines. At a May 1974 meeting in Manila devoted to the issues of minority races in Southeast Asia, the total ethnic-Chinese population in the region was placed at 14.5 million in 1974. The data by country, which have since appeared in *Pagkakaisa Research,* are given in Table 51.

It should be noted that none of these figures include the Chinese populations in Hong Kong and Macao. Ethnic Chinese make up approximately 95 percent of the total populations of these two cities. *Pagkakaisa Research* gave the absolute numbers for 1974 as 4,089,000 ethnic Chinese in Hong Kong and 292,000 in Macao. Since Hong Kong and Singapore play a particularly important role in the economic development of Southeast Asian countries, it is well to bear in mind that the ethnic-Chinese populations of Hong Kong and Singapore alone totaled 5.7 million in 1974.[52]

EMIGRANT AREAS, SPEECH GROUPS, AND OCCUPATIONAL DISTRIBUTION

We have already mentioned the predominance of the coastal areas in China, especially the provinces of Fukien and Kwangtung, as sources of supply for Chinese emigrants.

TABLE 51

GEOGRAPHICAL DISTRIBUTION OF ETHNIC CHINESE IN SOUTHEAST ASIA, 1974

Country	Chinese Residents (Thousands)	Total Population (Millions)	Percentage of Chinese in Population
Thailand	3,500.0	41.02	8.5
Peninsular Malaysia	3,687.0 (1975)	10.38	35.5
The Philippines	600.0	41.30	1.4
Indonesia	3,250.0	129.12	2.5
Singapore	1,579.9	2.22	72.0
North Vietnam	175.0	23.08	0.7
South Vietnam	2,000.0	20.40	0.9
Cambodia	425.0	7.89	5.3
Laos	60.7	3.26	1.8
Burma	500.0	29.52	1.7
Brunei	46.7	0.10	46.7
Portuguese Timor	9.5	0.61	1.5
Total	15,833.8	308.90	5.1

SOURCE: *Pagkakaisa Research* (Manila), no. 38, 1974. The sources cited by the compilers are: *Population and Housing Census of Malaysia, 1970*, published in Kuala Lumpur in 1972; Mely G. Tan of Indonesia, "Majority-Minority Situation: Indonesia" (Paper presented at the Manila conference organized by ASAIHL, May 8–10, 1974); *Philippines Statistics*, vol. 24, published in Manila in the third quarter of 1973; another ASAIHL paper by Boonsonong Punyodyana of Thailand; an interim release of the *1970 Population Census*, published in Singapore in 1971; *Third Malaysia Plan, 1976–1980* (Kuala Lumpur: Government Press, 1976), p. 142; and various United Nations sources. The figures of total population in the above table are taken from ADB, *Key Indicators*, vol. VII, no. 1 (April 1976): 3 and 111.

The two major centers in Fukien are in the vicinity of the port city of Amoy: Ch'üan-chou and its environs northeast of Amoy and Chang-chou, west of Amoy. The lower reaches of the Min River near Foochow (Fu-chou) and P'u-t'ien and Hsien-yü counties are also important areas of emigration.

In Kwangtung province, Chinese emigrants are mostly from (1) the Pearl River Delta near Canton, including in particular the counties of Hsin-hui, T'ai-shan (Toisan), K'ai-ping, and En-p'ing; (2) Ch'ao-chou (Teochiu in the local dialect) and Swatow (Shan-t'ou) along the Han River on the Kwangtung-Fukien border; (3) the Chia-ying area in northeast Kwangtung; and (4) Hainan Island, particularly the cities of Ch'iung-chou and Hai-k'ou (Hoikow).

Furthermore, sizable numbers of Chinese emigrants came from the provinces of Chekiang, Kiangsu, and Taiwan. Finally, there are seasonal migrant workers who cross over to Burma from Yunnan; some Yunnanese have also settled in northern Thailand and upper Burma.

Understandably, emigrants from the same province or speech group living in a foreign country have felt a special kinship and bond. There are five major Chinese speech or dialect groups in Southeast Asia. Their distribution, given by Wu Chu-hui in 1959, is shown in Table 52.

TABLE 52

CHINESE SPEECH GROUPS IN SOUTHEAST ASIA

Speech Group	Percentage of Persons in Each Group	Area of Origin in China
Hokkien (Fukien, Fukienese)	37	Southern and Eastern Fukien
Cantonese (Kwangtung)	24	Northern and Western Kwangtung
Hakka (Kechia, Khekka)	21	Eastern and Northwestern Kwangtung
Teochiu (Chaochow, Swatow)	15	Southeastern Kwangtung
Hainanese (Hailam, Hainanese)	3	Northern Hainan Island
Total	100	

SOURCE: Wu Chu-hui, *Kakyō honshitsu no bunseki* [Analysis of the Character of the Overseas Chinese Community] (Tokyo: Institute of Social Science, Toyo University, 1961), pp. 75 and 93.

Within the Fukienese group, a further distinction can be made among the Min-nan (southern Min or Amoy), Foochow, and P'u-t'ien dialects, not to mention a variation of the Amoy dialect spoken by persons from Ch'ao-an, Yün-hsiao, and Tung-shan that is very close to the Swatow dialect of the Teochiu people across the provincial border.

The dialect groups are not completely homogeneous. Many persons who speak a particular dialect are not from the part of China in which it is widely used, and many Chinese in Southeast Asia speak more than one dialect. In addition, Mandarin has been taught in virtually all Chinese schools in the area for many years. These factors and the decline in new immigration have tended to reduce the importance of the traditional dialect associations, but they still exert considerable influence in social and economic matters. Table 53 provides an overview of the distribution of Chinese by major speech group and by country.

Most of the economic strength of the ethnic Chinese in Thailand is controlled by the Teochiu- or Swatow-speaking group. In other Southeast Asian countries the economic leaders are mostly Fukienese, commonly known as Hokkiens, even in areas where the Fukien speech group is small. Members of this group, moreover, have consistently been in the majority in large enterprises. Major bases of Fukienese business operations are Malaysia, Singapore, Indonesia, and the Philippines. Large numbers of import-export firms and about half the local banking establishments and new industrial plants in these countries are run by Fukienese. In the Philippines, where the Fukienese account for 80 percent of the ethnic-Chinese population, their preponderant influence has never been challenged. Most Fukienese in Indonesia are concentrated either in the larger urban areas or in places in Java and Sumatra where specific natural resources are exploited. A prominent figure in Java's sugar industry from its beginning was

TABLE 53

DISTRIBUTION OF CHINESE IN SOUTHEAST ASIA BY COUNTRY AND SPEECH GROUP
(Percentage)

	Hokkien	Cantonese	Teochiu	Hakka	Hainanese	Other	Total
Thailand (1955)	7.0	7.0	56.0	16.0	12.0	2.0	100.0
Malaysia (1961)	31.7	21.7	12.1	21.8	5.3	7.4	100.0
Singapore (1963)	40.0	18.0	23.0	1.0	. . .	18.0	100.0
Indonesia (1930)	50.0	11.5	7.5	16.5	. . .	14.5	100.0
The Philippines (1965)	85.0	15.0	–	–	–	–	100.0
South Vietnam (1974)	7.0	60.0	20.0	6.0	7.0	–	100.0
Cambodia (1974)	6.5	15.0	60.0	4.5	9.0	5.0	100.0
Laos (1974)	. . .	15.0	70.0	. . .	10.0	5.0	100.0
Burma (1974)	25.0	25.0	. . .	. . .	. . .	50.0	100.0

SOURCES: Thailand: G. W. Skinner, *Chinese Society in Thailand* (Ithaca, N.Y.: Cornell University Press, 1957), p. 212;
Malaysia: *Federation of Malaya Official Year Book, 1961;*
Singapore: Huang Tien-chio, *Hua-ch'iao ching-chi wen-ti* [Problems of Overseas Chinese Economy] (Taipei: OCAC, 1963);
Indonesia: W. J. Cator, *The Economic Position of the Chinese in Netherlands Indies* (Oxford: Basil Blackwell, 1936), p. 31;
Philippines: See Chapter 3.
South Vietnam, Cambodia, and Laos: *Hua-ch iao ching-chi nien-chien, 1975,* p. 70;
Burma: Huang Tien-chio, *Hua-ch'iao ching-chi wen-t'i;* see also Purcell, *Chinese in Southeast Asia,* p. 45.

Oei Tiong Ham (Huang Chung-han), who came from Fukien. Oei became a sugar tycoon in Samarang in central Java a century ago. In March 1863, he founded the N. V. Handel Maatschappij Kian Guan, which dominated Indonesia's sugar industry for several decades.[53]

The economic strength of the Kwangtung speech group in Southeast Asia is second only to that of the Fukien group. Since Kwangtung borders on Indochina, large numbers of Cantonese-speaking emigrants have founded settlements in present-day Vietnam, Cambodia, and Laos. The rice trade in Vietnam was handled mostly by members of this group before the establishment of the communist regime. In Malaysia, the Kwangtung group holds important positions in the rubber and tin industries: it is surpassed only by the Fukienese among ethnic-Chinese groups. The Cantonese in Malaysia are found mostly in the southern and northern states, while a majority of the Fukienese live in Penang and Malacca.

Large concentrations of Teochiu-speaking persons have settled in Thailand, the three Indochina states, and Singapore. The Teochius owed their rise in Thailand to the brilliant exploits of General Phaya Tak Sin (also known as Chao Teh Sin), who was half Chinese. General Phaya was instrumental in reuniting Thailand after the Burmese invasion of 1767 and in founding a new Thai capital at Thonburi (Dhonburi), directly across the river from Bangkok. The Teochiu origin of the general's father was immensely helpful to the Teochius in reaching high positions in government, commerce, and industry, and this group controlled Thai external trade until British involvement increased in the mid-nineteenth century. The Teochius have continued to play an important role in the economic development of Thailand, although large numbers of newer arrivals from Fukien and Hainan in this century have weakened their dominant position.

Numerous Hakkas live in Malaysia, Indonesia, and Thailand. Their influence in Indonesia is second only to that of the Fukienese. Many are engaged in mining in Kalimantan; others are in farming in Sumatra; and there are many Hakka retailers—known to the local people as *warang*—in Indonesia's urban centers. The Hakkas rank second among the ethnic-Chinese communities in Thailand and third in Malaysia.

The Hainanese—relatively few in number—are found mostly in Indochina and Thailand, where many are employed as clerks, on rubber plantations, and in the fishing industry. Both the Hakkas and the Hainanese are known for their frugality and industry; a number have become highly successful and wealthy.

Although ethnic Chinese are widely distributed across various economic sectors in Southeast Asia, those engaged in commercial and industrial activities account for more than 50 percent of the total. Since World War II, they have made considerable progress in their fields, including manufacturing, mining, and transportation; their numbers in the technical and managerial professions have also risen significantly. Table 54 presents the occupational distribution of ethnic Chinese in four Southeast Asian countries.

TABLE 54

OCCUPATIONAL DISTRIBUTION OF ETHNIC CHINESE IN SOUTHEAST ASIA
(Percentages)

	Thailand (1955)	The Philippines (1954)	Malaysia (1970)	Indonesia (date unknown)
Government	0.02	–	–	0.6
Professions	1.59	40.0	–	1.5
Commerce and finance	50.84	41.0	24.0	36.6
Industry and handicraft	19.41	11.0	24.0	20.0
Domestic and other service	9.75	–	5.0	2.7
Agriculture	1.19	–	29.0	30.9
Unskilled	17.21	8.0	18.0	7.7
Total	100.00	100.0	100.0	100.0

SOURCES: Thailand: G. W. Skinner, *Chinese Society in Thailand*, p. 303;
Philippines: Data from The Federation of Filipino-Chinese Chambers of Commerce in 1954;
Malaysia: *Hsing-chiu jih-pao* (Singapore), December 2, 1975;
Indonesia: Shih Heng-san, "Tung-nan-ya hua-ch'iao chiu-yeh ch'ing-k'uang" [Occupations of Overseas Chinese in Southeast Asia], *Ching-chi tao-pao* [Economic Bulletin], September 18, 1961, p. 10.

SOCIAL ORGANIZATIONS

Speech groups provided a natural associative basis for Chinese in Southeast Asia, but self-protection through mutual assistance was another important motivation. Emigrants from China did not go to Southeast Asia in organized groups supported by the Chinese authorities or by other organizations. They went in search of opportunities, hoping to leave their misfortunes behind in China. Their choice of destination was based on distance, the presence of relations or friends, and the attractiveness of promised opportunities. The need to overcome obstacles made association for self-protection one way to make their lives easier. The new arrivals transplanted their South China habits and customs to Southeast Asia, and their settlements were as much as possible replicas of those they had left at home. The result was what some Western scholars have called a society within a society.

The ethnic Chinese in Southeast Asia could not escape contact with members of the larger society, however. It was up to the local populations to decide whether the Chinese among them were to be treated as guests or intruders. Language and cultural differences created political, economic, and social pressures, and numerous problems within the community could not be solved by individuals alone. The need to cope with external forces and solve community issues increased dependence on social organizations. Clubs and associations initially formed by small numbers of individuals from the same place of origin, speech group, or occupation soon grew into larger and then community-wide associations. In the early days these larger organizations were often independent of the judicial and administrative systems of the host countries, and in the absence of official support from China they never attempted to acquire the protective umbrella of Chinese law or requested official recognition from China. Their growth depended on the emigrants themselves.[54]

Many associations started as temples. The *Ch'i-fu Kung-so* (literally, the Seven-Prefecture Public Office) was, for instance, the earliest Southeast Asian Chinese association of a general nature. It was established in Vietnam in 1778 and had its origin in the *Ch'i-fu Erh-miao,* the Seven-Prefecture Second Temple. (Three of the seven prefectures are in Fukien, three are in Kwangtung, and one is in Chekiang.)[55] Similarly, four associations or *hui-kuan* (literally "houses of associations") in Singapore evolved from temples. All the association houses in use today have altars, even though their buildings no longer bear any resemblance to places of worship. Religious activities often provided opportunities for community meetings and the planning of welfare projects. The *kung-so* and *hui-kuan* have been supplemented by the *kung-si* (public companies). An early example is the I-an company, which was established by a Swatow-speaking group in Singapore in 1845.

The activities of the associations are varied; among them are medical care, relief, schooling, and burial assistance. Some large organizations operate both schools and hospitals. Medical and educational facilities run by the Chinese were common in Vietnam, and Chinese-operated hospitals are still found in the Philippines. Similar institutions were established in Singapore as early as 1870, as well as in other Southeast Asian countries.

Trade guilds are associations in another form. The *Hsüan-yüan Kuan* in Singapore, a tailors' union founded in 1865, was the earliest Chinese trade association in Southeast Asia. Following the example of the tailors, Chinese restaurant operators in Singapore established their own union in 1877.[56]

There were also political organizations. When Koxinga was busy harassing the Manchus in an attempt to revive the Ming dynasty, a group known as the *T'ien-ti Hui* (the Heaven and Earth Association) was organized by Chen Ying-nan. Branches of the association sprang up at various points in Southeast Asia under different names, including the *San-ho Hui* (the Triad Society) and the *San-tien Hui* (the Three Point Society). These branches were commonly referred to as *Hung-men* (meaning the Hung household) from *Hung-wu,* the imperial title assumed by the first Ming emperor. Perhaps the best example of the growth of the Hung-men was the establishment in 1770 of a republic called the *Ta-t'ang Tsung-hui* (General Association of the Great T'ang People) in Borneo by a Cantonese immigrant, Lo Fang-po, and a local sultan. The political activities of Hung-men organizations were never very extensive because of financial and manpower limitations, not to mention official efforts to suppress them. Many Hung-men establishments are still in existence today, but only as mutual-aid organizations.

The first truly revolutionary organization working against the Manchu government was founded by Sun Yat-sen in Honolulu in 1894. Known as the *Hsing Chung Hui* (Society for the Regeneration of China), it was formed to "overthrow the Manchus, restore the Chinese nation and establish a republic." Branches were set up in Hong Kong, in Taipei (a year after Taiwan was ceded to Japan following the first Sino-Japanese war), and in various places in Southeast Asia. In August 1905, when the organization was transformed into the *T'ung Meng Hui* (the Common Cause League) in Tokyo, its former branches became offshoots of the new association. In 1912, a year after the establishment of the Republic of China, the T'ung Meng Hui became an open political party and adopted its present name, the *Chung-kuo Kuomintang*—usually abbreviated as the Kuomintang or KMT. The former T'ung Meng Hui branches in Singapore, Malaya, Thailand, Burma, Indonesia, and the Philippines then became part of the Kuomintang.

Chinese organizations were sometimes set up as self-governing bodies for the Chinese. The first example was in Annam (modern Vietnam) during the reign of King Gia-long (1798–1820). Association offices were established for separate speech groups: Cantonese, Hokkien, Teochiu, and Hainanese. Members of these associations chose their own leaders, whose responsibilities were to settle disputes, handle matters of immigration, act as guarantors for newcomers, levy taxes, keep family registrations up to date, and carry out public-welfare projects. These administrative services for the Chinese were continued during the French occupation of Indochina and into the post–World War II years in Vietnam, Cambodia, and Laos. Elsewhere in Southeast Asia less systematic control of the Chinese by the Chinese was allowed, generally in the form of mutual-benefit societies based on common occupations or places of origin.

An association can be likened to a family that provides economic assistance and legal protection to its members. There are roughly five different kinds of associations among ethnic Chinese: (1) local dialect group associations; (2) surname or clan associations; (3) business associations; (4) clubs or recreational associations; and (5) religious and benevolent societies. Table 55 lists ethnic-Chinese organizations in Southeast Asia at the end of 1973.

Interorganizational relations between different Chinese associations are sometimes nonexistent. Conflicts and competition also arise among associations of a similar nature, such as those representing different dialect groups. On the other hand, since a person may belong simultaneously to two or more associations, a strong personality who serves as an officer in one stands a good chance of being elected to a post in another. Such interlocking directorships and other connections are useful in strengthening interassociation relations and in alleviating external and internal pressures.[57]

The importance of such associations to the ethnic Chinese in Southeast Asia is declining with the passage of years and the accelerating assimilation of Chinese residents into the native communities. These trends are not, as we have seen,

TABLE 55

CHINESE ORGANIZATIONS IN SOUTHEAST ASIA, DECEMBER 1973

Organizations	The Philippines	Vietnam	Laos	Cambodia	Thailand	Malaysia	Singapore	Brunei	Timor	Burma	Indonesia
General	16	32	13	–	19	37	2	1	–	25	1
Social	239	25	2	3	11	79	15	1	3	54	3
Regional	107	39	2	14	69	390	127	3	–	77	–
Religious	92	5	–	–	41	96	117	–	1	26	–
Trade	18	2	–	–	9	99	54	–	1	14	1
Industrial and commercial	350	2	–	–	50	380	125	5	5	16	4
Cultural and educational	41	10	1	1	41	80	30	–	2	22	–
Recreational	66	43	2	11	20	276	88	1	1	14	2
Youth	26	6	–	–	4	17	8	–	–	44	–
Women's	1	3	1	–	1	7	1	–	–	1	–
Political	49	3	–	–	–	–	–	–	–	4	–
Welfare	14	17	2	1	58	115	29	2	2	17	3
Charity	21	2	2	–	53	20	7	–	–	5	–
Other	20	33	–	–	3	59	14	1	–	9	1
Total	1,060	222	25	30	379	1,655	617	14	15	328	15

SOURCE: Overseas Chinese Affairs Commission, *Overseas Affairs Statistics* (Taipei, 1974).

uniform in all host countries, but it is apparent that all the problems we have considered represent a current stage in a long historical progression that is far from its end.

Southeast Asia in general is in the midst of what are probably the most tumultuous economic, political, and social changes the area has ever experienced. There is virtually no doubt that these changes will continue: the significant question is whether they will be for better or for worse. Whatever the outcome, however, the ethnic Chinese and the indigenous peoples among whom they live will share in either victory or defeat because their commitments, their hopes for the future, and their homelands are now the same.

3

Appendixes

A

Directions of Trade of ASEAN and Other Southeast Asian Countries, 1971–73 Average and 1974–75 Average

TABLE A-1

DIRECTIONS OF TRADE OF ASEAN AND OTHER SOUTHEAST ASIAN COUNTRIES: 1971–73 AVERAGE
(Percentage)

	Destination							
Exporting Countries	Indonesia	Malaysia	The Philippines	Thailand	Singapore	ASEAN Total	Hong Kong	Taiwan
Indonesia[a]		1.5 (1.5)	0.5 (0.5)	0.03 (0.03)	9.7 (9.8)	11.7 (11.8)	0.6 (0.6)	4.6 (4.6)
Malaysia	0.6 (0.6)		1.3 (1.3)	0.8 (0.8)	23.3 (23.6)	26.0 (26.3)	1.6 (1.6)	1.3 (1.3)
The Philippines	0.5 (0.5)	0.2 (0.2)		0.2 (0.2)	1.0 (1.0)	1.8 (1.8)	1.6 (1.6)	2.0 (2.0)
Thailand	3.4 (3.5)	5.3 (5.4)	1.8 (1.8)		8.1 (8.3)	18.5 (19.0)	7.2 (7.4)	3.7 (3.8)
Singapore	3.8 (3.9)	19.1 (19.5)	0.7 (0.7)	2.6 (2.7)		26.2 (26.8)	5.4 (5.5)	1.0 (1.0)
ASEAN Total	1.7 (1.7)	6.4 (6.5)	0.8 (0.8)	1.0 (1.0)	8.6 (8.6)	18.3 (18.6)	3.1 (3.2)	2.4 (2.4)
South Vietnam	3.8 (3.8)	– –	0.3 (0.3)	1.3 (1.3)	9.0 (9.0)	14.4 (14.4)	22.3 (22.3)	2.7 (2.7)
Laos[a]	–	39.5	–	50.0	1.6	91.1	2.6	–
Burma[a]	1 7 (1.8)	2.8 (2.8)	2.9 (3.0)	0.03 (0.03)	9.3 (9.4)	16.73 (17.03)	3.2 (3.2)	– –
Southeast Asia Total	1.7 (1.7)	6.3 (6.4)	0.8 (0.9)	1.0 (1.0)	8.6 (8.7)	18.4 (18.7)	3.2 (3.2)	2.3 (2.4)

SOURCE: (for all tables in this appendix): International Monetary Fund, *Direction of Trade Annual 1969–75* (Washington, D.C.: August 1976), pp. 84, 138, 154, 161, 194, 205, 208, 220, 221–48, 264, 266, 272, 275, 276.

				Destination				
Total of Singapore and Hong Kong	Total of Singapore, Hong Kong, and Taiwan	Japan	U.S.	EEC	Oil-Exporting Countries Except Indonesia	Other	Total World	Total World Excluding Oil-Exporting Countries and Indonesia
10.3	14.9	48.4	14.1	11.3	0.3	8.9	100.0	
(10.4)	(15.0)	(48.4)	(14.1)	(11.3)		(8.9)		(100.0)
24.8	26.0	18.1	12.3	21.0	1.1	18.6	100.0	
(25.2)	(25.5)	(18.3)	(12.4)	(21.3)		(18.8)		(100.0)
2.6	4.6	35.1	38.6	12.9	0.1	7.8	100.0	
(2.6)	(4.6)	(35.1)	(38.6)	(13.0)		(7.8)		(100.0)
15.3	19.0	24.1	11.7	16.5	2.0	16.2	100.0	
(15.7)	(19.5)	(24.6)	(11.9)	(16.8)		(16.5)		(100.0)
5.4	6.4	8.3	14.9	14.7	1.6	27.9	100.0	
(5.5)	(6.5)	(8.4)	(15.0)	(15.0)		(28.1)		(100.0)
11.7	14.1	25.5	17.1	15.3	1.0	17.1	100.0	
(11.8)	(14.2)	(25.8)	(17.3)	(15.5)		(17.2)		(100.0)
23.4	26.1	24.0	3.4	26.7	0.0	6.5	100.0	
(23.4)	(26.1)	(24.0)	(3.4)	(26.7)		(6.5)		(100.0)
4.2	4.2	0.7	0.05	0.1	–	5.2	100.0	
								(100.0)
12.5	12.5	16.3	0.9	26.1	1.1	35.5	100.0	
(12.6)	(12.6)	(16.5)	(1.0)	(26.4)		(35.9)		(100.0)
11.8	14.1	25.4	16.9	15.5	1.0	17.3	100.0	
(11.9)	(14.3)	(25.7)	(17.0)	(15.6)		(17.4)		(100.0)

NOTES: Figures in parentheses represent percentages in terms of the world total after excluding Indonesia and other oil-exporting countries.

[a]Components may not add to 100 because of rounding.

TABLE A-2

DIRECTIONS OF TRADE OF ASEAN AND OTHER SOUTHEAST ASIAN COUNTRIES: 1971–73 AVERAGE
(U.S. $ Million)

	Destination							
Exporting Countries	Indonesia	Malaysia	The Philippines	Thailand	Singapore	ASEAN Total	Hong Kong	Taiwan
Indonesia		32.0	11.7	0.6	211.8	256.1	12.8	99.5[a] (1972–73)
Malaysia	1.27		26.9	17.6	487.3	544.5	33.6	26.3
The Philippines	7.3	2.5		2.7	13.0	25.5	22.1	27.2
Thailand	39.8	61.0	20.5		94.0	215.3	83.5	42.9
Singapore	101.6[b]	506.0	19.3	70.2		697.1	142.4	26.5
ASEAN Total	161.4	601.5	78.4	91.1	806.1	1,738.5	294.4	222.4
South Vietnam	1.1 (1972–73)	–	0.1 (1972–73)	0.4	2.6	4.2	6.5	0.8
Laos	–	1.5	–	1.9	0.06	3.5	0.1	–
Burma	2.2	3.5	3.7 (1971–72)	0.04 (1971–72)	11.7	21.1	4.0	–
Southeast Asia Total[c]	164.7	606.5	82.2	93.4	820.5	1,767.3	305.0	223.2

[a]Chinese Chamber of Commerce in Jakarta, *Economic Data on the Republic of Indonesia,* July 1975, p. 17.
[b]This figure represents Indonesia's imports from Singapore
[c]Excluding Cambodia and, in some instances, Laos.

Destination									
Total of Singapore and Hong Kong	Total of Singapore, Hong Kong, and Taiwan	Japan	U.S.	EEC	Oil-Exporting Countries Except Indonesia	Other	Total World	Total World Excluding Oil-Exporting Countries and Indonesia
224.6	324.1	1,053.2	307.7	245.6	5.7 (1972)	193.2	2,173.8	2,168.1
520.9	547.2	377.8	256.2	440.3	23.1	389.3	2,091.1	2,068.0
35.1	62.3	476.4	524.6	175.1	1.9	105.8	1,358.6	1,356.7
177.5	220.4	279.2	134.6	191.3	23.5	187.3	1,157.6	1,134.1
142.4	168.9	218.9	389.2	388.6	43.2	730.1	2,636.0	2,592.8
1,100.5	1,322.9	2,405.5	1,612.3	1,440.9	97.4	1,605.7	9,417.1	9,319.7
9.1	9.9	7.0	1.0	7.8	0.0	1.9	29.2	29.2
0.2	0.2	0.03	0.002 (1973)	0.005 (1972–73)	–	0.2	3.8	3.8
15.7	15.7	20.5	1.2	32.9	1.4	44.7	125.8	124.4
1,125.5	1,348.7	2,433.0	1,614.5	1,481.6	98.8	1,652.5	9,575.9	9,473.3

TABLE A-3

DIRECTIONS OF TRADE OF ASEAN AND OTHER SOUTHEAST ASIAN COUNTRIES: 1971–73 AVERAGE
(Percentage)

	Source of Imports							
Importing Countries	Indonesia	Malaysia	The Philippines	Thailand	Singapore	ASEAN Total	Hong Kong	Taiwan
Indonesia		0.5	0.4	2.0	5.2	8.1	3.6	3.9
Malaysia	3.0 (3.0)		0.3 (0.3)	4.0 (4.0)	7.6 (7.8)	14.9 (15.1)	1.9 (2.0)	2.0 (2.1)
The Philippines	1.0 (1.1)	1.5 (1.6)		0.7 (0.8)	0.7 (0.7)	3.9 (4.2)	1.0 (1.1)	1.5 (1.7)
Thailand	0.4 (0.4)	1.2 (1.3)	0.2 (0.3)		1.3 (1.3)	3.1 (3.3)	1.3 (1.4)	3.2 (3.4)
Singapore	5.3 (5.8)	15.4 (16.9)	0.3 (0.3)	2.3 (2.5)		23.3 (25.5)	2.5 (2.7)	2.2 (2.5)
ASEAN Total	2.6 (2.8)	6.1 (6.5)	0.3 (0.3)	2.0 (2.1)	2.5 (2.6)	13.5 (14.3)	2.2 (2.3)	2.5 (2.7)
South Vietnam[a]	0.2 (0.2)	0.08 (0.1)	1.0 (1.0)	1.9 (2.0)	7.6 (7.7)	10.2 (11.0)	0.4 (0.5)	6.0 (6.0)
Laos[a]	5.7 (5.7)	0.01 (0.01)	0.2 (0.2)	40.5 (40.5)	5.6 (5.6)	52.01 (52.01)	1.9 (1.9)	1.7 (1.7)
Burma[a]	0.1 (0.1)	1.4 (1.4)	0.01 (0.01)	0.04 (0.04)	1.2 (1.2)	2.75 (2.75)	1.5 (1.5)	– –
Southeast Asia Total	2.5 (2.6)	5.7 (6.0)	0.3 (0.3)	2.1 (2.2)	2.8 (3.0)	13.4 (14.1)	2.1 (2.2)	2.7 (2.9)

NOTES: Figures in parentheses represent percentages of the world total after excluding Indonesia and the other oil-exporting countries.

[a]Components may not add to 100 due to rounding.

Source of Imports								
Total of Singapore and Hong Kong	Total of Singapore, Hong Kong, and Taiwan	Japan	U.S.	EEC	Oil-Exporting Countries Except Indonesia	Other	Total World	Total World Excluding Oil-Exporting Countries and Indonesia
9.1	13.0	29.1	15.8	17.1	–	22.4	100.0	
								(100.0)
9.5	11.5	20.8	8.0	22.1	2.6	27.7	100.0	
(9.8)	(11.9)	(21.4)	(8.3)	(22.7)		(28.4)		(100.0)
1.7	3.2	30.7	26.5	14.5	9.3	12.6	100.0	
(1.8)	(3.5)	(33.8)	(29.2)	(16.0)		(14.0)		(100.0)
2.6	5.8	36.7	14.3	19.6	5.5	16.3	100.0	
(2.7)	(6.1)	(38.8)	(15.1)	(20.8)		(17.2)		(100.0)
2.5	4.7	18.0	13.4	2.5	9.1	29.0	100.0	
(2.7)	(5.2)	(19.8)	(14.9)	(2.9)		(31.7)		(100.0)
4.7	7.2	25.0	14.9	12.6	5.9	23.4	100.0	
(4.9)	(7.6)	(26.5)	(15.8)	(13.4)		(25.0)		(100.0)
8.0	14.0	15.8	43.0	15.1	0.04	8.4	100.0	
(8.2)	(14.2)	(16.0)	(43.0)	(15.1)		(8.4)		(100.0)
7.5	9.2	13.2	12.4	12.0	0.01	6.7	100.0	
(7.5)	(9.2)	(13.2)	(12.4)	(12.0)		(6.7)		(100.0)
2.7	2.7	28.5	3.7	26.0	0.3	37.4	100.0	
(2.7)	(2.7)	(28.6)	(3.7)	(26.0)		(37.5)		(100.0)
4.9	7.6	20.1	16.3	13.0	5.4	27.0	100.0	
(5.2)	(8.1)	(21.3)	(17.3)	(13.7)		(28.5)		(100.0)

TABLE A-4

DIRECTIONS OF TRADE OF ASEAN AND OTHER SOUTHEAST ASIAN COUNTRIES: 1971–73 AVERAGE
(U.S. $ Million)

Source of Imports

Importing Countries	Indonesia	Malaysia	The Philippines	Thailand	Singapore	ASEAN Total	Hong Kong	Taiwan
Indonesia		9.2	7.6	38.2	101.6	156.6	69.5	76.1[a] (1972–73)
Malaysia	54.3		6.2	72.4	141.6	274.5	34.7	37.7
The Philippines	14.7	22.0		11.1	10.3	58.1	15.1	22.4
Thailand	6.1	19.8	3.6		20.1	49.6	21.2	51.3
Singapore	211.8[b]	616.0	14.1	93.6		935.5	99.3	90.0
ASEAN Total	286.9	667.0	31.5	215.3	273.6	1,474.3	239.8	277.5
South Vietnam	1.5	0.6	6.6	13.3	51.1	73.1	3.2	40.2
Laos	2.7	0.006	0.08	19.3	2.7	24.8	0.9	0.8
Burma	0.2 (1972)	1.9	0.02 (1972–73)	0.06	1.6	3.8	2.1	–
Southeast Asia Total[c]	291.3	669.5	38.2	248.0	329.0	1,576.0	246.0	318.5

[a]Chinese Chamber of Commerce in Jakarta, *Economic Data on the Republic of Indonesia,* July 1975, p. 17
[b]Figure obtained from Indonesia's exports to Singapore.
[c]Excluding Cambodia.

Source of Imports								
Total of Singapore and Hong Kong	Total of Singapore, Hong Kong, and Taiwan	Japan	U.S.	EEC	Oil-Exporting Countries Except Indonesia	Other	Total World	Total World Excluding Oil-Exporting Countries and Indonesia
171.1	247.2	567.1	309.9	333.9	–	437.2	1,950.3	
176.3	214.0	384.9	148.7	409.3	47.6	512.3	1,849.7	1,802.1
25.4	47.8	458.2	396.5	217.0	138.5	189.1	1,494.9	1,356.4
41.3	92.6	588.6	229.0	315.0	88.2	260.8	1,603.7	1,515.5
99.3	189.3	720.9	538.0	100.8	366.4	1,153.5	4,004.4	3,638.0
513.4	790.9	2,719.7	1,622.1	1,376.0	640.7	2,552.9	10,903.0	10,262.3
54.3	94.5	106.0	286.9	100.8	0.3	56.6	667.1	666.8
3.6	4.4	6.3	5.9	5.7	0.008	3.2	47.6	47.6
3.7	3.7	39.1	5.1	35.5	0.4	51.2	137.0	136.6
575.0	893.5	2,362.7	1,920.0	1,518.0	641.4	3,172.1	11,754.7	11,113.3

TABLE A-5

DIRECTIONS OF TRADE OF ASEAN AND OTHER SOUTHEAST ASIAN COUNTRIES: 1974–75 AVERAGE
(Percentage)

	Destination							
Exporting Countries	Indonesia	Malaysia	The Philippines	Thailand	Singapore	ASEAN Total	Hong Kong	Taiwan
Indonesia[a]		1.0 (1.0)	0.4 (0.4)	0.08 (0.09)	7.5 (7.5)	9.0 (8.9)	0.3 (0.3)	1.1 (1.1)
Malaysia	0.6 (0.6)		1.3 (1.3)	0.2 (0.2)	21.0 (21.3)	23.1 (23.4)	1.2 (1.2)	1.2 (1.2)
The Philippines	0.6 (0.6)	0.2 (0.2)		0.2 (0.2)	1.0 (1.0)	2.0 (1.9)	1.2 (1.2)	1.1 (1.1)
Thailand	2.9 (3.0)	4.7 (5.0)	1.2 (1.2)		7.8 (8.2)	16.6 (17.4)	8.7 (9.2)	4.4 (4.7)
Singapore	5.3 (5.5)	16.0 (16.5)	0.9 (0.9)	2.8 (2.9)		25.0 (25.8)	6.5 (6.8)	1.1 (1.1)
ASEAN Total	1.9 (2.0)	5.2 (5.3)	0.7 (0.7)	0.8 (0.8)	7.2 (7.4)	15.8 (16.1)	3.2 (3.2)	1.5 (1.5)
South Vietnam	3.0 (3.1)	3.6 (3.6)	0.1 (0.1)	2.0 (2.0)	12.0 (12.1)	20.7 (20.9)	14.7 (14.7)	4.4 (4.4)
Laos	–	16.4 (17.4)	–	34.5 (36.6)	5.3 (5.6)	56.2 (59.6)	1.8 (2.0)	3.5 (3.7)
Burma	11.1 (11.2)	10.5 (10.6)	0.4 (0.4)	0.8 (0.8)	6.7 (6.9)	29.5 (29.9)	4.1 (4.1)	0.6 (0.6)
Southeast Asia Total	2.0 (2.0)	5.2 (5.3)	0.7 (0.7)	0.8 (0.9)	7.3 (7.4)	15.9 (16.3)	3.2 (3.3)	1.5 (1.5)

NOTES: Figures in parentheses represent percentages of the world total after excluding Indonesia and the other oil-exporting countries.

[a]Components may not add to 100 due to rounding.

Destination								
Total of Singapore and Hong Kong	Total of Singapore, Hong Kong, and Taiwan	Japan	U.S.	EEC	Oil-Exporting Countries Except Indonesia	Other	Total World	Total World Excluding Oil-Exporting Countries and Indonesia
7.8	8.9	48.0	24.4	5.8	0.07	11.1	100.0	
(7.8)	(8.9)	(48.1)	(24.5)	(5.9)		(11.2)		(100.0)
22.2	23.4	15.6	15.0	22.1	1.7	20.1	100.0	
(22.5)	(23.7)	(16.0)	(15.2)	(22.5)		(20.5)		(100.0)
2.2	3.3	36.2	36.3	14.0	1.6	7.6	100.0	
(2.2)	(3.3)	(36.8)	(36.9)	(14.2)		(7.8)		(100.0)
16.5	20.9	26.2	9.4	15.1	5.2	14.4	100.0	
(17.4)	(22.1)	(27.6)	(10.0)	(16.0)		(15.1)		(100.0)
6.5	7.6	9.5	13.6	12.3	3.4	28.6	100.0	
(6.8)	(7.9)	(9.9)	(14.1)	(12.7)		(29.6)		(100.0)
10.4	11.9	28.1	19.5	12.5	2.0	17.4	100.0	
(10.6)	(12.1)	(28.6)	(20.0)	(12.7)		(17.8)		(100.0)
26.7	31.1	27.4	11.2	16.0	0.3	5.3	100.0	
(26.8)	(31.2)	(27.4)	(11.2)	(16.0)		(5.3)		(100.0)
7.1	10.6	11.1	8.5	1.2	5.8	11.9	100.0	
(7.6)	(11.3)	(11.8)	(9.0)	(1.2)		(12.7)		(100.0)
10.8	11.4	11.1	1.4	16.5	1.2	35.6	100.0	
(11.0)	(11.6)	(11.2)	(1.4)	(16.7)		(36.1)		(100.0)
10.5	12.0	27.9	19.3	12.5	2.0	17.6	100.0	
(10.7)	(12.2)	(28.4)	(19.7)	(12.8)		(18.0)		(100.0)

TABLE A-6

DIRECTIONS OF TRADE OF ASEAN AND OTHER SOUTHEAST ASIAN COUNTRIES: 1974–75 AVERAGE
(U.S. $ Million)

Destination

Exporting Countries	Indonesia	Malaysia	The Philippines	Thailand	Singapore	ASEAN Total	Hong Kong	Taiwan
Indonesia		74.2	27.2	6.2	539.3	646.9	25.6	79.5 (1975)
Malaysia	23.9		50.5	9.0[a] (1974)	844.3	927.7	47.6	50.0
The Philippines	14.5	4.8		3.8	25.0	48.1	29.5	28.0
Thailand	69.3	115.1	29.0		188.1	401.5	212.0	107.5
Singapore	312.0[b]	944.0	53.1	163.8		1,472.9	386.2	62.4
ASEAN Total	419.7	1,138.1	159.8	182.8	1,596.7	3,497.1	700.9	327.4
South Vietnam	2.3	2.7	0.1	1.5	9.0	15.6	11.0	3.3
Laos	–	2.8	–	5.9	0.9	9.6	0.3	0.6
Burma	23.3	22.0	0.8	1.7	14.2	62.0	8.6	1.2
Southeast Asia Total[c]	445.3	1,165.6	160.7	191.9	1,620.8	3,584.3	720.8	332.5

[a]The SGV Group, Thailand: *An Economic Profile* (Bangkok: SGV-NA Thailand and Co. Ltd., October 1975), p. 16.
[b]Estimate based on Indonesia's imports from Singapore.
[c]Excluding Cambodia and, in some instances, Laos.

				Destination				
Total of Singapore and Hong Kong	Total of Singapore, Hong Kong, and Taiwan	Japan	U.S.	EEC	Oil-Exporting Countries Except Indonesia	Other	Total World	Total World Excluding Oil-Exporting Countries and Indonesia
564.9	644.4	3,460.6	1,760.4	422.3	5.1	803.6	7,204.0	7,198.9
891.9	941.9	630.1	603.9	892.0	66.7	811.8	4,029.8	3,963.1
54.5	82.5	895.4	898.1	346.0	39.1	189.0	2,473.2	2,434.1
400.1	507.6	634.1	227.0	367.5	125.7	348.4	2,423.7	2,298.0
386.2	448.6	563.1	804.0	724.8	201.0	1,691.2	5,905.6	5,704.6
2,297.6	2,625.0	6,183.3	4,293.4	2,752.6	437.6	3,844.0	22,036.3	21,598.7
20.0	23.3	20.5	8.4	11.8	0.2	4.0	74.8	74.6
1.2	1.8	1.9	1.464 (1974)	0.2	1.0	2.04	17.1	16.1
22.8	24.0	23.3	3.0	34.8	2.5	75.0	210.4	207.9
2,341.6	2,674.1	6,229.0	4,306.3	2,799.4	441.3	3,925.0	22,338.6	21,897.3

TABLE A-7

DIRECTIONS OF TRADE OF ASEAN AND OTHER SOUTHEAST ASEAN COUNTRIES: 1974–75 AVERAGE
(Percentage)

	Source of Imports							
Importing Countries	Indonesia	Malaysia	The Philippines	Thailand	Singapore	ASEAN Total	Hong Kong	Taiwan
Indonesia		0.47 (0.5)	0.33 (0.3)	1.5 (1.5)	6.9 (6.9)	9.2 (9.2)	2.7 (2.8)	2.0 (2.1)
Malaysia	2.2 (2.4)		0.7 (0.5)	3.7 (3.9)	8.4 (8.8)	1.5 (15.6)	1.7 (1.8)	2.0 (2.1)
The Philippines	1.0 (1.2)	1.2 (1.4)		0.7 (0.9)	0.7 (0.8)	3.6 (4.3)	0.9 (1.0)	2.3 (2.8)
Thailand	0.1 (0.1)	0.6 (0.7)	0.1 (0.2)		2.4 (2.9)	3.2 (3.9)	1.4 (1.7)	2.4 (2.9)
Singapore	7.3 (8.8)	11.4 (13.9)	0.3 (0.3)	2.2 (2.7)		21.2 (25.7)	2.1 (2.6)	1.7 (2.1)
ASEAN Total	3.2 (3.6)	4.5 (5.2)	0.3 (0.3)	1.8 (2.0)	3.1 (3.5)	12.9 (14.6)	1.9 (2.2)	2.0 (2.3)
South Vietnam	0.3 (0.3)	0.1 (0.1)	0.2 (0.2)	0.5 (0.5)	17.3 (17.3)	18.4 (18.4)	1.4 (1.4)	2.8 (2.8)
Laos	0.9 (0.9)	0.001 (0.001)	0.3 (0.3)	33.7 (33.8)	3.4 (3.4)	38.4 (38.4)	3.5 (3.5)	0.3 (0.3)
Burma	5.8 (5.8)	2.6 (2.6)	0.08 (0.08)	0.6 (0.6)	9.1 (9.1)	18.18 (18.18)	1.6 (1.6)	0.01 (0.01)
Southeast Asia Total	3.1 (3.5)	4.4 (5.0)	0.3 (0.3)	1.8 (2.1)	3.6 (4.1)	13.2 (15.0)	1.9 (2.1)	2.0 (2.3)

NOTE: Figures in parentheses represent percentages of the world total after excluding Indonesia and the other oil-exporting countries.

Source of Imports								
Total of Singapore and Hong Kong	Total of Singapore, Hong Kong, and Taiwan	Japan	U.S.	EEC	Oil-Exporting Countries Except Indonesia	Other	Total World	Total World Excluding Oil-Exporting Countries and Indonesia
9.6	11.6	32.0	14.8	18.3	0.3	20.7	100.0	
(9.6)	(11.6)	(32.1)	(14.8)	(18.3)		(20.7)		(100.0)
10.1	12.1	21.1	10.0	20.7	5.5	24.0	100.0	
(10.6)	(12.7)	(22.4)	(10.7)	(22.0)		(25.4)		(100.0)
1.6	3.9	27.0	23.0	12.5	17.0	13.7	100.0	
(1.8)	(4.6)	(32.6)	(27.7)	(15.1)		(16.5)		(100.0)
3.8	6.2	31.5	13.7	17.9	16.7	13.2	100.0	
(4.6)	(7.5)	(37.9)	(16.4)	(21.4)		(15.8)		(100.0)
2.1	3.8	16.2	13.8	12.1	17.6	15.3	100.0	
(2.6)	(4.7)	(19.6)	(16.7)	(14.7)		(18.6)		(100.0)
5.0	7.0	23.6	14.7	15.5	12.2	17.2	100.0	
(5.7)	(8.0)	(26.9)	(16.8)	(17.6)		(19.6)		(100.0)
18.7	21.5	8.6	55.7	6.6	0.1	6.4	100.0	
(18.7)	(21.5)	(8.6)	(55.8)	(6.6)		(6.4)		(100.0)
6.9	7.2	11.24	18.5	16.0	0.06	12.0	100.0	
(6.9)	(7.2)	(11.24)	(18.5)	(16.0)		(12.0)		(100.0)
10.7	10.71	29.0	6.6	21.0	0.01	23.6	100.0	
(10.7)	(10.71)	(29.01)	(6.6)	(21.0)		(23.6)		(100.0)
5.5	7.5	23.1	16.2	15.2	11.6	16.8	100.0	
(6.2)	(8.5)	(26.1)	(18.3)	(17.2)		(19.0)		(100.0)

TABLE A-8

DIRECTIONS OF TRADE OF ASEAN AND OTHER SOUTHEAST ASIAN COUNTRIES: 1974–75 AVERAGE
(U.S. $ Million)

	Source of Imports							
Importing Countries	Indonesia	Malaysia	The Philippines	Thailand	Singapore	ASEAN Total	Hong Kong	Taiwan
Indonesia		21.4	15.2	67.7	312.0	416.3	125.7	93.9 (1975)
Malaysia	87.5		17.7	142.0	321.4	568.6	65.6	77.2
The Philippines	35.3	42.2		26.0	24.7	128.2	31.5	82.7
Thailand	3.0	19.7	4.7		77.7	105.1	44.7	76.8
Singapore	646.9[a]	1,016.5	25.4	196.3		1,885.1	186.6	151.8
ASEAN Total	772.7	1,099.8	63.0	432.0	735.8	3,103.3	454.1	482.4
South Vietnam	2.5	0.5 (1974)	1.5	4.6	159.3	168.4	12.7	25.8
Laos	0.6	0.001	0.2	23.1	2.3	26.2	2.4	0.2
Burma	13.0	5.8	0.2	1.3	20.2	40.5	3.5	0.03
Southeast Asia Total[b]	788.8	1,106.1	64.9	461.0	917.6	3,338.4	472.7	508.4

[a]Estimate based on Indonesia's exports to Singapore.
[b]Excluding Cambodia.

Source of Imports								
Total of Singapore and Hong Kong	Total of Singapore, Hong Kong, and Taiwan	Japan	U.S.	EEC	Oil-Exporting Countries Except Indonesia	Other	Total World	Total World Excluding Oil-Exporting Countries and Indonesia
437.7	531.6	1,442.0	666.0	823.6	1.5	931.6	4,500.6	4,499.1
387.0	464.2	811.4	387.0	796.5	212.4	922.5	3,841.2	3,628.8
56.2	139.0	965.4	822.7	446.2	608.1	488.6	3,573.4	2,965.3
122.4	199.2	1,019.5	441.9	577.6	539.4	426.8	3,231.8	2,692.4
186.6	338.4	1,438.1	1,226.6	1,080.0	1,564.4	1,362.6	8,895.2	7,330.8
1,189.9	1,672.4	5,676.4	3,544.2	3,723.9	2,925.8	4,132.1	24,042.2	21,116.4
172.0	197.8	78.7	511.9	60.5	1.3	58.8	918.1	916.8
4.7	4.9	7.7	12.7	11.0	0.04	8.2	68.44	68.4
5.5	5.6	64.6	14.7	46.6	0.03	52.7	222.7	222.7
1,372.1	1,880.7	5,827.4	4,083.5	3,842.0	2,927.2	4,251.8	25,251.4	22,324.2

FIGURE A-1

FOREIGN PRIVATE DIRECT INVESTMENT AND EXPORT EXPANSION, THAILAND, 1965–73

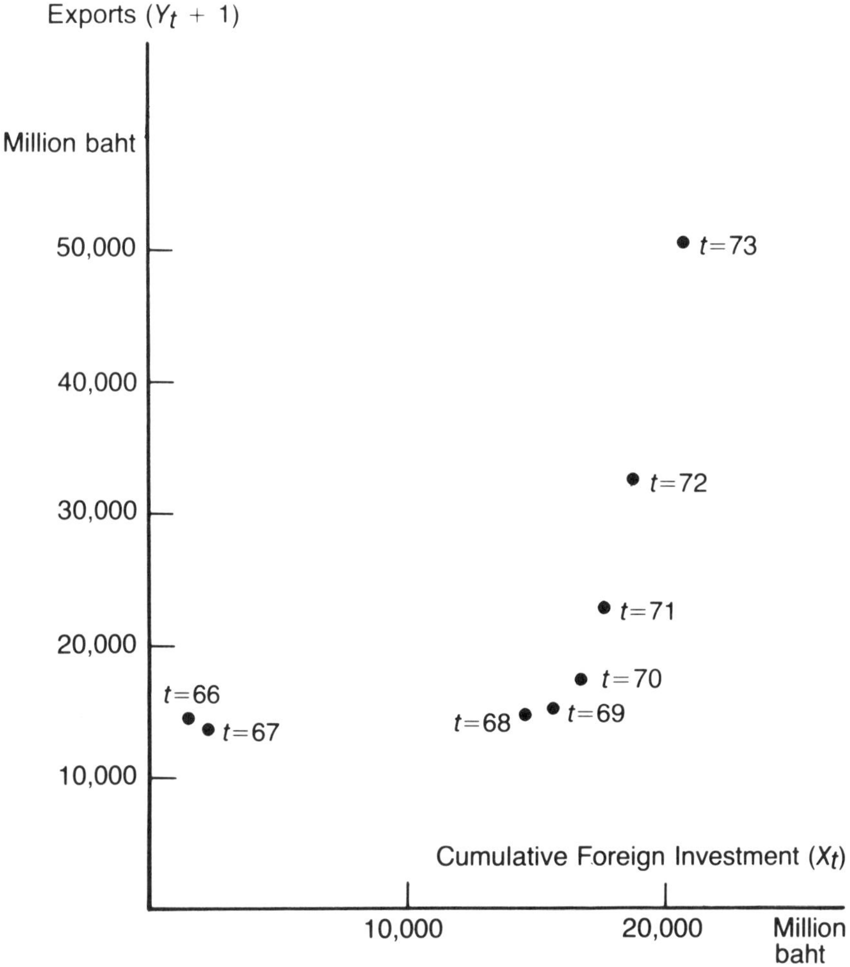

SOURCES: ADB, *Key Indicators*, vol. VII, no. 1 (April 1976):169; the Economic Cooperation Center for the Asian and Pacific Region (ECOCEN), *Thai-Japanese Economic Relations: Trade and Investment* (Bangkok, 1974), p. 98.

NOTE: The cumulative value of foreign investment as of year t is plotted with the export value of year $(t+1)$.

FIGURE A-2

FOREIGN PRIVATE DIRECT INVESTMENT AND EXPORT EXPANSION, THE PHILIPPINES, 1968–75

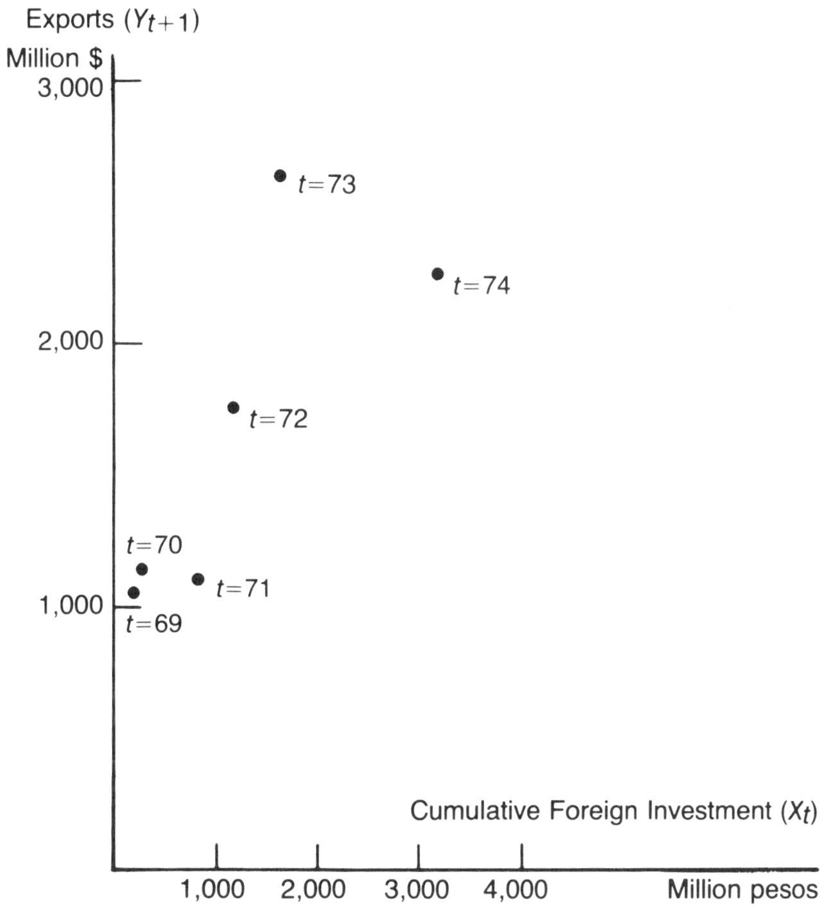

SOURCES: ADB, *Key Indicators*, vol. VII, no. 1 (April 1976):137; *Philippine Progress* (Board of Investments, Republic of the Philippines) 10 (4th Quarter 1975), p. 11.

FIGURE A-3

FOREIGN PRIVATE DIRECT INVESTMENT AND EXPORT EXPANSION, MALAYSIA, 1970–75

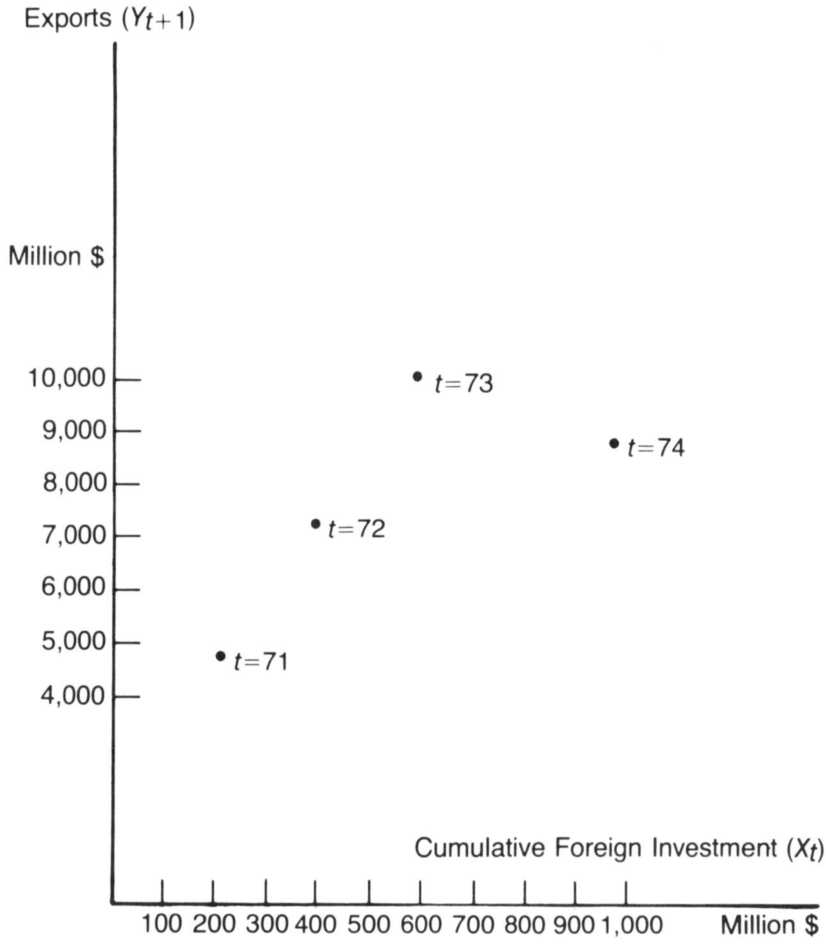

SOURCES: ADB, *Key Indicators*, vol. VII, no. 1 (April 1976): 113; 1970–74: International Monetary Fund, *Financial Statistics*, February 1976.

FIGURE A-4

FOREIGN PRIVATE DIRECT INVESTMENT AND EXPORT EXPANSION, INDONESIA, 1970–74

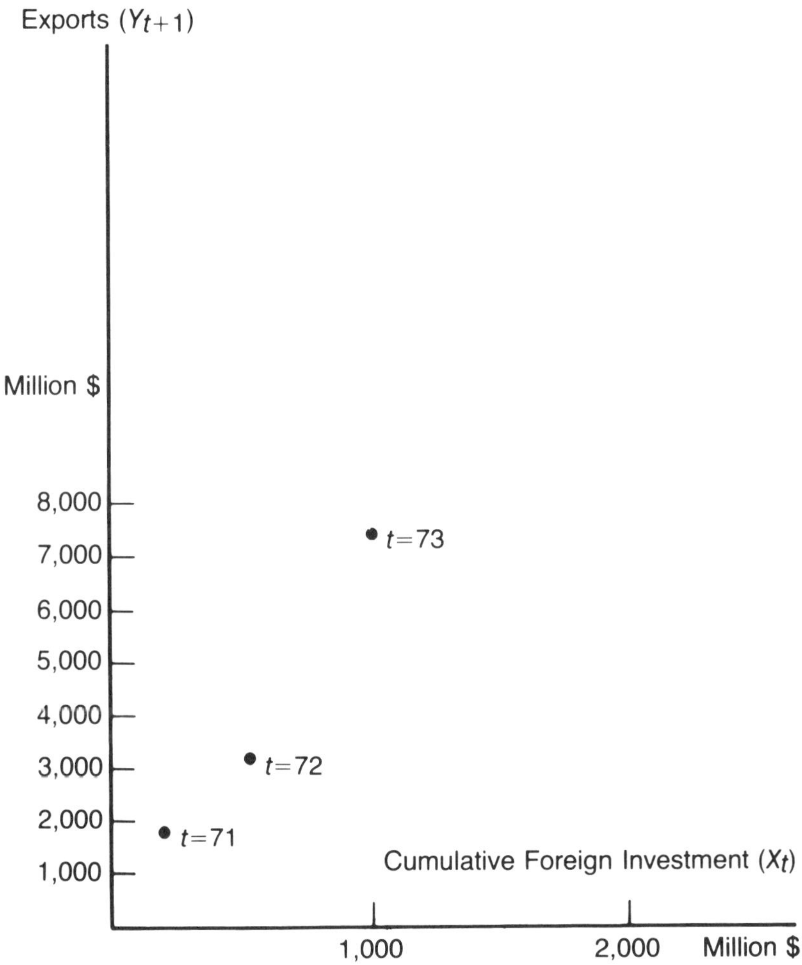

SOURCES: ADB, *Key Indicators*, vol. VII, no. 1 (April 1976): 96; International Monetary Fund, *Financial Statistics*, February 1976.

FIGURE A-5

CORRELATION BETWEEN CUMULATIVE VALUE OF U.S. DIRECT INVESTMENT IN TAIWAN AND ROC EXPORTS TO THE UNITED STATES

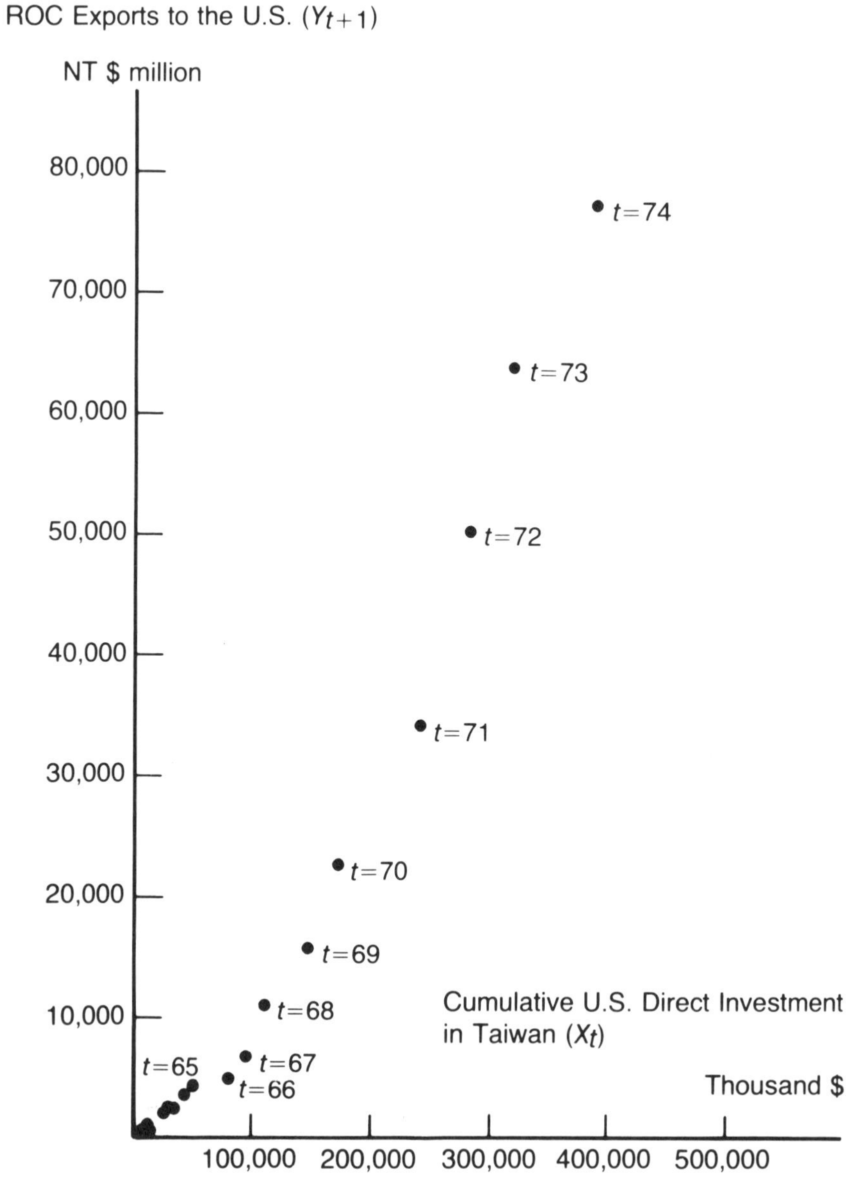

SOURCES: Economic Planning Council, Executive Yuan, Republic of China, *Taiwan Statistical Data Book, 1976* (Taiwan, 1976); American Embassy, Taipei, *Economic Summary of the Republic of China* (Taipei, Taiwan, 1976).

B

An Estimate of Chinese-Owned Capital Stock in ASEAN Member Countries as of the End of 1975

In this appendix we shall attempt to describe schematically a new estimate of Chinese-owned capital stock in the five ASEAN countries. The term capital stock, or capital, is used in the sense of productive capital, excluding personal effects and residential housing. Our approach begins with certain basic estimates that are obtained by adding estimated minimal new investments during 1970–75

$$\left(\sum_{t=1970}^{t=1975} k_t\right)$$

to a set of initial figures representing the capital stock as of 1969 (K_{1969}) or, for Thailand, the end of 1972 (K_{1972}). Adjustments are then made to allow for other available information and for special circumstances surrounding the estimates for some of the countries. A few alternative estimates are presented at this point as an independent check and for comparison.

STEP ONE: THE BASIC ESTIMATES

K_{1975}, the capital stock to be estimated for each of the ASEAN countries, is derived from

$$K_{1975} = K_{1969} + \sum_{t=1970}^{t=1975} k_t$$

or, for Thailand,

$$K_{1975} = K_{1972} + \sum_{t=1973}^{t=1975} k_t \quad ,$$

where k_t is new net investment in year t. (For Indonesia the estimate is for K_{1974} since data for GDP growth in 1975 are not available.)

The amount of new net investment each year is assumed to be a given proportion (s) of the income received by the ethnic-Chinese population in that year (Y_t). Here, s is the average propensity to invest. Thus,

$$\sum k_t = s \sum Y_t .$$

The level of income received by the Chinese population in any year (Y_t) is related to that of the preceding year (Y_{t-1}) by an annual growth rate (r_t) so that

$$Y_t = (1 + r_t)\, Y_{t-1}$$

where r_t is assumed to be equal to the GDP (gross domestic product) growth rate for that year. The level of income the Chinese population received in 1970 (Y_{1970}), or for Thailand in 1973 (Y_{1973}), is obtained from the product of the size of the ethnic-Chinese population and the estimated per-capita income of the Chinese.

The various initial estimates and parameters employed are as follows:

1. K_{1969} (K_{1972} for Thailand)
   For Peninsular or West Malaysia, Singapore, Indonesia, and the Philippines, the initial capital-stock estimates are those of Ho I-wu.[1] Ho's estimates, based on data from various survey and other sources from each of the individual countries, are as follows:

	U.S. $ million
Singapore	770
Peninsular Malaysia	700
Indonesia	704
The Philippines	573

In the case of Thailand, we are fortunate to have an estimate from Thai financial circles reported in the *Hua-ch'iao ching-chi nien-chien* of 1974/75;[2] it gives a total of U.S. $1,640.5 million for, we believe, the year 1972.

2. Y_{1970} (Y_{1973} for Thailand)
   a) *Peninsular Malaysia.* Y_{1970} is obtained from an ethnic-Chinese population of 3,274,000[3] and a per-capita annual income of M $816,[4] which was twice the corresponding figure for Malays. At an exchange rate of M $2.58 to U.S. $1, Y_{1970} = $1,036 million.
   b) *Singapore.* Y_{1970} is estimated as the product of per-capita GDP (S $2,804)[5] and the ethnic-Chinese population (1,579,000).[6] At an exchange rate of S $3.00 to U.S. $1, Y_{1970} = $1,477 million.
   c) *Indonesia.* The per-capita income for ethnic Chinese in 1970 is assumed to equal the corresponding figure in West Malaysia, which was M $816 or U.S. $316. This would compare with a per-capita GDP of $75[7] in 1970 and of $183 in 1974. The ethnic-Chinese population in 1970 was 3 million. Thus, Y_{1970} = $316 × 3,000,000 = $948 million.
   d) *Thailand.* The value of GDP per capita in 1973 was 5,408 baht[8] or U.S. $270 at the rate of 20 baht to U.S. $1. Of the 3.5 million ethnic Chinese in Thailand in 1973,[9] 2 million lived in Bangkok where their per-capita annual income, according to an earlier UN report, was 2.45 times the national average.[10] In the smaller towns and other areas outside Bangkok where the remaining 1.5 million ethnic Chinese lived, the Chinese had a per-capita income averaging 1.69 times the national average. Thus, the per-capita annual income of the Chinese population in 1973 is estimated at [(2 × 2.45) + (1.5 × 1.69)] × $270 ÷ 3.5 = $574. Y_{1973} then = 574 × 3,500,000 = $2,009 million.
   e) *The Philippines.* The 1969 GDP per-capita income was 945 pesos[11] or U.S. $242 at the exchange rate at that time of 3.9 pesos to U.S. $1. The average annual per-capita income of the Chinese in 1969 is estimated at twice this level.[12] Given an ethnic-Chinese population of 600,000,[13] Y_{1969} = 600,000 × 484 = $290 million. Y_{1970}, estimated at the 1970 GDP growth rate, would be $307 million.
3. The GDP growth rates (r_t). For r_t the data employed are given in Table 19.
4. The average investment-income ratio (s). According to a Japanese report, the traditional practice of Chinese in Southeast Asia is to allot a third of their income to living expenses, including luxuries; a third to education of their children; and the last third to reinvestment.[14] Hence s can be estimated at one third. Some of the funds marked for reinvestment may be placed in nonproductive hoards, however, including personal cash reserves. Therefore a minimum estimate of s may be as low as one sixth.

In addition, we may assume an in-between value of one fourth (that is, one sixth + one half of one sixth). These alternative values of s are used below in deriving $\Sigma k_t = s(\Sigma Y_t)$.

STEP TWO: ADJUSTMENTS AND ALTERNATIVE ESTIMATES

1. An adjustment of the initial capital stock (K_{1969}) for the Philippines. Ho I-wu's estimate for K_{1969} was the sum of three sectoral estimates:

Sectors	U.S. $ Million
Commercial	274.72
Industrial	288.75
Other	10.00
Total	573.47

The commercial-sector estimate was based on the existence of 13,700 Chinese-owned stores.[15] Later information indicates that the correct number was closer to 30,000. Assuming that the missing establishments were of comparable size, K_{1969} should be raised to 1,253.4. This would make the alternative K_{1975} estimates (1) 1,611, (2) 1,790, and (3) 1,969 million dollars.

2. An alternative estimate for K_{1975} for Malaysia. According to the Third Malaysian Plan (1976–80), the accumulated capital of Chinese in corporate business enterprises in Malaysia amounted to M $2,755.9 million.[16] At the same time, 30 percent of the country's GDP was produced by these limited companies. If Chinese ownership in the unincorporated businesses, as well as their capital-output ratio, was the same as in the corporate sector, the amount of Chinese capital in unincorporated businesses would be M $6,430.4 million, making the total value of K_{1975} M $9,186.3 million or U.S. $3,501 million.

CONCLUSION

Our basic estimates tend to be underestimates for the following reasons:

First, the initial capital-stock data are generally based on the registered capital of the individual businesses. Since some of the concerns were established many years ago and prices have risen considerably in the meantime, the amount of capital is necessarily understated without asset revaluation.

Second, a common practice of certain Chinese businesses is to understate their actual assets and capital, primarily for tax reasons.

Third, new investment can be and has been financed with bank or other credit rather than with savings out of personal income. Borrowings from abroad, which may or may not be registered as foreign capital, can also take place. Hence it appears probable that Chinese-owned capital stock may have grown at a much faster rate than estimated new investments would indicate.

Fourth, the rate of growth of Chinese income from year to year may differ from the average rate of growth of GDP. For the most part, the ASEAN countries enjoyed a period of fair to rapid expansion during the first half of the 1970s. During this period, Chinese business probably expanded faster than the national GDP average growth rates. A possible exception to this rule was Malaysia, where Chinese business was adversely affected by the May 1969 riot. Even here, however, it is not certain that the increase in Chinese income fell below the GDP growth rate.

Fifth, if there has been a net outflow of Chinese capital from any country, it would make actual capital assets in 1975 lower than our basic estimate for K_{1975}. Between 1970 and 1975, however, several countries, including Indonesia and the Philippines, that had discriminated against ethnic-Chinese enterprise either softened their policy or seemed about to do so. In addition, net outflows from one or two ASEAN countries probably were offset by net inflows enjoyed by others, particularly Singapore. If there was a net outflow for ASEAN as a whole, the total amount, part of which went to Hong Kong, would probably still be lower than the underestimate contained in the set of basic estimates presented above.

Finally, the basic estimates for Malaysia are for Peninsular or West Malaysia only.

All in all, therefore, we are inclined to regard the highest of the alternative K_{1975} estimates as the closest to the truth. These estimates, which yield an aggregate of $16.6 billion for ASEAN as a whole, are underscored in Table B-1. They are referred to in the text as our estimates.

ESTIMATE BASED ON WU KU'S CAPITAL-STOCK ESTIMATE FOR 1960

For those who are curious, we can provide still another set of estimates of K_{1975} on the basis of Wu Ku's estimate of Chinese-owned capital stock in 1960. Wu Ku's figures, which appeared in the Hong Kong publication *Ching-chi tao-pao* [Economic Bulletin], no. 657, 1960, are:

	U.S. $ Million
Singapore and Malaysia	1,200
Indonesia	900
Philippines	400
Thailand	600

TABLE B-1

ESTIMATE OF ETHNIC-CHINESE CAPITAL IN ASEAN

(CURRENT U.S. $ MILLION)

	Singapore	Thailand	Malaysia	The Philippines	Indonesia[a]	Total ASEAN
I. *Basic Estimate*						
K_{1969}	770	1,641 (1972)	700	573	704	**4,388**
Y_{1970}	1,477	2,009 (1973)	1,036	307	948	**5,482**
$\sum_{1970}^{1975} k_t$						
1. $s = 1/6$	1,945	1,048 (Σk_t where t = 1973–1975)	1,243	358	934	**5,509**
2. $s = 1/4$	2,917	1,572	1,864	537	1,400	**8,261**
3. $s = 1/3$	3,889	2,096	2,486	716	1,866	**11,053**
K_{1975} (Basic estimate)						
1.	2,715	2,689	1,943	931	1,638	**9,897**
2.	3,687	3,213	2,564	1,110	2,104	**12,649**
3.	*4,659*	*3,737*	3,186	1,289	*2,570*	**15,441**
II. *Alternative Estimates of K_{1975}*			*3,674*	1,611		***16,609***
				1,790		
				1,969		

[a]For Indonesia the relevant preliminary estimates are $\sum_{1970}^{1974} k_t$ and K_{1974}.

Here K_{1975} is obtained from $K_{1960} + \sum_{1961}^{1971} k_{t_1} + \sum_{1972}^{1975} k_{t2}$ where

1. K_{1960} is given by Wu Ku and the \$1,200 for Singapore and Malaysia combined is divided between Singapore (\$629 million) and Malaysia (\$571 million), at the ratio of 11 to 10, which corresponds to the ratio of Ho I-wu's figures noted earlier:
2. $\sum_{1961}^{1971} k_{t1}$ is based on $s \sum_{1961}^{1971} Y_{t1}$;
3. $\sum_{1972}^{1975} k_{t2}$ is obtained from $s \sum_{1972}^{1975} Y_{t2}$, with (a) $Y_{t1} = Y_{t1-1}\,(1+r_{t1})$ and $Y_{t2} = Y_{t2-1}\,(1+r_{t2})$, with r_{t1} taken from Table 2 and r_{t2} from Table 19 of Chapter 1 and (b) $Y_{t2} = Y_{1972}$ (Y_{1970} for Malaysia) estimated as follows:

Peninsular Malaysia:	Y_{1970} = \$1,036 million,	same as before.
Singapore:	Y_{1972} = \$2,125 million,	estimated from per-capita GNP (1,300 multiplied by the ethnic-Chinese population—1,634,640, as given by the *Yearbook of Statistics, Singapore 1973/74*).
Indonesia:	Y_{1972} = \$1,155 million,	estimated from an ethnic-Chinese per-capita income of \$385 (Yu Chung-hsün, *Kakyō seiji keizai ron* [The Overseas Chinese Political Economy] [Tokyo, 1976], p. 173) and a Chinese population of 3 million.
Thailand:	Y_{1972} = \$1,631 million,	estimated from a Chinese population of 3.5 million and an ethnic-Chinese per-capita income of \$466, which is derived from a per-capita income of \$220 for all Thailand (ADB, *Key Indicators*,

vol. V, no. 2 [October 1974] : 7), weighted in the same manner as in the previous case for Thailand.

The Philippines: Y_{1972} = \$664.5 million, estimated from an ethnic-Chinese population of one-half million (*Hua-ch'iao ching-chi nien-chien, 1973* [Overseas Chinese Economy Yearbook], p. 202) and a per-capita Chinese income of \$1,329 (Yu Chung-hsün, *Kakyō seiji keizai ron*).

If the average propensity to invest is assumed to be only one sixth, then the estimated

$$1.\ \sum_{1961}^{1975} k_t \text{ and } 2.\ K_{1975},$$

would be

	U.S. \$ Million	
	(1)	(2)
Singapore	3,852	4,481
Thailand	3,166	3,766
Malaysia	2,354	2,925
Indonesia	2,235	3,135
The Philippines	1,343	1,743
Total ASEAN	12,950	16,050

These estimates are essentially in the same order of magnitude as our earlier estimates.

The interested reader can obtain additional comparisons by using the estimates of Callis (1937) and Fukuda (1930) although many more years have passed since their time than since the reference points we have used. In making comparisons with such pre–World War II estimates, a crucial question would be the rates of growth in 1930–37, 1937–41, and 1941–45, bearing in mind that the Sino-Japanese war broke out in 1937 and the Pacific War began in 1941. Because of the uncertainties brought on by these large-scale hostilities that embroiled the entire region, we have chosen not to pursue the subject further. However, test projections based on both the Callis and the Fukuda estimates have given us estimates of ethnic-Chinese capital stock in 1975 of about \$17 billion.

C

Restrictions on Ethnic-Chinese Economic Activities

The following chronological account describes the development of restrictions on the economic activities of ethnic Chinese in four Southeast Asian countries; it is focused primarily on the post–World War II period. The account is not meant to be exhaustive.

INDONESIA

Scope of Activity

1950	A number of commodities were placed under the *Benteng* (fortress) import program and only program members were allowed to import these items. Members were limited to firms with predominantly indigenous Indonesian managements that owned at least 70 percent of the equity The 1950 list was expanded in 1952, and in 1954–55, textiles were added to it.
March 1955	Ownership of rice mills was limited to indigenous Indonesians. Nonindigenous owners of existing mills were required to transfer ownership to indigenous citizens within a two-year period. In January 1957, more than

SOURCES: The SGV Group, *Doing Business in Thailand, February 1974* (Bangkok: SGV-NA Thalang & Co., Ltd., 1974); the SVG Group, *Doing Business in Malaysia, March 1975* (Kuala Lumpur: SGV-Kassim Chan Sdn. Bhd., 1975); the SGV Group, *Doing Business in the Philippines, August 1975* (Manila: Sycip, Gorres, Velayo & Co., 1975); the SGV Group, *Doing Business in Indonesia, December 1974* (Jakarta: P. T. SGV-Utomo, 1974); *Hai-wai hua-ch'iao ching-chi fa-chan ch'ü-shih chih yen-chiu* [Trends of Overseas Chinese Economic Development] (Taipei, 1974), pp. 42–63; SRI International, *Business in Indonesia* (Menlo Park, Ca.: Stanford Research Institute, August 1974); and U. S. Embassy, Kuala Lumpur, Malaysia.

thirty Chinese-owned rice mills in Medang, Sumatra, were taken over by local authorities and sold to indigenous buyers.

March 1957 Fifteen industries, mostly in light manufacturing, were reserved for operation by Indonesian citizens only. A number of businesses in the proscribed fields owned by alien Chinese were transferred to Indonesian citizens of Chinese descent and managed to stay in operation. All firms in the fifteen industries were to be reregistered.

May 1959 A May 14, 1959, decision of the minister of trade, implemented in November 1959 under Government Regulation No. 10, stated that as of January 1, 1960, aliens would no longer be allowed to engage in retailing in rural areas below the regency level. (The service industry was exempted.) Agitation for this move had begun two years earlier.

February 1977 The trade minister announced the compulsory sale of sixteen thousand alien-Chinese businesses to Indonesians by the end of the year.

Capital Participation

1957 The indigenization of the fifteen industries ordered in May was to be implemented by transferring equity in businesses belonging to nonindigenous owners to indigenous Indonesians. Half the equity was to be owned by the latter within a five-year period. At the end of this grace period, the remaining equity (no more than 50 percent) would also have to be sold to indigenous buyers. Such sales should use installment payments over a ten-year period. If necessary, even the initial 50 percent was to be paid for gradually out of the anticipated profits of the new indigenous owners.

March 1972 In an address before the Indonesian Chamber of Commerce on March 29, 1972, President Suharto urged the nonindigenous Indonesian citizens to sell 50 percent of their stock to the Pribumi (indigenous Indonesians).

Regulations Governing Labor

1957 The indigenization of industry required Chinese firms to appoint indigenous Indonesians as directors and to employ and train Indonesian labor.

1958 A March 9, 1958, ministry of labor regulation prohibited the employment of aliens without work permits. Such work permits were issued for periods of six months to two years. Permits were not to be issued if the work could be performed by Indonesians. As of mid-1959, 144,000 applications had been filed, according to the employment office of the ministry.

Other Discriminatory Treatment

1950 National banks were required to give special credit to indigenous Indonesian businessmen.

1951 Payment of large deposits was required of foreign importers. Only four Chinese importers could make the stipulated deposit of Rp 5 million each. More than one thousand Chinese importers were forced to close.

June 1967 According to a June 1, 1967, instruction of the presidium of the cabinet, "capital that is acquired and accumulated within the territory of Indonesia, i.e., foreign domestic capital, is basically national wealth that is in the hands of aliens [*read Chinese*] and should therefore be recruited, developed and utilized for the benefit of rehabilitation and development."* Such capital was not to be allowed to be transferred abroad.

1973–74 Special credits were offered to small indigenous Indonesian businessmen, including those in rural areas, to set them up in business.

MALAYSIA

Malaysian restrictions on ethnic-Chinese economic activities are based on a 1948 understanding with the British concerning the organization of a plural society in Malaysia. The special position of the Malays was to be respected along with the legitimate acquired rights of the Chinese and Indian communities. Malays who hold political power have determined that the acquisition and maintenance of their special position requires giving the Malay community greater opportunities by adopting a quota system. The source of conflict between Malays and Chinese is the lack of an agreed definition of where the Malays' special position begins to infringe on the acquired rights of the other communities and vice versa.

*Instruction of the Presidium of the Cabinet No. 37/U/IN/6/1967, The Basic Policy to Resolve the Chinese Problem.

Scope of Activity

Article 89 of the constitution guarantees the continuation for the Malays of the land-reservation system, which existed before independence. Land now owned by nonindigenous Malaysians could, with their approval, be added to the existing Malay reservation.

According to a 1971 plan for rubber planting, 99.3 percent of the 14,860 rubber planters permitted to be in business were to be Malays, 0.1 percent Chinese, and 0.6 percent Indians.

Capital Participation

Nonindigenous enterprises are to be acquired initially by government-sponsored trusts for subsequent transfer to Malays and other natives. Malays are to have at least a 30 percent interest and 30 percent participation in every occupation and industry. Special lending agencies have been set up to aid Malays in this respect. The same principle is followed in forming joint ventures with foreign investors.

Regulations Governing Labor

Employment Quotas. Fifty percent of private industrial and commercial employment must consist of Malays. Appointments to high-grade government posts must be apportioned as follows:

RATIO OF MALAYS TO NON-MALAYS

Foreign affairs and the interior department	4:1
Justice department	3:1
Customs	3:1
Police	4:1
Armed forces	4:1

Of those appointed to federal-government service from 1969 to 1972, non-Malays constituted only 2 percent. The rest were Malays and some members of the indigenous population of East Malaysia (Sabah and Sarawak).

Other Discriminatory Treatment

Business-License Quotas. Discriminatory quotas favorable to Malays have been set administratively in issuing licenses for truck and taxi drivers, operators of market stalls, and so on (Article 89 of the Constitution).

Educational Quotas. Discretionary admission quotas are reserved for Malays in institutions of higher learning (Article 153 of the Constitution).

THE PHILIPPINES

Scope of Activity

January 1947 — Republic Act No. 37 gave Philippine citizens preference in renting public stalls in Manila street markets. Alien-Chinese stall operators were denied further access to the stalls.

May 1954 — Republic Act No. 1180, generally known as the Retail Trade Nationalization Law, was adopted by the Congress on May 29, 1954, and signed by President Magsaysay on June 19. Under the law all alien-owned retail stores established after May 15, 1954, were to close down upon the expiration of their corporate charters or articles of partnership. In no case, however, could they operate more than ten more years. Where the stores were proprietorships, continued operation was permitted until the owners' death or retirement. There were 16,245 Chinese-operated retail stores in 1945, but the number had dwindled to 13,000 in 1960.

May 1960 — Republic Act No. 3018 stipulated that all alien-operated businesses in the retail and wholesale trade, cultivation, and transportation of rice and corn were to cease operation within two years (mills and warehouses within three years). The law was first adopted by the Philippine Congress on May 20, 1960. Following a presidential veto on June 19, it was amended and again passed Congress on July 18. Signed by President Garcia on August 2, it came into effect on January 1, 1961. There were twenty-six hundred alien-Chinese firms in the proscribed fields as of mid-June, 1960.

According to what was then the Chinese Chamber of Commerce in the Philippines, in 1948 Chinese residents owned a hundred large and thirty small rice mills, together with forty corn mills. Their total investment amounted to ten million pesos (then equivalent to U.S. $5 million). Two thousand Chinese were employed in rice milling; five hundred in corn milling; and ten thousand in other activities related to the rice and corn trades.

The January 1961 law was abolished by President Marcos in 1973.

These limitations were obstensibly directed at aliens, but in analyzing their impact one should bear in mind that alien Chinese could not obtain Philippine citizenship easily. The cost of naturalization was often prohibitive. The conditions were eased on the eve of President Marcos's decision to establish diplomatic relations with Peking, and again in late 1976.

Under Presidential Instruction No. 491, dated December 29, 1976, the qualifications of an applicant for naturalization previously laid down in Presidential Instruction No. 270 were relaxed. Both the language and the financial requirements were lowered and the minimum age was reduced from twenty-one to eighteen. Applicants who failed to qualify earlier could now reapply. Application for collective naturalization was reopened in January–March 1977.

Regulations Governing Labor

May 1961 — Alien employees of retail stores were permitted to work only through December 31, 1961. (This measure was partially aimed at alien retail-store owners operating in the guise of employees after turning nominal ownership over to a family member who was a Philippine citizen). The subsequent Anti-Dummy Act was of the same nature.

Other Discriminatory Treatment

December 1949–January 1962 — Under exchange controls in force during this period, the amount of foreign-exchange allocation granted to Chinese importers was progressively reduced. Since 1961 the Filipinos have had the largest share.

June 1956 — The National Marketing Corporation (NAMARCO) was organized to supply Filipino-owned retail stores at subsidized prices. After some initial success NAMARCO incurred serious indebtedness to the government which it could not repay. The corporation was abolished by President Marcos in March 1967.

THAILAND

Scope of Activity

June 1942	Twenty-seven industries and occupations were reserved for the employment of Thai citizens only. The list was reduced to seven in 1949, but two were added in 1952. Since 1952 administrative discretion has been employed to favor Thais. An attempt in 1968 to add another fourteen categories to the list was postponed. Current restrictions now apply to industry categories A and B (see Appendix C).

Capital Participation

1972	An Alien Enterprise Law made joint ventures with Thai nationals a condition for continuation in business. Thai nationals must hold 51 percent of stock. This restriction does not apply to investments under the Foreign Investment Law.

Regulations Governing Labor

1956	Thai citizens were to constitute more than 50 percent of the employees of factories with more than ten persons on the payroll in thirty designated industries.

Other Discriminatory Treatment

December 1951	Remittance of funds to China was forbidden.
January 1952	The annual cost of an alien registration card was raised to 400 baht (U.S. $20) a year from the previous level of 20 baht (then U.S. $8), which was set in 1949.

D

Restrictions on Foreign Investors versus Inducements Offered

INDONESIA

Scope of Activity

Industries from which foreign investors are barred are: harbor operation; shipping; domestic aviation; nuclear energy; retailing and distribution; production, transmission, and distribution of electric power to the public; telecommunications; supply of drinking water; public railways; mass media; and industries performing vital functions in national defense, such as the production of arms, ammunition, and explosives.

In contrast, foreign investment in the following types of industries is favored: industries that process more domestic than imported raw materials; industries that produce input for other industries; basic industries such as iron and steel and shipbuilding; infrastructure projects; fully integrated textile industries; industries that produce specified essential commodities (oil excluded); industries that produce synthetic fibers; industries that export more than 50 percent of their products; chemical industries; manufacturers of medicine and health equipment; transportation and tourism (with the exceptions noted above).

Capital Participation

1. All foreign investments must be in the form of joint ventures with local owners (except in very special cases and with the approval of the minister of trade and industry).
2. Within a specified time period, Indonesians should be allowed gradually to increase their holdings to 51 percent of the company's stock.

SOURCES: Same as those for Appendix C.

3. In the case of joint ventures between foreigners and nonindigenous Indonesians, provision must be made to promote the transfer of at least half the nonindigenous shares to indigenous Indonesians.

Regulations Governing Labor

1. Foreign staff (managerial or technical) may be appointed if local personnel cannot fill the positions.
2. Foreigners working in Indonesia must have work permits. Such work permits cannot be loaned to persons holding tourist or short-visit visas.

Other Restrictions

1. Representative offices of foreign companies are not allowed to handle purchases or sales, or to open branch offices outside their initial domicile. They are limited to sales promotion and supply of technical information.
2. Transfer permits for capital repatriation cannot be granted as long as concessions concerning taxes are still in effect.
3. Permits for investment of foreign capital are granted for a specified period not to exceed thirty years. Extension or renewal of the permit can be granted upon application to and negotiation with the government at least two years prior to the termination of the initial thirty-year period.

Benefits

1. New enterprises or businesses established under the Foreign Investment Law are exempted from corporation and dividend taxes for two years provided that dividends declared and paid during the tax-free period are not subject to profit or income taxes in the recipient country.
2. This tax-free period can be extended by another year under the following conditions:
   a) The investment in question will increase or save foreign-exchange earnings by at least U.S. $250,000 a year for three consecutive years.
   b) The investment is outside Java. (This condition also varies with the type of industry.)
   c) The investment has previously required a substantial amount of capital (U.S. $15 million or more) due to the need to provide adequate infrastructure facilities and the great risks involved.
3. The same enterprises are exempted from import duties and the import sales tax on permanent fixtures and capital equipment imported into Indonesia.

4. These enterprises are also exempted from the capital stamp duty for funds derived from foreign investment.
5. Losses in the first six years can be deducted from profits earned in subsequent years.
6. Land grants will be made by the state for building purposes.
7. Credit is available from the state bank on favorable terms to joint ventures in the production of exports and essential goods and services (usually up to 20 percent of capital).
8. Owners of previously nationalized enterprises are given a waiver of the minimum capital requirement, as well as a moratorium on overdue taxes.
9. The right of repatriation is extended to:
   a) Profits after deduction of taxes and other financial obligations in Indonesia;
   b) An amount equivalent to costs incurred in connection with the employment of foreign personnel working in Indonesia;
   c) An amount equivalent to the depreciation of capital assets;
   d) Compensation received in case of naturalization.
10. Mining of strategic minerals (oil, tin, nickel, uranium, and other radioactive minerals) can only be undertaken by the state, but arrangements have been worked out to permit domestic and foreign private companies to operate under product-sharing agreements (for oil) and work contracts (for other minerals).

MALAYSIA

Scope of Activity

Foreign investors are encouraged to engage in:

1. Labor-intensive projects;
2. Export-oriented industries;
3. Industries that are conducive to backward and forward integration;
4. Industries that use a high proportion of local raw materials as input.

Capital Participation

1. There are no strict limitations on capital ownership that are inflexibly enforced, but the government encourages local-equity participation.
2. In general, companies that sell all their products in the local market are required to have majority local-equity participation.

3. If the projects depend substantially on the domestic market, foreign participation, if necessary, will be allowed up to 30 percent of the total equity of the project.
4. Foreign ownership of export-oriented companies may be as high as 100 percent depending upon the extent of export business and negotiations with government authorities.
5. If the projects are substantially export-oriented and independent of Malaysia's depleting resources, foreign majority ownership can be considered.
6. Of the projects that are export-oriented and dependent upon Malaysia's renewable natural resources, anywhere from 51 to 70 percent or more of equity must be held by Malaysians, with the extent of foreign ownership dependent upon the merit of the case.

   These equity proportions are only general guidelines; more liberal or more stringent measures may be adopted at the discretion of the government. The government of Malaysia aims to require equity to be held in the following proportions by 1990: 30 percent foreign, and 70 percent Malaysian–30 percent to Bumiputras and 40 percent to non-Bumiputras.

Regulations Governing Labor

1. All foreigners employed in Malaysia must obtain work permits:
   a) Employment passes for those earning salaries in excess of $1,200, valid for two years or more;
   b) Visit passes for those not qualified for the employment pass, valid for no more than a year at a time; and
   c) Professional visit passes for those who are employed and paid by foreign investors.
2. The government has adopted a Malaysianization program aimed at replacing foreigners by Malaysians. However, foreigners are allowed to retain key positions in foreign industrial enterprises.
3. The composition of a company's board of directors must reflect its equity structure.
4. The work force of a company must contain no less than 30 percent Bumiputras at all levels.

Benefits

The following major tax incentives are available:

1. Pioneer Status: A firm is granted pioneer status if it meets the following conditions:

a) It is a joint venture with significant local participation;
b) The industry is based in Malaysia and is essential to the country's industrialization;
c) It has great employment potential in Malaysia;
d) It has to use the products or by-products of existing industries in Malaysia.

Firms enjoying pioneer status are exempt from:

a) The company tax and the supplementary development tax (for two to eight years);
b) The income tax on dividends.

Carrying forward of losses and special depreciation allowances are permitted.

2. Labor Utilization Relief: The exemption period for company taxes and supplementary-development taxes varies from two to five years depending on the number of employees:

50–100 employees: two years
101–200 employees: three years
201–350 employees: four years
More than 350 employees: five years

The exemptions mentioned above for pioneer status are also applicable to this incentive.

3. Investment Tax Credit: This applies to companies that are not qualified for pioneer status or labor-utilization relief.

The amount of tax credit given will not be less than 25 percent of the total capital expenditure incurred on the plant or machinery of the approved projects.

4. Exports: For companies that export at least 20 percent, by value, of their locally manufactured products, the following expenditures are tax deductible:

a) Overseas advertising;
b) Cost of supplying and delivering free samples overseas;
c) Expenses on market research;
d) Costs incurred in the preparation and negotiation of contracts;
e) Expenses incurred in supplying technical information overseas.

In order to meet the 1990 goals of its New Economic Policy (NEP), the government of Malaysia has adopted the ICA (Industrial Coordination Act) rules for regulating and supervising the orderly industrial development of Malaysia. Its conditions are as follows:

a) All companies must adopt concrete measures over a reasonable period of time to use Bumiputra distributors to the maximum extent possible. (The minimum is 30 percent.)
b) All companies must install new and modern machinery in an efficient layout.
c) All companies must take into consideration atmospheric, water, and noise pollution of the environment (Environment Quality Act of 1974).
d) Companies must use local raw materials, components, and parts at least to the level indicated in their approved licenses, but this rule seems to be flexible.
e) All agreements (including those involving the employment of expatriate personnel) for starting-up operations, technical know-how and assistance, trademarks and services, royalties, and marketing must receive prior approval from the ministry of trade and industry (MTI) in writing before becoming effective.
f) The companies' products must meet the standards approved by the Standards Institution of Malaysia (SIM).
g) Companies may not be restricted by their foreign partners, licensors, or suppliers of technical know-how with regard to the sale of their products outside Malaysia.
h) The ex-factory price of products sold in Malaysia may not exceed the prevailing cost, insurance, and freight (c.i.f.) prices of equivalent imported products. In addition, companies are not permitted to increase their prices unless the MTI approves such a move.
i) All companies will be encouraged to export as many of their products as possible.
j) Companies incorporated in Malaysia are required to keep statutory books and registers (minute books of members' meetings, register of members, register of charges, and so on). They are also required to keep in Malaysia other accounting records that sufficiently explain the transactions and financial position of the company.

THE PHILIPPINES

Scope of Activity

1. Industries in which investment is favored include export-oriented indusries; industries producing substitutes for imports; domestic banks; areas

of crucial importance to the nation's development, such as agriculture, mining, timber products for export, electronics, and garment manufacturing; labor-intensive industries; shipbuilding and ship repairs; exploration and development of Philippine petroleum resources; shipping; and cottage industries.

2. Preferred firms may have either pioneer or nonpioneer status; both types are open to foreign investors.
3. Registered tourist enterprises are permitted subject to certain ownership restrictions.
4. The preferred pioneer status involves the manufacture or production of commodities or rare materials that are not produced on a commercial scale in the Philippines, or the use of a new and untried design, formula, or process for producing or transforming raw materials into finished products.
5. Aliens or companies not wholly owned by Philippine citizens are not allowed to engage in retail trade, except as manufacturers or processors selling to industrial or commercial consumers who will use the goods to render a service to the general public or who will produce goods that they also sell.

Capital Participation

1. Preferred nonpioneer firms: At least 60 percent of the capital stock must be owned and held by Philippine nationals.
2. Preferred pioneer firms: There is no nationality requirement for registrants in this area. (A foreign firm is a firm with greater than 40 percent ownership by foreigners.)

   In order to expand the mining industry, a domestic or foreign mining corporation and its stockholders are permitted to own up to 40 percent of the voting capital stock of another mining corporation. A domestic or foreign nonmining corporation is allowed to own up to 30 percent of the outstanding stock of three other mining corporations. An individual may own stock in any number of mining corporations as long as his holding is less than 15 percent in any two companies.
3. Registered tourist enterprises.

   Ownership: The applicant must be a Filipino partnership or association; 60 percent of its capital must be Filipino-owned.

   Corporation: Sixty percent of its voting stock must be owned by Philippine nationals.
4. At least 60 percent Filipino ownership is required for finance companies; 70 percent for commercial and private development banks; and 100 percent for banks and mass-media corporations or associations.

5. The interisland shipping industry is reserved to firms that are at least 60 percent Filipino-owned.
6. Export:

   The same capital-holding requirements that apply to registered tourist enterprises are also in force here, with the following exceptions in the case of a corporation:

   a) A pioneer enterprise or
   b) An export producer, at least 70 percent of whose products are exported.

   Under these exceptions, an enterprise need not meet the nationality requirement, but an applicant from a registered enterprise must undertake to attain the minimum required Filipino ownership within thirty to forty years.

Regulations Governing Labor

1. Preferred nonpioneer firms:
   a) At least 60 percent of the members of the board of directors must be Filipino citizens.
   b) Such firms can employ foreign nationals in supervisory, technical, or advisory positions within five years of registration. Dependents of these aliens may enter the country, including children under twenty-one years of age.
2. Preferred pioneer firms: No nationality requirement.
3. A foreigner can obtain a multiple-entry visa for one year, renewable annually, if his salary is at least U.S. $12,000 and he is employed at regional or area headquarters.
4. Foreign stockbrokers, investors, representatives of investment houses, land developers, and so on, are very welcome.
5. A permit from the department of labor is required for the employment of aliens.
6. Technicians may be admitted to the country on a prearranged basis. Preference is to be given to Filipino citizens in awarding government contracts.

Benefits

1. Incentives to foreign personnel:
   a) Foreigners are exempt from all immigration and alien-registration fees, all types of clearance requirements, contractor's tax, customs duties, and compensating tax.

b) The withholding tax amounts only to 15 percent of gross income received from the regional office.

c) Foreigners are exempt from customs duty and import tax on one motor vehicle.

d) Foreign investors are permitted to remit earnings on investments and to repatriate their investments in the currency in which they were originally made.

2. Incentives to business:

a) Preferred pioneer enterprise

(1) Pioneer enterprises are exempt from all taxes except the income tax (National Internal Revenue Code) as follows: 100 percent for the first five years; 75 percent for the sixth to eighth years; 50 percent for the ninth and tenth years; 20 percent for the eleventh and twelfth years; 10 percent for the thirteenth through fifteenth years.

When the total project costs exceed 100 million pesos, the duration of the period of tax exemption in any bracket may be extended, but the total period of exemption shall not exceed twenty years.

(2) Pioneer enterprises are completely exempt from duties and import taxes on machinery and equipment.

(3) Pioneer enterprises receive postoperative tariff protection not exceeding 50 percent of the dutiable value of imported goods similar to those manufactured by the enterprise.

b) Preferred nonpioneer enterprises:

(1) Can deduct from taxable income:

- Organizational and preoperating expenses for the establishment of a registered enterprise, for a period less than ten years from the day of operation;
- Certain amounts, determined by the Board of Investments (BOI), of undistributed profits reinvested for the procurement or expansion of machinery and equipment;
- 50 percent of labor training expenses up to 10 percent of the direct labor payroll.

(2) Receive the following tax credits:

- Credit for taxes withheld on interest payments on foreign loans under certain conditions;
- 100 percent of the value of the compensating tax and customs duties on machinery, equipment, and spare parts purchased from a domestic manufacturer;

- 50 percent of the compensating tax and customs duties (to the domestic manufacturer).

(3) Receive protection from government competition.

(4) Can take accelerated depreciation of fixed assets at a rate not more than twice the normal rate.

(5) Can carry over operating losses in any of the first ten years of operation for the following six years.

c) Export businesses:

(1) Can take tax credits equal to sales, compensations, and other specific taxes and duties paid on materials and supplies used in the manufacture of export products.

(2) Can deduct from taxable income, for the first five years of registration, direct labor costs and local raw materials used in the manufacture of export products but not exceeding 25 percent of total export revenue.

d) Registered tourist enterprises:

(1) Can deduct from taxable income 50 percent of the foreign exchange earned in the first five years of operation;

(2) Are exempt from real-estate taxes on land improvements for the first five years of operation;

(3) Are fully exempt from tariff duties and compensatory taxes on imported capital equipment (importation must be within seven years from date of registration);

(4) Can deduct from taxable income undistributed reinvested profits (the percentage varies with the geographical area);

(5) If the enterprise's sphere of activity is in greater Manila, 70 percent of its revenues must be in foreign currency. This share must never fall below 50 percent in any given year within the period for which incentives are granted. If the enterprise is outside greater Manila, its revenues must be 50 percent in foreign currency and must never fall below 35 percent.

e) Export processing zones:

(1) Are exempt from customs duties, national taxes, local taxes on foreign and domestic merchandise, raw materials, equipment, export taxes, local-government fees, licenses or taxes except real-estate taxes.

(2) Receive priority in allocation of foreign exchange from the Central Bank and in obtaining financial assistance from governmental financial institutions.

f) General businesses:

(1) Reinsurance premiums received by nonresident foreign corporations are exempt from income taxes.

(2) The Philippine Foreign Loan Guarantee Corporation has been created to guarantee foreign loans to any domestic Philippine enterprise—that is, one with majority stock ownership by Philippine citizens.

(3) Partnerships or individuals may construct specific public-works projects and be paid by certificates of indebtedness that can be used in tax payment.

THAILAND

Scope of Activity

The Alien Business Control Law (Decree No. 281) of November 26, 1972, provided three lists of selected business activities.

Category A consists of business activities that are reserved for Thai nationals or for juristic companies that are majority-owned and managed by Thais. No foreign national may engage in such activities in his personal capacity. There are twelve such items: rice farming; salt farming; internal trade of local agricultural products; trade in real property; accountancy; practice of law; architecture; advertising; brokerage; auctioning; hairdressing; and building construction.

Category B consists of thirty-six business activities operating in Thailand, but the majority of the firms are owned by aliens. No new business owned by aliens is allowed in these fields, but those established before November 1972 may continue to operate. The thirty-six activities are: farming; fruit and vegetable growing; livestock raising; forestry; fishery; rice milling; manufacture of flour from rice and field crops; manufacture of sugar; manufacture of beverages with or without alcoholic blending; manufacture of ice; manufacture of medicine; cold storage; wood processing; manufacture of products from gold, silver, niello, or bronze; manufacture of lacquerware; manufacture of wood carvings; manufacture of all types of matches; manufacture of lime and cement; stone blasting or crushing; manufacture of plywood, wood veneer, chipboard, or hardboard; manufacture of garments or shoes except for export; printing, newspaper publication; silk combing, weaving, or printing patterns on silk materials; manufacture of products from silk, silk thread, or silk cocoon; retailing of all products except those specified in Category C; sale of mining products except those specified in Category C; sale of all types of foods and beverages except those specified in Category C; sale of antiques, period antiques, or works of art; tour agencies; hotel business except hotel management; all businesses defined by law as service premises; photography, photographic developing, and printing; laundry; tailoring; and internal transportation by land, water, or air.

Category C consists of fourteen fields in which alien-owned business enterprises are operating and other nonspecified fields in which both existing and new alien enterprises are permitted. They are: wholesale of all types of products within the country except those specified in Category A; export of all types of products; retail of machines, engines, and tools; sale of food and beverages for the promotion of tourism; manufacture of animal feeds; extraction of vegetable oil; manufacture of embroidery and knitting products including weaving, dyeing, and pattern printing; manufacture of glass containers including light bulbs; manufacture of crockery; manufacture of writing and printing paper; rock-salt mining; mining; all other services not specified under Category A and B; other constructions except those specified in Category A.

Companies engaged in petroleum survey and exploration are the most favored.

Ten promoted areas are: transportation, agriculture, industry, fishery, animal husbandry, tourist facilities, production for export, exporting, land improvement as industrial areas, and machine-repair services for the preceding activities.

Capital Participation

If a foreign entity is an investor in a Category A business, or a non-Thai occupies a managerial position in the enterprise, the majority-share holdings and managerial positions should be held by Thai nationals.

Alien enterprises in this category, as of November 26, 1972, are given until November 26, 1974, to wind up their operations or convert to at least 51 percent Thai ownership.

Regulations Governing Labor

1. Alien technicians and experts must not engage in activities other than duties specified before their entry into the country.
2. With a few exceptions, non-Thai nationals should have work permits. They are restricted to the particular occupation, employer, and locality specified.
3. For those who worked before March 14, 1973, work permits are automatically issued and are valid for life.
4. Aliens who entered Thailand after March 13, 1973, and who are working with a nonpromoted firm will be permitted to apply for a work permit if the occupation applied for is not banned and if they hold a resident or nonimmigrant visa. They cannot work without a permit.

Other Restrictions

Conditions promoted companies must observe:

1. Land owned as a part of a promoted firm's investment privileges must be used for the promoted activity.
2. On machinery of the promoted firm:
   a) Machinery exempt from import duties or business taxes must be imported within twenty-four months, and used only for the promoted activity within five years after importation.
   b) Machinery used in the promoted business must be modern and of high efficiency.
   c) For five years the firm is forbidden to mortgage, dispose of, transfer, or permit others to use its machinery except with the prior approval of the Board of Investments (BOI).
3. Unless a company has the approval of the BOI to do otherwise, it must use other necessary goods exempted from import duty and business taxes for the promoted activity.
4. The promoted firms must start work within six months from issuance of the promotion certificate, and within thirty months they must finish all preliminary work and be ready for business.
5. Before engaging in the promoted activity, the company must give the BOI at least fifteen days, written notice so that the BOI can inspect the firm's preparations and give its approval to start operations.
6. After starting operations, the promoted firm must furnish the following reports:
   a) Production, use of raw materials, labor, sale of services rendered, expenditures and acquisition of foreign exchange;
   b) Financial status and results of business activities.
   c) Other matters according to deadlines set by the BOI.
7. The company must take into consideration all kinds of environmental problems and attempt to protect nearby communities from them.

Benefits

1. All industries are guaranteed against naturalization or expropriation without just compensation.
2. The state promises not to engage in any new industrial activity in direct competition with a promoted company.
3. The promoted companies are exempt from import duties and business taxes on machinery, equipment, and component parts and accessories that are required by the industry.

4. The promoted companies are guaranteed their right to remit in foreign exchange profits, repayment of invested foreign capital, and interest on foreign loans.
5. If the promoted company is a limited company registered in Thailand, it is permitted to own land for purposes of industrial activity.
6. Export of the promoted company's products is permitted as long as it does not threaten the security or economic interests of Thailand.
7. New promoted industries can be exempted from the income tax on net profit for a period determined by the BOI varying from three to eight years, effective from the date of the first sale.
8. Reductions of as much as 50 percent of import duties and business taxes on raw materials or necessary goods for the promoted industries are granted for not more than five years from the date of operation.
9. Reductions by as much as 90 percent of the business tax on the sale of the promoted companies' products are granted for a period of not more than five years from the date of the first sale.
10. For income tax purposes, permission is given to deduct two times the actual costs of transportation, electricity, and water supply for a period of time specified by the BOI.
11. In addition to the normal rate of depreciation, for income tax purposes, a promoted company may deduct as much as 25 percent of its investment in facilities it has installed or constructed. (This refers to a single year over a period of ten years from the date of first sale.)
12. A promoted company may reduce by 50 percent the income tax on net profit, for a period of five years after the expiration of the original three to eight years' tax exemption period granted by the BOI.

E

Wholly or Partially Chinese-Owned Banks in ASEAN and Hong Kong

Location of Head Office	Name of Bank
Singapore	Overseas Chinese Banking Corp.
	Lee Wah Bank, Ltd.
	Overseas Union Bank, Ltd.
	Industrial and Commercial Bank, Ltd.
	Far Eastern Bank, Ltd.
	Development Bank of Singapore
	Tat Lee Bank, Ltd.
	Bank of Canton, Ltd.
	Four Seas Communication Bank, Ltd.
	United Overseas Bank, Ltd.
	Chung Khiaw Bank, Ltd.
	Bank of Singapore, Ltd.
	Asia Commercial Bank Corporation
	International Bank of Singapore, Ltd.
Malaysia	The Kwong Yik (SEL) Banking Corp., Berhad
	Ban Hsin Lee Bank, Berhad, Penang
	Wah Tat Bank
	Malayan Banking, Berhad (Kuala Lumpur, Sarawak, and Sabah)
	Hoch Hua Bank (Kuala Lumpur, Sarawak, and Sabah)
	Development and Commercial Bank, Berhad
	The Oriental Bank of Malaya, Berhad
	The Pacific Bank, Berhad
	Kwong Lee Bank, Ltd.
	United Malayan Banking Corp., Berhad
	Public Bank, Berhad
	Kong Ming Bank, Ltd.
	The United Commercial Bank, Ltd.
	Bian Chiang Bank, Ltd.
	Southern Banking, Berhad
	United Asia Bank, Berhad
	Bank of Canton, Ltd.

Location of Head Office	Name of Bank	
Thailand	Bangkok Bank, Ltd.	Bank of Canton
	The Bank of Ayudhya, Ltd.	Bangkok Metropolitan Bank
	Bank of Asia for Industry & Commerce	The Thai Development Bank, Ltd.
	Siam City Bank	Wang Lee Bank
	Thai Farmers Bank	Bangkok Bank of Commerce
	Asia Trust Bank	Union Bank of Bangkok
The Philippines	China Banking Corporation	Consolidated Bank & Trust Corp.
	Equitable Banking Corp.	Pacific Banking Corp.
	Philippine Bank of Communications	Bank of Asia
	Associated Banking Corp.	Rizal Commercial Banking Corp.
	The Metropolitan Bank, Ltd.	Producers' Bank of the Philippines
	Insular Bank of Asia and America	
Indonesia	Mualin Bank, Ltd.	Bank Surakarta MAI
	P. T. Bank Kredit	Bank Umum National
	Bank Angkasa Putra	Bank Umum Servitia
	Industrial Development Bank	Bank Danamon Indonesia
	Bank of Central Asia	Bank Tani Nasional
	Asia Africa Banking Corp. Ltd.	Central Nationalities Economy Bank
	Bank Buana Indonesia	Commissary of Mualin Bank, Ltd.
	Bank Bhumi Bahari	Bank Pancha Dewa
	Bank Central Dagang	Overseas Express Bank
	Bank Dewa Rutji	Bank Arta Pusara
	Bank Indonesia Raya	Bank Bali
	Bank Kesedjahteraan Angkatan Perang	Bank Bumi Arta Indonesia
	Bank NISP	Central Sumatera Djawa Bank
	Bank Patriot Pusat	Bank Dirgahaju
	Bank Pertiwi	Bank Daya Indonesia
	Bank Perkembangan Asia	Bank International Indonesia
	South East Asia Bank	Natin Bank

Location of Head Office	Name of Bank	
Indonesia (Continued)	Pan Indonesia Bank	Bank Toni National
	Bank Patriot Cabang	United City Bank
	Bank Petita Jacatra	Bank Windu Kentjana
	Bank Perkembangan Pelayan Indonesia	Bank Perkembangan Ekonomi Indonesia
	Sejahtera Bank Umum	United City Bank
Hong Kong	The Shanghai Commercial Bank	Tai Sang Bank, Ltd.
	Dah Sing Bank, Ltd.	United Chinese Bank
	The Wing On Bank	Wing Lung Bank
	The Bank of East Asia, Ltd.	Hang Seng Bank, Ltd.
	Hong Kong Industrial and Commercial Bank, Ltd.	Union Bank of Hong Kong, Ltd.
	The Commercial Bank of Hong Kong	The Hong Kong Chinese Bank, Ltd.
	Overseas Trust Bank, Ltd.	Chekiang First Bank, Ltd.
	Kang Ping Bank, Ltd.	Dao Heng Bank, Ltd.
	Liu Chong Hing Bank, Ltd.	Far East Bank, Ltd.
	The Ka Wah Bank	Kwong On Bank, Ltd.
	The Bank of Canton, Ltd.	The United Commercial Bank, Ltd.
	Wing Hang Bank, Ltd.	Hang Lung Bank, Ltd.

Notes

CHAPTER 1

1. See G. Ngyuyen Tien Hung, *Economic Development of Socialist Vietnam, 1955–80* (New York: Praeger Special Studies), 1977.

2. As we will show later in this chapter, several Southeast Asian countries exhibited somewhat faster growth in the early 1970s, especially in 1973, before the onset of the oil crisis in October of that year. The data of 1960–73, however, probably present a better long-term perspective.

3. Supply is here defined as net imports plus domestic production.

4. The Taiwan ratio in 1974 was higher than usual because of heavy borrowing for ten major construction projects designed to expand the economic infrastructure, which had become strained after a decade of fast economic growth. The relatively lower ratio for Thailand reflected the concentration of foreign capital in the form of direct investment rather than loans plus U.S. offshore spending in Thailand.

5. See Asian Development Bank (ADB), Economic Office, *Key Indicators of Developing Member Countries of ADB* vol. VII, no. 1 (April 1976), country tables, pp. 96, 113, 137, and 169.

6. This has been the case especially for U.S. and Japanese investors.

7. Available foreign-investment data for Thailand begin with 1965. For the Philippines the corresponding data begin with 1968. A large increase in foreign investment in the Philippines in 1974 was due to the sharp rise of foreign capital in financial institutions following a change in the law. This increase, which put the 1975 point significantly to the right of the scatter diagram, did not therefore have much direct short-run effect on Philippine exports. The available foreign direct-investment data for Malaysia and Indonesia begin with 1970.

8. The resource-poor fast-growing countries of the 1960–73 period have generally fared much better than the figures for 1974–75 in Table 19 indicate. Although published data for 1976–77 are still unavailable in many cases, private information indicates that they have performed far better than expected in weathering the aftermath of the oil crisis and the worldwide recession.

9. When the cost of capital investment is inflated by the practice of making payments to government officials and others and when these payments are used for consumption by their recipients, real productive investment expenditure is overestimated. This overestimate is less, however, if the same payments are used by their recipients for capital investment in their own enterprises.

CHAPTER 2

1. *The Economist*, June 1, 1974, p. 92.

2. See Louis Kraar, "The Wealth and Power of the Overseas Chinese," *Fortune*, March 1971, p. 165. See also Garth Alexander, *The Silent Invasion: The Chinese in Southeast Asia* (London: Macdonald & Co., 1973), pp. 51–52. The term overseas Chinese used by *The Economist* is somewhat vague.

3. Atan bin Long (University of Malaya), "Majority-Minority Situation: Malaysia" (Paper presented at the Manila conference on the Majority-Minority Situation in Southeast Asia organized by ASAIHL, May 8–10, 1974 [ASAIHL stands for the Association of Southeast Asian Institutes for Higher Learning, which sponsored the meeting]). Original data from the Malaysian Second Plan.

4. *The Economist*, June 1, 1974.

5. Alexander, *Silent Invasion*.

6. Ibid.

7. See Kraar, "Wealth and Power."

8. *The Economist*, June 1, 1974.

9. Schubert S. C. Liao, ed., *Chinese Participation in Philippine Culture and Economy* (Manila: Published by the Author, 1964), p. 229. Note that the Chinese referred to here by Liao include alien Chinese only. Some of the Filipino investors are actually ethnic Chinese.

10. As of September 1975, the cumulative total of authorized Japanese foreign investment in all countries was U.S. $14.2 billion. This information is given by Toshiro H. Shimanouchi of Keidanren in "Japan's Growing Role in the Pacific" (Speech delivered on March 3, 1976, at Fresno, California), reprinted in the *ACCJ Journal of the American Chamber of Commerce in Japan* 13, no. 6, 1976, pp. 38–46.

11. For data on the occupational distribution of ethnic Chinese and Thai in Thailand in 1952, see G. W. Skinner, *Chinese Society in Thailand* (Ithaca, N.Y.: Cornell University Press, 1957), p. 302.

12. It is interesting to note that some indigenous businessmen have, in recent years, become full-fledged members of the local Chinese business organizations. This is the case in Thailand.

13. See Appendix C.

14. See Part II for an explanation of the term peranakan.

15. See Appendix D.

16. See Part II.

17. This is especially true in cases where local sales are an important part of the undertaking.

CHAPTER 3

1. See Yuan-li Wu, *The Strategic Land Ridge* (Stanford, Ca.: Hoover Institution Press, 1975).

2. Included among the alien Asiatics are the Indians.

3. A more comprehensive discussion is reserved for Part II.

4. See John S. Furnivall, *Netherlands India: A Study of Plural Economy* (Cambridge: Cambridge University Press, 1939); and J. H. Bocke, *Economics and Economic Policy of Dual Societies as Exemplified by Indonesia* (New York: Institute of Pacific Relations, 1953).

5. As Jan O. M. Broke wrote, "Generally speaking, the natives form the agrarian base, the Chinese and Arabs the commercial middle class, and the Westerners the small but ruling apex of the socio-economic pyramid" (*The Economic Development of the Netherlands Indies* [New York: Institute of Pacific Relations, 1942], p. 5).

6. Kao Shih-heng, *Nan-yang lun* [Southeast Asia] (Shanghai: Nan-yang ching-chi yen-chiu-so [Institute of Economic Research on Southeast Asia], 1948), p. 225.

7. Community associations have contributed significantly to capital accumulation by the Chinese. M. Freedman, a British social anthropologist and sinologist, has attempted to explain the economic sophistication of the overseas Chinese in handling money by the widespread existence of, and their participation in, diverse loan associations. Lacking modern banks or large credit associations, these organizations were established to provide large sums of money for personal commercial investments at low or even zero interest. C. Geertz, another anthropologist, in a cross-cultural analysis of rotating credit associations, has argued in a similar vein that such institutions probably represent a middle rung in development. See Chen Yi-lin, "Some Socio-Cultural Factors in Chinese Economic Organization," *Asian Culture Quarterly* 5, no. 2 (Summer 1977), p. 22.

8. Wu Chu-hui, *Kakyō honshitsu no bunseki* [Analysis of the Character of the Overseas Chinese Community] (Tokyo: Institute of Social Science, Toyo University, 1961), p. 32.

9. Shōzō Fukuda, *Kakyō keizai ron* [Treatise on Overseas Chinese Economy] (Tokyo: Ganshōdō, 1940), p. 101. Fukuda gave the prewar distribution of Chinese employment and investment as follows (p. 88 and 101):

CHINESE EMPLOYMENT IN SOUTHEAST ASIA BY SECTOR, 1930
(PERCENTAGES)

	Malaya and Singapore	Indochina	Thailand	Indonesia	The Philippines
Primary[a]	39	16	10	21	. . .
Secondary[b]	23	28	20	30	25
Tertiary[c]	38	56	70	49	75
Total	100	100	100	100	100

NOTES: [a]Agriculture.
[b]Mining and manufacturing.
[c]Wholesale and retail trade, banking, and other areas.

CHINESE INVESTMENT IN SOUTHEAST ASIA BY SECTOR, 1930
(PERCENTAGES)

	Malaya and Singapore	Indochina	Thailand	Indonesia	The Philippines	Total (U.S. $ Million)
Primary	49.5	4.9	...	30.5	0.1	238.7
Secondary	14.8	13.1	8.3	2.4	18.8	103.9
Tertiary	35.7	82.0	91.7	67.1	81.1	734.8
Total	100.0	100.0	100.0	100.0	100.0	1,077.4
Total (U.S. $ million)	264.0	126.9	251.3	333.3	101.0	1,077.4

NOTE: Exchange rate: U.S. $1 : ¥ 3.77

The Chinese employment pattern meant that the ethnic-Chinese communities were concentrated in urban areas. One fifth of the ethnic Chinese in Thailand lived in Bangkok and more than half the total Chinese population was scattered within a 50-mile radius of that city (see Skinner, *Chinese Society in Thailand*, p. 203). A comparable situation existed in Manila, the Cholon section of Saigon, Phnom Penh, Jakarta, and Rangoon. In Malaysia the trend toward urbanization for ethnic Chinese has continued to the present (see J. C. Calwell, "The Demographic Background," in T. H. Silcock and E. K. Fisk, eds., *The Political Economy of Independent Malaya: A Study on Development* [Singapore, Eastern Universities Press, 1963], p. 87).

10. *The Economist*, July 1, 1974, p. 92.

11. See the following section.

12. Taku Suyama, *Kakyō* [Overseas Chinese] (Tokyo: NHK Press, 1974), p. 54.

13. Nai Ho, "Singapore ti hua-ch'iao yü hua-ch'iao ching-chi" [Overseas Chinese Economy in Singapore], *Ching-chi tao-pao* [Economic Bulletin] (Hong Kong), no. 691, October 17, 1960, p. 12.

14. Nan Jen, "Pei-mo-shou ch'ung-kung ti Huang-chung-han Kung-ssu" [The Confiscation of Gian Yuan], *Ching-chi tao-pao*, no. 773, 1970, pp. 21–22.

15. Liu Chi-hsüan and Shu Shih-cheng, *Chung-kuo min-tsu t'o-chih nan-yang shih* [A History of Chinese Settlements in Southeast Asia] (Taipei: Commercial Press, 1971), p. 4. Also Victor Purcell, *The Chinese in Southeast Asia*, 2nd ed. (London: Oxford University Press, 1965), p. 235.

16. See the section "Penang and Singapore, 1786–1900," chapter 27 in Purcell, *Chinese in Southeast Asia*, pp. 243–56.

17. The following statistics are abstracted from the 1957 census:

	Number of Females per Thousand Males				
	1911	1921	1931	1947	1957
Malays	...	...	973	1,010	1,013
Chinese	215	371	486	815	926
Indians	320	424	514	707	746

SOURCE: *Malaysia Official Year Book* (Kuala Lumpur: Government Printing Office, 1964).

18. The percentages of the population, by race, born in the Federated States of Malaya or in Singapore, according to official Malaysian statistics, are as follows:

	1921	1931	1947	1957[a]
All races	56.4	58.9	78.3	84.8
Malaysians	. . .	. . .	96.0	97.4
Chinese	20.9	29.9	63.5	75.5
Indians	12.1	21.4	51.6	65.0

SOURCE: *Malaysia Official Year Book* (Kuala Lumpur: Government Printing Office, 1964).

[a]Figures for 1957 probably do not include Singapore.

19. According to 1931 data on the ownership of rubber estates of a hundred or more planted acres, Chinese in the Straits Settlements and Federated Malay Estates owned 12.5 percent of the total; non-Asians (including Britons, Frenchmen, Belgians, and Americans) owned 84 percent; and Indians held 2.3 percent. See also *Malaya Rubber Statistics Handbook* (Singapore: no publisher, 1932), p. 15.

20. Shōzō Fukuda, *Kakyō keizai ron*, p. 101.

21. In 1920, 64 percent of the tin mines were operated by Chinese, compared with 36 percent by Europeans. The corresponding proportions in 1938 were reversed: 33 percent by Chinese and 67 percent by Europeans. See *Quarterly Bulletin of Statistics Relating to the Mining Industry in the Federated Malay States* (Kuala Lumpur: Government Printing Office, 1939) 11, no. 4, p. 11.

22. For details see the table below:

CHINESE BY SPEECH GROUP, 1947 AND 1957

	1947		*1957*		
Specific Community	Thousands of persons	Percentage	Thousands of persons	Percentage	Percentage of Increase
Hokkien	538.2	28.6	740.6	31.7	37.6
Hakka (Kheh)	397.4	21.1	508.8	21.8	28.0
Cantonese	484.0	25.7	505.2	21.7	4.4
Teochiu	207.0	11.0	283.1	12.1	36.7
Hainanese	105.0	5.6	123.0	5.3	16.6
Kwongsai	71.1	3.8	69.1	3.0	2.8
Hokchiu	38.6	2.0	46.1	2.0	19.4
Henghua	9.6	0.5	11.9	0.5	23.8
Hokchia	6.4	0.3	9.8	0.4	52.1
Other	26.7	1.4	34.3	1.5	28.6
Total	1,884.0	100.0	2,331.9	100.0	23.8

SOURCE: *Federation of Malaya Official Year Book* (Kuala Lumpur: Government Printing Office, 1961).

23. Shōzō Fukuda, *Kakyō keizai ron*, p. 88.

24. See Helmut G. Callis, *Foreign Capital in Southeast Asia* (New York: Institute of Pacific Relations, 1942), p. 57.

25. For an official view, see Tunku Abdul Rahman, *May 13th: Before and After* (Kuala Lumpur: Government Printing Office, 1969.)

26. Student enrollment in the University of Malaya, 1971–1972 by faculty:

Faculties	Malayan	Chinese	Indian	Other	Total
Arts	2,481	723	324	50	3,578
Economics and administration	590	674	188	18	1,470
Education	185	266	67	6	524
Engineering	29	448	19	4	500
Agriculture	149	203	30	1	383
Medicine	157	409	78	10	654
Sciences	147	1,169	108	13	1,437
Total	3,738	3,892	814	102	8,546
Percentage	43.73	45.55	9.53	1.19	100.00

27. The following data are indicative of the prevailing disparities:

PERCENTAGE DISTRIBUTION OF HOUSEHOLDS BY INCOME AND RACE IN PENINSULAR MALAYSIA, 1970

Monthly Income Range	Malays	Chinese	Indians	Others
$ 1 - 99	40.3	8.3	11.6	25.0
$ 100 - 199	33.7	25.0	39.3	12.5
$ 200 - 399	18.3	38.0	31.3	12.5
$ 400 - 699	5.3	17.0	10.7	12.5
$ 700 - 1,499	2.0	9.2	5.3	12.5
$1,500 - 2,999	0.4	2.2	0.9	12.5
$3,000 or more	neg.	0.3	0.9	12.5
Total	100.0	100.0	100.0	100.0

SOURCE: *Mid-Term Review of the Second Malaysia Plan, 1971–1975* (Malaysia: Government Press, 1973), p. 3.

28. See *Third Malaysia Plan, 1976–1980* (Kuala Lumpur: Government Press, 1976), pp. 5 and 160–161.

29. Shih Hsi, "Malaysia ti hua-jen ching-chi" [The Chinese Economy in Malaysia] *Ssu-hai-i-chia* [Universal Brotherhood Monthly] (Taipei), no. 12, August 15, 1975, p. 40.

30. See *Third Malaysia Plan*, p. 117.

31. See *Third Malaysia Plan*, p. 184, Table 9-9.

32. See the account of the major Singapore and Malaysian industrialists in Chapter 4.

33. See *Second Malaysia Plan, 1971–1975* (Kuala Lumpur: Government Press, 1971), pp. 41–42.

34. For example, stocks of a Japanese steel firm in Malaysia valued at M $17 million were acquired in June 1975 by the State Economic Development Corporation (SEDC).

35. In 1740 the Dutch decided to send as slaves to Ceylon all Chinese who could not prove that they were making an honest living. The action brought to a head the rising discontent among the Chinese and resulted in rebellion, followed by a massacre. See

Purcell, *Chinese in Southeast Asia*, p. 404, and the *Hua-ch'iao chih tsung-chih* [General Gazetteer of the Overseas Chinese], p. 73.

36. See W. J. Cator, *The Economic Position of the Chinese in Netherlands Indies* (Oxford: Basil Blackwell, 1936), p. 231.

37. See D. M. Campbell, *Java: Past and Present* (London: Heinemann, 1915), 2: 1095, and Ta Chen, *Chinese Migrations, With Special Reference to Labor Conditions* (Washington, D.C.: Government Printing Office, 1923), p. 60.

38. Victor Purcell, *Chinese in Southeast Asia*, p. 480.

39. The following are results of the 1930 census:

Race	Born in the Netherlands Indies	Born Elsewhere	Born Elsewhere (Percentage)
Hokkiens	427,962	125,204	22
Hakkas	121,734	78,505	39
Teochius	32,822	54,700	62
Kwong Fus	45,636	90,007	66
Other Races	110,082	77,616	41
Unknown	17,936	1,649	8
Total	756,172	427,681	36

SOURCE: W. J. Cator, *Economic Position of Chinese*, p. 31.

40. Mely G. Tan, "Majority-Minority Situation: Indonesia" (Paper presented at the Manila conference on the Majority-Minority Situation in Southeast Asia organized by ASAIHL, May 8–10, 1974).

41. Victor Purcell, *Chinese in Southeast Asia*, p. 384.

42. In late 1959 an anti-Chinese storm broke out in Indonesia. Although the Peking regime had friendly relations with Indonesia at that time, it could do nothing to protect its nationals there. In February 1960, however, a Committee for Reception and Resettlement of Returned Overseas Chinese was established under the state council. Communist Chinese reports indicated that in one year's time, Peking resettled about ninety-four thousand overseas Chinese from Indonesia See Chun-hsi Wu, "Overseas Chinese" in Yuan-li Wu, ed., *China Handbook* (New York: Praeger, 1973), p. 424.

43. Kraar, "Wealth and Power," p. 78.

44. *Hua-ch'iao ching-chi nien-chien, 1974* [Overseas Chinese Economy Yearbook] (Taipei: World Chinese Traders Convention Liaison Office, 1974), p. 171.

45. Ibid., 1973, p. 174.

46. Ibid., 1971, p. 175.

47. See Appendix C.

48. Lie Tek Tjeng, "The Chinese Problem," *International Spectator* 24, no. 12 (June 1970), quoted by Hugh and Ping-ching Mabbett, *The Chinese Community in Indonesia* (London: Report No. 10 of the Minority Rights Group, June 1972), p. 14.

49. Phya Tak Sin, who was of mixed Chinese-Siamese ancestry, united the Siamese kingdom under his rule after the Burmese had destroyed Ayuthia in 1767. Five years later he established his capital at Dhonburi across the Bangkok river, now a part of Bangkok. See K. P. Landon, *The Chinese in Thailand* (London: Oxford University Press, 1941), pp. 7–8.

50. See Purcell, *Chinese in Southeast Asia*, p. 102.

51. Ibid., p. 104.

52. Skinner estimated a total of 2,315,000 for 1955, distributed as follows: Teochius, 56 percent; Hakka, 16 percent; Hainanese, 12 percent; the rest being Cantonese, Hokkien and others. See Skinner, *Chinese Society in Thailand*, p. 212.

53. The ROC's estimates referred to above are taken from *Ch'iao-wu t'ung-chi* [Overseas Chinese Affairs Statistics, 1973] (Taipei: OCAC, 1974). See also Numbers and Distribution of Ethnic Chinese in Southeast Asia in Part II.

54. Nihon bōeki shinkōkai chōsa hōkoku [A Report by JETRO], *Kaigai Shijō* [Overseas Market] (Tokyo: 1964).

55. *Hua-ch'iao ching-chi nien-chien, 1976*, p. 46.

56. Wu Chu-hui, *Kakyō honshitsu no bunseki*, p. 185.

57. *Ching-hua tao-pao* [Bangkok Metropolitan Bank Bulletin] 4, no. 4 (April 1974): 14–17.

58. Gregorio F. Zaide, "Contributions of Aliens to the Philippine Economy," in Schubert S. C. Liao, ed., *Chinese Participation in Philippine Culture and Economy* (Manila, 1964), pp. 151–154. See also Liu Chi-hsüan and Shu Shih-cheng, *Chung-kuo min-tsu t'o-chih nan-yang shih*, pp. 84–85.

59. See Juan de la Conception, *Historia General de Philippines*, 18: 53, as quoted by Liao, *Chinese Participation*, pp. 19–25.

60. See Liu Tzu-tien, "Chiu-shih-nien-lai Fei-li-pin yü hua-ch'iao" [The Philippines and Overseas Chinese since 1877], in *90th Anniversary Yearbook of the Philippine-Chinese Charitable Association 1877–1967* (Manila: Philippine-Chinese Charitable Association, 1968), pt. 6, p. 13.

61. Ibid., p. 14.

62. Huang Ming-teh, *Fei-lü-pin hai-wai hua-ch'iao ching-chi* [Overseas Chinese Economy in the Philippines] (Taipei: Hai-wai ch'u-pan-she, 1956), p. 21.

63. A second step in the relaxation was promised by Marcos at the end of 1976. See Persons of Mixed Parentage in Part II.

64. Huang Ming-teh, *Fei-lü-pin hai-wai hua-ch'iao ching-chi*, p. 119.

65. Ibid., p. 146.

66. According to the *Manila Post* (March 11, 1947), the foreign trade of the Philippines in 1946 was carried on by firms of different nationalities in the following percentages:

	Imports	Exports	Total
American	28.00	42.57	33.59
Chinese	39.14	24.48	33.51
Filipino	23.48	21.38	22.70
Other	9.38	11.57	10.20
Total	100.00	100.00	100.00

67. The requirement was slightly different for proprietorships on the one hand and partnerships and corporate organizations on the other. For details see Appendix C.

68. JETRO, *Kaigai shijō*.

69. *Hua-ch'iao ching-chi nien-chien, 1974*, p. 193.

70. Li Ch'ang-fu, *Chung-kuo chih-min shih* [History of Chinese Settlements in Southeast Asia] (Taipei: Commercial Press, 1970), pp. 81–89.

71. Purcell, *Chinese in Southeast Asia*, p. 3.

72. Ibid., p. 47. According to Purcell, the occupational distribution of Chinese in Burma in 1931 was as follows:

Traders and merchants	41
Carpenters and workers in metal and leather	38
Semiskilled workers	9
Clerical workers	5
Miscellaneous	7

73. Jiang Lu-mou, "Mien-tien hua-ch'iao ching-chi ti o-yün" [Misfortune of the Chinese Economic Conditions in Burma], *Ch'iao-tzu hui-shu* [Overseas Chinese Investment Bulletin], Taipei, no. 3, pp. 18–19.

74. Josef Silverstein, "Burma," in Kahin, ed., *Government and Politics of Southeast Asia*, (Ithaca: Cornell University Press, 1962), pp. 134–136.

75. In 1963 nationalization began with 31 banks, together with the foreign-export industry, tobacco manufacturing, the cultured-pearl industry, ocean fishing, and rice milling. In 1964 all commercial firms were added to the list, including wholesalers, brokers, trade agents, and department stores and merchants selling native products. The mines and oil wells were nationalized in 1965. In 1968 the program of nationalization was further extended to include 114 theaters, 49 lumberyards, 116 factories (including 60 textile mills, 23 chemical manufacturers, and 28 food-processing plants) and 30 other businesses. A year later, 2 newspapers, 28 shipping companies, and 17 printing firms as well as the miners of precious stones and 56 theaters were nationalized. These data are based on Overseas Chinese Affairs Commission (OCAC) reports from Taipei.

76. Denzil Peiris, "Socialism without Commitment," *Far Eastern Economic Review*, (Hong Kong), September 13, 1974, p. 29.

77. See H. F. MacHair, *The Chinese Abroad* (Shanghai: The Commercial Press, 1924), p. 49. These territories were under the direct rule of China from 36 B.C. to A.D. 968. Tongking was regarded by China as a vassal state until 1884.

78. Ordinance No. 48 automatically conferring Vietnamese citizenship on all Chinese born in Vietnam was promulgated on August 21, 1956.

79. Victor Purcell, *Chinese in Southeast Asia*, p. 3.

80. Ryuzō Okamoto, *Kakyō shūdan* [Overseas Chinese Groups] (Tokyo: Ban-cho Bookstore, 1973), p. 176.

81. *Hua-ch'iao ching-chi nien-chien, 1976*, p. 85. Okamoto, however, estimated the Cantonese group at 415,000 persons (34.6 percent) and the Teochius at 370,000 persons (30 percent).

82. Decree No. 53 was promulgated on September 6, 1956, prohibiting non Vietnamese nationals from engaging in eleven occupations. These were mostly in the retail trade (fishmongers; butchers; general storemen; coal and firewood merchants; dealers in petroleum products, secondhand goods, and scrap metal; and transporters of persons and merchandise) and the entire intermediary trade in rice. Those aliens engaged in the first seven of these occupations had to liquidate their businesses within six months; those in the last four categories had to close within one year.

83. Lung Chih-i, "Vietnam lun-hsien-hou hua-ch'iao ching-chi so-chao-shou ti sun-shih" [Chinese Losses in 1975], *Ssu-hai I-chia* [Universal Brotherhood Monthly] (Taipei), no. 12, August 15, 1975; and *Hua-ch'iao ching-chi nien-chien, 1976*, pp. 60–61.

84. W. E. Willmott, *The Chinese in Cambodia* (Vancouver, Canada: University of British Columbia, 1967), p. 15, table 2.

85. Victor Purcell, *Chinese in Southeast Asia*, p. 221.

86. According to Willmott, *Chinese in Cambodia*, p. 63, table 15, 90 percent of Chinese employment was in commerce.

87. Ibid., pp. 52–53.

CHAPTER 4

1. In 1973, 18,948 ships of over 75 net registered tons, totaling 93,564,000 NRT, entered Singapore. During the same year 18,884 vessels of 92,518,000 tons cleared port; the corresponding figure for Hong Kong in the same year was 7,358 vessels. Singapore was reputed to be the fourth busiest port in the world. See *Yearbook of Statistics, Singapore 1975/6*, pp. 118–122, and *Hong Kong Yearbook 1975*, p. 91.

2. Hong Kong was declared a free port in October 1843. Singapore became a free port when the British acquired it from the Malay rulers in 1824. As the following statistics show, British Malaya (including Singapore) and what was then the Netherlands East Indies registered comparable values of exports and imports both in 1929, before the worldwide depression, and in 1936, on the eve of the Sino-Japanese war. The exports of these two areas together would have either equaled or surpassed Japan's exports.

	Imports (U.S. $ Million)		*Exports (U.S. $ Million)*	
	1929	1936	1929	1936
Siam	86	27	94	46
British Malaya	498	175	521	217
The Philippines	146	60	163	81
Netherlands Indies	446	108	581	231
Korea	194	131	160	102
Formosa	94	50	129	67
Japan	995	464	970	452
French Indochina	105	35	106	59

SOURCE: League of Nations, Economic Intelligence Service, *Review on World Trade 1936–1937* (Geneva, 1938), p. 24.

3. Singapore residents are required to go through foreign-exchange control for their foreign-currency requirements. Because of Singapore's large exchange reserves, however, the control process serves more as a monitoring device than as a restriction. Local residents are not permitted to make deposits with Singapore currency (S $) in the offshore banking arrangement known as the Asian Currency Unit (ACU). Hong Kong, on the other hand, has a totally free exchange market. Both residents and nonresidents can hold and maintain deposits in all currencies.

4. See Ta Chen, *Chinese Migration*, pp. 79–86.

5. In 1953, remittances from Thailand were limited to 2,000 baht per family per month. Similarly, the monthly limits in Malaya and Singapore in 1946 were M$ 45 per person. On the role of arbitrage in remittances, see Cheng Lin-k'uan, *Fukken kakyō no sōkin* [Fukien Overseas Chinese Remittances] (Tokyo: Mantetsu Tōakeizai Chōsa Kyoku, 1943), pp. 158–62.

6. Singapore Ministry of Finance, *Economic Survey of Singapore, 1975*, pp. 67–68. Since Singapore does not publish its trade returns with Indonesia, actual re-exports should be larger than the reported figures. However, the declining trend is unmistakable.

7. Derived from trade statistics of the Hong Kong government and estimates of PRC trade in *People's Republic of China: International Trade Handbook* (Washington, D.C., October 1976), p. 13.

8. Mainland China's total imports from Hong Kong were HK $63.9 million in 1970 and HK $271.2 million in 1973. Exports to Hong Kong, on the other hand, were HK $2,830 million in 1970 and HK $5,634 million in 1973.

9. Far Eastern Economic Review, *Asia 1976 Yearbook* (Hong Kong), p. 164, and Singapore Ministry of Labor, *Yearbook of Statistics, 1975–76*, p. 43.

10. Singapore Ministry of Labor, *Yearbook of Statistics, 1973–74*, p. 28; Hong Kong government, *1975–1976 Fiscal, Financial and Budgetary Bill*, p. 31.

11. See Iain Buchanan, *Singapore in Southeast Asia* (London: G. Bell & Sons, 1972), pp. 96–97.

12. See Chun-hsi Wu, *Dollars, Dependents and Dogma* (Stanford, Ca.: Hoover Institution Press, 1967), pp. 84–89.

13. *Hong Kong ching-chi nien-chien, 1976* [Hong Kong Economic Yearbook] (Hong Kong: Ching-chi tao-pao-she, 1976), part 1, p. 228.

14. Chun-hsi Wu, *Dollars, Dependents and Dogma*, p. 91, table 16.

15. The Monetary Authority of Singapore, *Monthly Statistical Release* (Singapore) 1, no. 6 (June 1976): 7.

16. See *Far Eastern Economic Review* (Hong Kong), December 3, 1976, pp. 38–42.

17. The distribution by country is as follows:

	$ Million
Thailand	4.32
Malaysia	1.19
Singapore	3.26
Indonesia	2.42
Hong Kong	2.35
Total	13.54

SOURCE: *Hua-ch'iao chingchi nien-chien, 1976*, p. 576.

18. Data from the Foreign Investment Commission, Taiwan, Republic of China.

19. In this respect Taiwan has the advantage of size over both Singapore and Hong Kong. The potential of its domestic market is substantially larger.

CHAPTER 5

1. See Wang Gung-wu, "Chinese in Malaya," *China Quarterly*, no. 43, July–Sept. 1970, pp. 1–7.

2. Chiao's talk on the present world situation and foreign policy was delivered in Tientsin on May 20, 1975. See *China News Analysis* (Hong Kong), April 9, 1976, pp. 3–4.

3. See *Ching-chi tao-pao*, (Hong Kong), June 18, 1961, p. 5.

4. See Stanford Research Institute, "International Business Principles-Codes," *SRI International*, no. 24, and "Company Codes," *SRI International*, no. 25, 1975.

PART 2

1. See Narita Setsuo, *Kakyōshi* [A History of Overseas Chinese], rev. ed. (Tokyo: Keisetsu shoin, 1942), p. 3.

2. Ch'en Lun-chiung, *Hai-kuo wen-chien lu* [A Record of Personal Experiences in Maritime Countries], reprinted by the Institute of Economic Research, Bank of Taiwan, Taipei, 1958. In his work Ch'en defined Nanyang as including Annam (Central Vietnam), Champa (Cambodia), and Malaya (Peninsular Malaysia and Singapore).

3. Wu Chu-hui, *Kakyō honshitsu no bunseki* [Analysis of the Character of the Overseas Chinese Community] (Tokyo: Institute of Social Science, Toyo University, 1961), pp. 17–19.

4. See Purcell, *Chinese in Southeast Asia*, p. 1.

5. Ordinance No. 48 conferring Vietnamese citizenship automatically on all Chinese born in Vietnam was promulgated on August 21, 1956. Since the measure was retroactive, all Chinese born in Vietnam either before or after that date were to be regarded as Vietnamese nationals and had to take Vietnamese names. This was generally regarded as the most drastic action yet taken by any Asian country to absorb an alien minority. Ibid., pp. 215–16.

6. Mabbett, *Chinese Community in Indonesia*, p. 4.

7. *Jen-min jih-pao* [People's Daily] (Peking), October 13, 1956.

8. *Ching-chi tao-pao* [Economic Bulletin] (Hong Kong), no. 726, June 3, 1961, p. 12.

9. Mely G. Tan, "Majority-Minority Situation: Indonesia," p. 13.

10. *Hua-ch'iao-chih tsung-chih* [General Gazetteer of the Overseas Chinese] (Taipei: Hua-ch'iao chih pien-tsuan wei-yüan-hui, 1964), pp. 124–26.

11. The following diagram shows how intermarriage and mixed parentage affect the concept of Overseas Chinese in the opinion of Wu Chu-hui, *Minzoku Soziologie* [Ethnological Sociology] (Tokyo: Tokyo University Press: 1958), pp. 231–33.

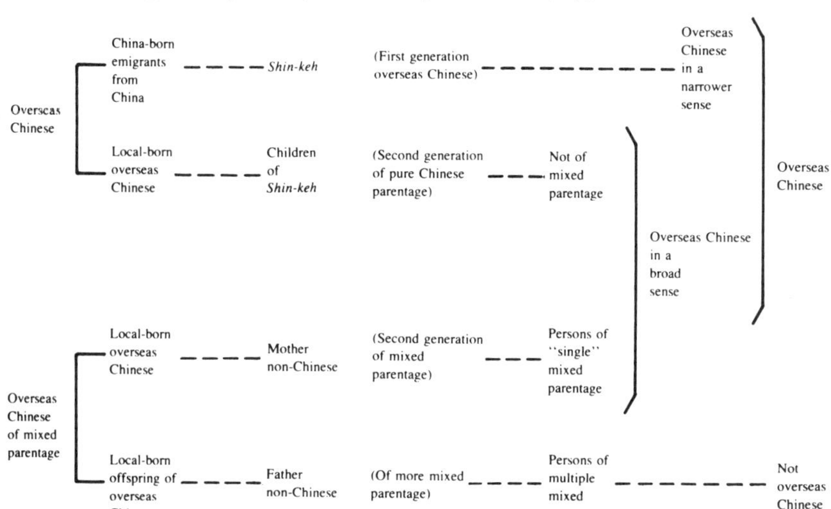

12. *Information Malaysia 1975/76* (Kuala Lumpur: Government Printing Office, 1976), pp. 26–27.

13. Purcell, *Chinese in Southeast Asia*, p. 180.

14. *Chung-yang jih-pao* [Central Daily News] (Taipei), January 13, 1977.

15. Mabbett, *Chinese Community in Indonesia*, pp. 3–4.

16. Li Ch'ang-fu, *Hua-ch'iao* [The Overseas Chinese] (Shanghai: Chung-hua shu-chü, 1927), p. 1.

17. Wu Chun-tsai, *Tung-nan-ya shih* [History of Southeast Asia] (Taipei: Chung-hua wen-hua ch'u-pan shih-yeh she, 1963), 3d ed. pp. 28–29.

18. According to Janes, "It can be assumed that the first Chinese who ventured into the country and mingled with the natives were journeying merchants or artisans. Even today Chinese peddlers are highly regarded among natives because of their skill in commerce and craftsmanship." Quoted in Purcell, *Chinese in Southeast Asia*, p. 10.

19. This was mentioned in the *Han Shu*, vol. 28. Voyages in the Han dynasty to Jihnan and Hsuwenhopo took five months; it took four months to reach Touyuankuo, and twenty days to get to Ilumeikuo. See Feng Ch'eng-chün, *Chung-kuo nan-yang chiao-t'ung shih* [A History of China's Intercourse with Southeast Asia] (Shanghai: The Commercial Press, 1934), p. 1.

20. Purcell, *Chinese in Southeast Asia*, p. 11.

21. Li Ch'ang-fu, *Chung-kuo chih-min shih*, p. 28.

22. *Fa-hsien Fu-Kuo-Chi*, the record of Fa Hsien's voyages reprinted by the Commercial Press, Taipei, 1974.

23. Sun Pao, *T'ang Sung Yüan hai-shang shang-yeh cheng-tse* [Policy on Seaborne Trade in the Tang, Sung, and Yüan Dynasties] (Taipei: Cheng-chung Press: 1969), pp. 1–3.

24. Ibid., p. 11.

25. See Feng Ch'eng-chün, *Chung-kuo nan-yang chiao-t'ung shih*, p. 2.

26. A fictionalized story based on his travels appeared in the sixteenth century under the title *Hsi Yu Chi* [Record of a Journey to the West], subsequently translated into English as *The Adventures of the Monkey*.

27. Li Ch'ang-fu, *Chung-kuo chih-min shih*, pp. 54–55.

28. *Chau Ju-kua (Late Sung Dynasty): His Work on the Chinese and Arab Trade in the Twelfth and Thirteenth Centuries*, translated from Chinese and annotated by Friedrich Hirth and W. W. Rockhill (St. Petersburg, 1911). The name of the work in Chinese is *Chu Fan Chi*.

29. Wang Gung-wu, *A Short History of the Nanyang Chinese* (Singapore: Eastern Universities Press, 1959), p. 4.

30. Ch'en Cheng-hsiang, *Chen la feng t'u chi ti yen-chiu* [A Study of the Chen La Feng Tu Chi], Research Report No. 22 (Hong Kong: The Chinese University, June, 1969).

31. Feng Ch'eng-chün, *Chung-kuo nan-yang chiao-t'ung shih*, p. 84.

32. Liu Chi-hsüan and Shu Shih-cheng, *Chung-kuo min-tsu t'o-chih nan-yang shih*, p. 276.

33. Ibid., pp. 63–64.

34. In Wang Gung-wu's view, "The voyages of Cheng Ho represented a policy of state trading. This policy was grafted on to the restrictive policy revived by the Ming

founder in 1367 of trading only through tribute missions sent by Nanyang countries. Evidently, the Chinese court found this form of trading inadequate for its needs and decided that it would be worth while to send officials out to the Nanyang in order to buy the products in demand at the source" (Wang Gung-wu, *Short History of Nanyang Chinese*, p. 7).

35. Li Ch'ang-fu, *Chung-kuo chih-min shih*, p. 14.

36. See Liu Chi-hsüan and Shu Shih-cheng, *Chung-kuo min-tsu t'o-chih nan-yang shih*, p. 24.

37. *Hua-ch'iao-chih tsung-chih*, Chapter 6, pp. 632–42.

38. Ibid., p. 640.

39. The following brief account and bench-mark dates may be useful for reference:

Indonesia: Early in the 1500s the Portuguese who had come in search of spices built fortresses in the Moluccas. One hundred years later they were replaced by the Dutch. Indonesia first came under Dutch control in 1596 and won independence on August 15, 1950.

Philippines: After centuries of Spanish rule (1571–1898), the Philippines fell quickly into the hands of the United States in 1898. After the Pacific War, the Republic of the Philippines was proclaimed on July 4, 1946.

Malaysia: The Malay States were under Portuguese and Dutch influence from the sixteenth century until the British arrival in 1786. The latter acquired Penang by treaty from the sultan of Kedah and established British rule in the last quarter of the nineteenth century. In 1957 Malaya gained independence within the British Commonwealth. The Federation of Malaysia came into existence on September 16, 1963.

Singapore: Singapore was pioneered by Sir Thomas Raffles in 1819–24. It gained self-governing status in 1959 and formed a part of Malaysia from 1963 to August 9, 1965, when it became a separate independent state. Since April 1959 Singapore has been governed by the People's Action Party led by Lee Kuan Yew.

Burma: Burma was annexed in stages up to 1885, when it became a province of British India. It was separated from India in 1937 and became self-governing. The Union of Burma won independence on January 4, 1948; it became the Socialist Republic of the Union of Burma on January 3, 1974.

Vietnam: France established a protectorate over Vietnam in 1885. The south became the Republic of Vietnam on October 26, 1955; the north was known as the Democratic Republic of Vietnam. Reunification under communist rule was achieved in 1975.

Cambodia: Cambodia became a French protectorate in 1864. Independence was declared in March 1945.

Laos: France established a protectorate in the 1890s. Independence was declared in 1953.

40. P. C. Campbell, *Chinese Coolie Emigration to Countries within the British Empire* (London: P. S. King & Son, 1923), pp. 94–135.

41. *Hua-ch'iao-chih tsung-chih*, pp. 639–40.

42. Li Ch'ang-fu, *Chung-kuo chih-min shih*, p. 267.

43. See Liu Chi-hsüan and Shu Shih-cheng, *Chung-kuo min-tsu t'o-chih nan-yang shih*, pp. 136–40.

44. The number of escapees to Hong Kong from 1949 to 1964 was 1,047,000, according to Egashira Kazuma, "Gekidō no kakyō sekai" [Upheaval of Overseas Chinese Communities], *Economist Weekly* (Tokyo) December 8, 1964, p. 38.

45. Government Statistics, Hong Kong, 1976.

46. Ta Chen, *Migrant Community in South China* (New York: Institute of Pacific Relations, 1940), p. 25.

47. Ko Hsiang-feng, *Chung-kuo p'in-ch'iung wen-t'i* [Poverty Problems in China] (Shanghai: Cheng-chung Shu-chü, 1937), pp. 153–54.

48. Approximately 23.4 million lives were lost during three major famines:

1846	225,000
1849	13,750,000
1877	9,500,000
Total	23,375,000

SOURCE: Li-Ch'ang-fu, *Chung-kuo chih-min shih*, p. 12.

49. Purcell, *Chinese in Southeast Asia*, p. 3.

50. Ibid., pp. 2–3.

51. *Ch'iao-wu t'ung-chi* [Overseas Chinese Affairs Statistics, 1973] (Taipei: OCAC, 1974).

52. The 1975 ethnic-Chinese population in Singapore was 1,712,000 out of a total population of 2,249,000, according to official statistics.

53. See Yusuf Panglaykim, *Trends in Marketing* (Jakarta: Center for Strategic and International Studies, 1974), p. 105 n. 18.

54. H. B. Morse, *The Gilds of China* (London: Longmans, Green & Co., 1909), p. 27.

55. *Hua-ch'iao-chih tsung-chih*, p. 385.

56. Ibid., p. 368.

57. Li Yih-yüan, "Tung-nan-ya chu-kuo hsien-tai ti jo-kan wen-t'i" [Problems of Modernization in Southeast Asian Countries], *Ssu yü Monthly* (Taipei) 3, no. 4 (1965): 4.

APPENDIX B

1. Ho I-wu, *Hua-ch'iao ching-chi yen-chiu* [A Study on Overseas Chinese Economy] (Taipei: Overseas Chinese Affairs Commission, 1966), p. 50.

2. See Table 34, Chapter 3.

3. Data from *Third Malaysia Plan, 1976–1980* (Kuala Lumpur: Government Press, 1976), p. 142.

4. In terms of per-capita income, the Malays received M$ 34 per month or one half as much as the Chinese at M$ 68, while the Indians obtained M$ 57, some 70 percent more than the Malays. See *Third Malaysia Plan, 1976–1980*, p. 5.

5. Asian Development Bank (ADB), *Key Indicators of Developing Member Countries of ADB*, vol. VII, no. 1 (April 1976): 149.

6. Chief Statistician, Department of Statistics, *Yearbook of Statistics, Singapore 1975/76* (Singapore, 1976), p. 11.

7. ADB, *Key Indicators* vol. VII, no. 1 (1976): 98.

8. Ibid., p. 172.

9. See *UN Economic Survey of Asia and the Far East, 1970* (Bangkok, 1971), pp. 308–9.

10. Ibid.

11. ADB, *Key Indicators*, vol. VII, no. 1 (April 1976): 140.

12. The wage differential between Chinese and Filipinos in Chinese business establishments is 2:1.

13. There was some migration of Chinese during 1967–70, before the imposition of martial law. Some left the Philippines for North America, Hong Kong, and elsewhere. We assume that this outflow was sufficient to offset any natural growth between 1969 and 1974, thus keeping the Chinese population in 1969 at about the same level—about six hundred thousand—as in 1974.

14. *Shūkan Post* [Post Weekly] (Tokyo) 7, no. 44 (November 7, 1976): 185.

15. Ho I-wu, *Hua-ch'iao ching-chi yen-chiu*, p. 50.

16. *Third Malaysia Plan, 1976–1980*, table 9-9, p. 184.

Index